KU-485-045

Contents

Sue Ward
Organising
things

A guide to successful
political action

Press

Sue Ward is a freelance researcher and writer. She lives in London and previously worked for the TUC where, among other things, she organised the national demonstration for health service employees in September 1982. Her previous publications include *Pensions: A Workers' Handbook* and *Social Security at Work.* She is currently writing a book on the procedure and practice of meetings, also to be published by Pluto.

First published in 1984 by Pluto Press Limited,
The Works, 105a Torriano Avenue, London NW5 2RX
and Pluto Press Australia Limited, PO Box 199, Leichhardt,
New South Wales 2040, Australia

Cover designed by Colin Bailey
Text designed by Claudine Meissner and Robin Kinross

Phototypeset by *Sunrise Setting,* Torquay, Devon
Printed in Great Britain by Guernsey Press, Guernsey C.I.

British Library Cataloguing in Publication Data

Ward, Sue
    Organising things
    1. Campaign management
    I. Title
    324   JFV2112.C3

ISBN 0-86104-799-0

Acknowledgements

I have spent large amounts of time over the last few years in meetings deciding how to organise one thing and another, and then at the event, and in the resulting post-mortem. Many of the things I have helped organise have been wildly unsuccessful; a few have been successful. I have learnt as much from the bad ones as from the good; above all it is the people that I have worked with who have contributed, directly or indirectly, to this book, but they are too many to name. Specific thanks, though, should go to Mike Barley, Jane Allen, Ann Creighton, Tess Woodcraft, Caroline Hartnell, Camden Playbox, Pat and Barbara Roche, NCCL, Megan Dobney, Sonia Markham, Jane Winter, Ernest Rodker, the Islington Bus Company, Nicki North, Judith Watt, Abdul Choudry, and Dick Muskett, for their help, and Mike Cunningham for reading much of the manuscript and making helpful suggestions.

Also I would like to thank the authors of the books in the 'Useful books' list, most of which I have consulted extensively; and Richard Kuper and Paul Crane of Pluto Press. All the mistakes, of course, are my own.

1.

Introduction

In the autumn of 1982 I found myself organising a major national demonstration. The day I was given the job, I did not know where to start. I sat and panicked quietly to myself and then went and panicked noisily to other people.

Once I started talking to them, though, I found that I knew a lot of people who had each organised something, and who had ideas to contribute. The trouble was that none of them had ever written down what happened last time. Before any event people were too busy; afterwards they were too tired. So the next time something came up, someone had to go around again, finding out what was already in someone else's head, and wasting time they could not afford to waste.

This book aims to put at least some of this information down on paper, to give ideas about what has to be done when an event is decided on.

Who this book is for

Some people who start organising things have an easy source of equipment and help to hand, but others will have to hunt around to find a telephone that does not swallow 5p's. Well-equipped groups will not need to be given ideas about, for instance, how to find a printer, and can skip those bits, but I have tried to look at things from the point of view of the least knowledgeable person, with the fewest resources, except, inevitably, of time and energy. I have assumed this person is starting pretty much from scratch. Even if your big event is not the first one you have organised, it may well be the first of its type. So there will be new things to find out, and new things to go wrong. Although you may feel you are a fairly experienced organiser, you may still find for instance the checklists useful.

What this book is not

The campaigns you run, and the way you decide to run them, is your own affair. This book is not intended to indicate which campaigns are good and which are bad, or to give political guidance about who or what you should support.

Nor does it tell you how to run a committee, a community group, or a campaign from start to finish. There are other books that do that (see 'Useful books' for details). The idea is to provide a sort of workshop manual on the mechanism of running one-off events, from small meetings to major demonstrations.

It was only in writing it, though, that I realised the mistakes that I, and a lot of other people, had been making over the years: we had not thought about **our aims**; and we had not thought afterwards about **the gains and losses**. So chapter 2, which you should read whatever you are organising, goes into this.

How this book is organised

No one expects you to read this book straight through from page 1 to the end. It is for dipping in and out of, pulling out the bits that are useful to you. So it is divided into three parts.

Part 1 contains things you need to know for all sorts of events, for instance where you can go for information, help with finding office space, printing and duplicating facilities, the law on public assemblies, and flyposting.

Part 2 covers a number of specific events, like public meetings, petitions, and festivals.

Each chapter asks you to start by defining your aims and priorities, in the way explained in chapter 2. It is then split into subsections with explanations of different things. The same basic points apply to several events. For instance, you might need to book a hall for a public meeting, a conference, or a festival. To avoid repeating the same information, there are cross-references between the chapters. At the end of each chapter there is a comprehensive checklist for the event covered in that chapter, and this tells you where to look for the items that are covered elsewhere in the book. There is space for you to tick, or to write down dates when you did something, and to put in names, phone numbers and contact addresses. You might want to turn one of these lists into a large wall chart, or to copy it into the front of a file you carry round with you.

The chances are that you will not be able to do every single thing on the lists. There will be things you can safely leave out because local circumstances make them unnecessary, and other things you will just not have time to do. But with this book you may be able to work out what you can afford to miss sensibly, rather than haphazardly. There is no need to feel guilty if you do not do things according to the book – you may well have worked out better methods for yourself. But if you do, let people know, so they can use your ideas too.

Part 3 is the 'disasters' section – what to do when something goes wrong. This book should cut down the risks, but you cannot avoid them altogether, and you will probably be blamed for it, whether fairly or not. So this section is to give you a few ideas about rescuing the situation and clearing up the bits.

The topics the book covers only briefly are: using the press, television, and radio; and fund-raising strategies. They are mentioned in a number of places and several of the events covered in Part 2 are to do with fund-raising. But to deal with either topic fully needs a whole book each. In the case of press and publicity, Denis MacShane's book (*Using the Media*, Pluto 1979) is excellent and I would advise any activist to read it.

2.

Why are you doing it?

The most usual reason that people have an event of the sort described in this book, is that they are sitting round at a committee meeting and someone says something like, 'We've got to do something to move on the campaign.' Someone else says, 'Let's have a demonstration/lobby/petition,' and suddenly you are committed.

This is the wrong way round. The first question should be, 'What is the most important thing our campaign needs at this stage?' For instance, you may need:

- publicity for the arguments;
- an illustration that there is massive public support;
- something to make your supporters feel good about the campaign;
- the assistance of influential politicians and others in getting across complicated facts to those who make the decisions;
- to convince local, non-political, people that your cause is important.

Having worked out whether it is one of these things, or something else, that your campaign needs most just now, you should be able to see what event will suit you best. For example if you **need publicity** most, that means you need something that will catch the eye of the press. A march of 500 people on a rainy Wednesday evening probably will not do this; they've seen it before. Stopping the traffic outside the town hall with a bit of street theatre might succeed in interesting them.

If you need **to illustrate your massive public support**, you've got to get a lot of people involved. If you can be sure that a demonstration will be big, this will do it, but you are taking a risk. A big petition or letter-writing campaign, or a public meeting that is packed to the doors would all make the same point.

If you want **to convince the politicians** who are actually going to decide the issue, then you need to organise a place where the arguments can be put in detail. This would mean a lobby or a public meeting.

If you want **to convince ordinary non-political people** about an issue, you need a chance to talk to them, not patronisingly or as if they are already converted, but going through all the points in detail. So you need an excuse to knock on doors, or to go up to people in the street. This might mean organising a public meeting on an estate, and putting a lot of effort into going round and handing out leaflets; or running a market stall with a petition, so you can approach people as they do their shopping.

Sorting out your aims will also show you what to avoid. If your public meeting is to convince local people, you will not want to advertise it in *New Statesman* so that people come from all over the place. If the meeting is to get publicity for a national campaign, perhaps you do advertise it. If you are anxious to get support from the clergy, you will not want to do anything that will shock them.

Image

Decide at this stage, also, what sort of image your group want to get across to people seeing your event, or reading about it in the papers. The easiest way to think about this is to imagine what descriptions you want to see of yourselves in the newspapers.

Look at the examples in chapter 10 on petitions. Two groups described there need to have very different stories about themselves appearing, if they want to achieve their aims. First, there is Debbie's **youth group**, who want to start a youth club on their estate. They need to be seen as responsible people to whom the council can entrust money. Second, there is Olly's **group of pensioners**, campaigning for better pensions, who want people to see them as 'battling grannies' not old folk who will sit down quietly and accept charity.

In both cases, they've got to go against the standard ideas about their groups – of troublesome youth or shy retiring pensioners. In other cases, you may want to go with the standard pattern. Nurses might want to encourage public sympathy for them in a battle to keep the local hospital open, for instance.

So when working out your aims and priorities, think about this as well. Do you want to appear respectable? Aggressive? Sympathetic? In each case, you will need to make sure that the way you run your event fits in with this, and nothing contradicts it.

Priorities

The next step is to use your understanding of the aims to decide what is the most important thing about the event. For any activity, there are several reasons why you might have decided that this was the right one. For instance, the reason for holding a public meeting might be: to get **publicity**; to **build up the numbers** in your organisation locally; to **put the case** to ordinary people; or to **have a slanging match** with your opponents.

The purpose will affect the way you organise the meeting, and how you publicise it. If your main aim is publicity for your cause, then you want a big-name speaker, and you might want to spend money on advertising in the local paper, as well as printing posters and leaflets. On the other hand, if you want to build up the numbers in, for instance, your tenants' association, you will want speakers from your area, publicity on the estate only, and to put a good deal of effort beforehand into knocking on doors persuading people to come. Your leaflets will still have to be decently produced, but they will be a different kind of leaflet.

If having worked it out, you seem to be aiming to do everything at once at your event, think again. Some events are incompatible with each other. You cannot, for instance, have big-name speakers and the press at a meeting, and also get down to detailed discussion of the small print of a constitution. You need to decide which is the more important.

You may at this stage decide that the event you first decided on is quite wrong for your purpose. Demonstrations particularly are very often held just because people think they are the right thing to do – but much of the time they are not. They can draw attention to a cause; they can show the strength of support; they can get publicity. But they do not do any of these things if they are only small; and they do not convince people who are not converted already. Indeed, they *can* do the opposite and put people off, because this is not the way ordinary people behave. They can also be a considerable nuisance, if they hold up the traffic, and so annoy people who might otherwise be sympathetic.

If you realise that the idea you started out with is wrong do not hesitate to change it. It will waste less time and energy in the long run.

Delegating

The last stage is to divide up the jobs. Delegating responsibility is important. If you have a very small group slogging themselves to death, this increases the danger of things going wrong because they will just not be able to cover everything. They also deny other people the opportunity of learning for themselves. The more people involved, the more you can spread the responsibility out. But avoid endless vague meetings which decide to do all sorts of things without deciding who is to do them. Split the organising tasks up into clearly-defined pieces, let people go away and do them, and then have another meeting to report back and check progress. Some groups use a pyramid structure, with two or three people acting as liaison points, each with three or four others under their wing. The liaison people are responsible not just for their jobs, but for checking on progress and reporting back on everything in their subgroup. Page 218 shows the notes of an early planning meeting for a festival covering the crucial job of sorting out people's tasks.

Use the checklists at the end of each chapter in Part 2 as a way of splitting up the work. Some jobs will be finished before the event actually starts; the persons involved can then be re-allocated to something on the day itself. Do not forget to allocate the jobs for afterwards as well.

There is often a temptation to keep things in very few hands, because those few do not trust anyone else to do the job properly and because, if they are honest, they get a kick out of being the important people with the knowledge. It does not help the campaign as a whole, though.

Coming unstuck

As well as the 'nuts and bolts' there are some important points on which you, and your campaign with you, can easily come unstuck.

Do not let the event overshadow, or even take over the campaign. A demonstration, or a meeting, is only a means to an end, not the end in itself. The point is to win the industrial dispute or the zebra crossing, and having 500 people outside the town hall is only **one way** of getting there. If you devote all your energies to the event, and lose sight of the real aim, you run the danger of being so exhausted afterwards, without any energy to carry on the struggle, that the campaign falls to pieces. **Events can damage campaigns.** Keep them in perspective, to make sure they help instead.

Get to thinking beyond the day. Make your plans for what to do next **before** the big event, on the assumption that it will not have an immediate effect. After all, you can always cancel things if you win. In the Bible, people marched round the walls of Jericho blowing horns, and the walls fell down; in real life, they would probably have had to come back another day and wave banners as well.

Do not kill yourself over it. No one ever died of a sleepless night or two, and whoever has the main responsibility is bound to worry about it. But if the worry turns you into a nervous wreck, or makes you ill, you are not helping the campaign. The event may be a disaster anyway; it certainly *will* be if you go into hospital the week before. Remember that you are only human. When you feel the pressure building up, stop. Take a night off, go out for a meal, spend an evening with a friend who knows nothing about your obsession and doesn't care either.

Afterwards

When you have had your event and cleared up, all you will want is to go home and collapse. Do; but get together a bit later and go over the event in detail.

First, the practical points: which hire firm didn't turn up and should not be relied on in the future? Who was wonderful at looking after the children? What went wrong when the banner had no one to carry it?

Second, tie up your loose ends, especially the results of things going wrong. If something has got damaged, how are you going to replace it? If you have mortally offended someone, how can you put it right? There will also be unexpected bonuses. Perhaps you have made far more members than you thought you would. Who is going to follow them up and collect the subs?

Third, and very important, **go back to your reasons for having the event** in the first place, and **compare them** with what you have achieved and what you have not. You might want to draw up a balance sheet of your gains and losses. For instance, 'We got 20,000 people, but we got a bad press out of the punch-up at the beginning of the march.' If your aim was to get a good press, then that must be a minus. In planning the next stage of your campaign, you will have to work out how to put it right.

If you have had a failure, face up to it; do not kid yourselves, but try to work out why. Was it poorly advertised? Was it not clear to people what message you were trying to get across? Is it an unpopular cause? If you can work it out you should be able to decide how you need to change your approach next time.

This all sounds very scientific and calculating, and it may put some people off. But if we are trying to win the fight **we have to plan properly**. Even so, events can still be enjoyable. A campaign that is fun to join in with will have more supporters than one that is dull and uninspiring.

Part 1
Hints for all events

3.

Resources and information

You have had a meeting of your group in the secretary's front room one evening, and decided to organise, for instance, a public meeting. It would take work to do so, and you do not even know who your local councillor is. Where do you start?

Information

Directories

The first place to look for addresses, dates, and places, are the ordinary telephone directories, Yellow Pages, and Thomson Local Directories.

Thomson's now cover almost all the country; they have half a dozen 'community pages' at the beginning which give phone numbers and addresses for local organisations and official bodies; and also tell you where the local markets are, what day is early closing, and the names of local newspapers. The 'Helplines' pages give numbers for the organisations that cover your area, like the NSPCC and Shelter, and there is also a street map and an index of streets. The maps have schools, open spaces, health centres and other public buildings marked on them, which is useful if you are looking for ideas on where to hold a meeting or a rally.

When you look at the entries themselves, remember that this is a commercial service, and groups that do not pay for an entry will not be in it. So for instance in the Middletown directory, the only entries under 'Political organisations' are the Conservative and the Constitutional Clubs. The Labour Party does exist in Middletown, but it doesn't think it is worth paying for an advertisement, or no one has suggested it to them.

The main telephone directory, issued by British Telecom, is

comprehensive except for the people who have asked to go ex-directory, but you do need to know what to look up. If you cannot find the group you want, look at the entries under the name of your area, to see if it is listed there. Try both the **immediate local area** and the name of the **larger district**. For instance, for Brixton you could look up both 'Brixton' and the borough it is part of, which is Lambeth.

Suppliers

If you want to find a supplier of say, badges or catering for a conference:

- **Start with Yellow Pages.** If there is nothing under what you think is the correct heading, go through the index at the back and see if there is any other category you might find useful. For instance there may be no entry for balloon shops but there is one for 'Novelties and carnival goods'. This might include balloons; ring these people and find out.
- Look in a **local trade directory in the library.**
- **Buy a copy of** *Exchange and Mart* from a newsagent and look in the back pages, under 'Business and technical'.
- **Look in local and national** left-wing or radical magazines, like *Marxism Today* or *City Limits.* There may also be local alternative directories; London has a directory of co-ops published by London ICOM (see 'Useful addresses') with addresses of a number of catering and printing co-ops.
- Ask other groups, or the National Council for Voluntary Organisations (see 'Useful addresses') whether there is a community group doing this work, or other firms they have found reliable.

Commercial firms may well be sweatshops, and non-unionised. If they advertise in left magazines they are probably OK. If you are not sure, check with the Trades Council that at least they are not currently in industrial dispute.

Libraries

These are a very useful, and underestimated souce of information about all sorts of things.

In many areas, libraries are divided into small branch libraries, and a much larger Central Library which will have a big reference section. This is usually in the main shopping centre or, in the countryside, in the main county town, so it could be some distance from you. But you can ask for information at any library, and they can always phone up a larger one if they do not have what you want, so start by going to whatever library is most convenient to you.

Make sure that **you talk to the right person**. Most libraries have an issue desk, where books are checked in and out. This may be staffed by a rather junior assistant, but there is also an **enquiries desk**, with a more fully trained librarian, and this is where you should go.

Ask for the specific information you want; if they cannot help, ask them to phone up a larger branch to see if they have got it, to save you wasting your journey. If they cannot do this right away, because they are too busy, they will probably take your number and phone you, or make a note for you to pick up later. You should be able to find out the following, for instance:

- the names of your local councillor, county councillor, and MP, their addresses, and what party they belong to;
- whether they run surgeries, and if so, where;
- which council department deals with which subject;
- when the council and its committees meet;
- contact names and addresses for major local organisations;
- the address of the local police station, and also of the police headquarters that covers your area;
- addresses of local hospitals, of the District Health Authority, and the members;
- addresses of schools locally, the names of head teachers, and of the school governors;
- addresses of advice services like those listed on page 17.

In some cases you will be able to find out what political parties the various local worthies belong to.

The library may also be able to tell you what halls are available for hire, and how to go about booking them. A main library should have a big ordnance survey map of the area, which is useful if you are planning a march, an A–Z of the town, and a Chamber of Commerce directory for local businesses, if these are published. The notice board may have advertisements for local organisations and events.

Libraries are good at handing out hard facts; names, addresses, dates, books on subjects you want to know about. They will be able to find a reference book, and show you how to look something up (for instance, what your MP said in parliament about the issue you are campaigning on). If they have time, and you ask for help, they may be able to go through information in detail with you and explain it. Often librarians are very helpful, but they are too busy to be able to stop and talk for a long time with someone who only vaguely knows what s/he wants. They are also liable to be interrupted by people wanting to borrow books or to know where the railway station is. So spend a few minutes before you go there writing a shopping list of the facts you need. Having found the right person, if s/he is friendly, explain why you need the information. S/he may have ideas of sources and contacts that you have not yet thought of.

Citizen's Advice Bureaux

For more detailed explanations of your rights and the procedures to follow, try the Citizens' Advice Bureau (CAB). Unfortunately, these vary a lot in quality. Some are well-staffed, with professionals who really know their stuff, but others are run in their spare time by well-meaning middle-class people, and are often only open a couple of mornings a week. But all of them are linked to their national centre, called NACAB, which sends out regular information bulletins about, for instance, changes in the law. It also runs a telephone enquiry service. Given time, a bureau can find out almost anything, though you may need to make an appointment and return for an answer. Examples of information might be the law on selling things on a Sunday; or what the local by-laws are.

The CAB is a sensible place to go if you are in **legal trouble over the event**, for instance if you are threatened with being sued for damaging something on a march. Many CABs have a panel of lawyers who give free advice on a rota basis at evening sessions, so you could make an appointment to talk to one about the problem. Even if your CAB does not do this, it will have a list of local lawyers to take legal aid cases, and what they specialise in. His/her politics may be quite different from yours, but s/he is likely to have some sort of social conscience otherwise s/he would not be giving up free time. So you stand a better chance of finding a sympathetic lawyer this way than simply by walking off the street into a solicitor's office.

Help

The following organisations may be able to help in practical ways, as well as by giving information and advice. These are the various groups with resources, for instance, to put together and duplicate your first leaflet; to give you a room to meet in; to help find a sympathetic printer.

Organisations

Most areas have some sort of co-ordinating body, linking the various community groups in their area. They are usually paid for, mainly or partly, by the local council or the government. They may be called the **Council of Voluntary Service**; the **Council of Social Service**; or in the countryside, the **Rural Community Council**. In some parts of large cities, there are **Resource Centres**. These tend to be more radical and respond readily to people who are campaigning rather than organising coffee mornings.

Any of these should have some basic equipment, meeting rooms, and helpful people with experience of doing things. They often have odd opening hours – they might be open one or two evenings a week, for instance, and shut an equal number of mornings – so ring up to check before you waste a journey.

In towns with a university or a polytechnic, the student organisation might be able to help. There may be a branch of **Student Community Action**, or there may be someone in the **students' union** with a specific job of making links with organisations in the town. Again, ring up and make enquiries first. Student unions can be very daunting places for a stranger to wander round looking for the right office, since they are full of young people taking not the slightest notice of you. Ring the main university or polytechnic number and ask for the secretary or president of the students' union.

Remember, though, that students have long holidays, especially in the summer. They may not be able to help much between July and the end of September, or over Christmas, although there will still be students around.

If yours is an industrial dispute, or something that might affect jobs, like the closing of a hospital or a school, the local **Trades Council** might help with resources. Some of them have an office with a typewriter, duplicator, telephone, and so on; some use the resources of a particular union. Others are run from the home of the secretary, but they will still know of places where you can get duplicating done and a leaflet sorted out. The library may be able to tell you the secretary's address. If not, try your own union's branch secretary or regional office; or another union. If you cannot find one in the phone book, or do not know of one, ring up the town hall and ask to speak to the NALGO branch secretary, or a large hospital or factory and ask to speak to the union convenor.

Political parties can also be useful, but remember that they have their own policies and programmes and will not help if you are campaigning against them. You will not get help from the Labour Party, if you are campaigning for the sale of council houses, for instance. Political party organisations are likely to use you to help them promote their wider aims, and they may try to take credit for your successes. If you are linking with any of these groups, it is wise to insist on the following:

- writing your own leaflets and press releases;
- having your group's name and address on them, not theirs;
- only having their speakers at meetings if you agree before-hand, and are happy with, what they will say.

You can find out where these political organisations are based by:

- looking in the phone book;
- looking on the notice board in the library to see if any meetings are advertised there;
- asking the librarian;
- phoning their head office; or
- contacting a local MP or councillor of the right party, and asking for a contact in your local branch.

Another source of help may be **groups like your own** – that is, other groups of tenants, pensioners, pre-school playgroup parents; or people whose campaign is about a different thing but on the same principle. A campaign to stop the closure of an old people's home might well learn a lot from the people fighting to stop a hospital closing, for instance.

As well as being sympathetic to your cause, if they have been involved in a similar event elsewhere they could give you some practical advice. They may on the other hand be pessimistic, and tell you all your ideas have been tried before and do not work; but do not be discouraged. To find out about other groups:

- ask people who seem active in politics or their union;
- try the same sources as for political parties;
- look in a few back numbers of the local papers to see if there are groups that have been active in your area recently.

There is also a **Directory of Self-Help Organisations** (see 'Useful books') which your library should have, with useful addresses for national organisations.

If there is not a helpful group in your area, try another area nearby, where you might have better luck. They may not be able to help you officially, but one or two of their members might give their time informally to help you along.

How to use the help

In a big city there will probably be a number of organisations you can turn to, once you have found where they are. Don't confuse the issue by chopping and changing between different groups; **find out who can be most help and stick to them**. Otherwise, there is a risk of getting some things done twice and others not at all, and people will be annoyed and not trust you.

What sort of help you can ask for depends very much on what sort of organisation you are, and what you are planning. You are unlikely to be able to say, 'We want a meeting organised', and leave them to get on with it; or if they do, it may turn out to be quite different from your plans, because it will be their meeting not yours. More often, they will offer assistance so that you can do the work. They may offer:

- office space, use of a typewriter and a telephone (but see page 23 about paying for this);
- help with drafting letters, petitions, and so on;
- cheap photocopying, and cheap or free duplicating;
- help with drawing up leaflets that get the message across;
- possibly cheap printing – or knowledge of where to get it;
- use of a room to meet in;
- help with silk-screening posters;
- help sorting out a bank account, and drawing up accounts.

And, if the place is lively and well used, there will be endless cups of coffee and distracting conversations, and ideas about what you should be doing. If you want to make the best use of your contacts, be considerate and use your common sense. For instance, if you arrange to see someone, or to be shown how to use a machine, or to get help organising something, **turn up on time. If you cannot make it, ring up and say so**. The person may have put someone else off for you, or have arranged to see you in their spare time. If you let them down and then stroll in carelessly the next day, do not expect a very friendly reception!

Give people enough time to do the things you are asking them to do. However willing and efficient they are, it is impossible to type, run off, and put together a five-page document in the half-hour before a meeting. If there is a good reason why something is going to have to be done in a rush, **tell them in advance about it**, if possible, so that they are ready for it.

Clear up after yourself (especially dirty coffee cups and half-eaten hamburgers) and confess if you break or damage something, or do something stupid like leaving the photocopier running all night.

Money

Get enough cash to get going

This section is intended to give a few ideas on how to raise enough money to get your organisation off the ground, to cover postage and the first leaflet. After that, if it is going to be a long drawn-out struggle, you need to plan fund-raising seriously, and this book does not cover the issue (see 'Useful books' for some that do). To start with, you need a launch fund. Possible ways to do this are:

- have a whip round at your first meeting; get everyone to put in a pound to get things going;
- ask a sympathetic organisation – like the Labour Party or Trades Council – to let you speak and take a collection at their next meeting. In an industrial dispute, or if the issue is urgent, they will probably let you do this even if it is at very short notice. For other things, they might say you have to wait until they can fit you in.
- write to all the sympathetic organisations you can think of, both locally and in other parts of the country, and ask other groups if you can include a leaflet or a letter in their mailing, appealing for money. Even if only half a dozen groups respond, it will give you enough to get started.

■ When people in Wandsworth were fighting to save their Law Centres, they asked the national Law Centres Federation to put a letter in their next mailing asking for help, and got several hundred pounds in donations to get the campaign going.

Making a speech

If you can get yourself invited to speak at a meeting of the Trades Council or the Labour Party, it can be a bit daunting when you actually get there, if you are not used to public speaking. Remember that you are bound to have some sympathisers, otherwise they would not have invited you. They have heard people before in a similar position, so they are not expecting a great speaker, but someone who cares about the subject. It helps, if you are nervous, to write down every word you are going to say. Once you get used to it, you will be able to use notes instead. Take along other members of the group, to give support. If you like, you can each do a short stint, rather than one person talking the whole time. In any case, keep it short and concise, and get across your main points, which will include:

- what your campaign is about;
- why it is important;
- what help they can give (resolutions of support, letters to local papers, joining your picket, coming to your meeting);
- why you need money, and how much.

Try to get them to take a collection then and there, or to make a donation from their funds (a collection raises more).

Fund-raising letter

You need to put in a first letter:

- what you are trying to do;
- brief background information about when you were formed, what it is you are campaigning about;
- what you want to do, and what would be a 'success' – keeping your school open, taking 20 people away on holiday;
- what you need the money for, and how much you need, both as a whole and from each group. For instance, you could say, 'We need £100 to produce a leaflet and hold our first public meeting. If each group gives £5 we will have enough.'

Keep your letter short – at most two sides. Put the vital information about who you are and what you want to do, in the first paragraph. Do not assume they know anything about your campaign – it may be hot news in Southend, but it probably has not made the front page in Billericay. Don't use jargon, and be optimistic, even if you are not, because no one wants to give money to a cause that is bound to fail. Give a name and phone number that people can contact if they want to know more.

If your cause is a popular one, you could try writing to the local paper with the same sort of appeal. If it is controversial, though, you may get some abusive replies, which could be upsetting.

Looking after the money

Having got some money, you also need to keep track of it. Even if you do not bother with officers like chairperson or secretary, you *will* need a treasurer, who must be reliable and trustworthy. More campaigns have been ruined by arguments over where the money has gone than by anything else. The treasurer does not need fancy book-keeping skills, but there are some basic rules.

Keep a piece of paper that accounts for every transaction. Never pay anything out without either having a bill which you can mark PAID and the date, or a receipt which the person you have given the money to signs. If you have both, clip them firmly together and write on one that it refers to the other, so you know you have not paid a bill twice.

Buy a book of numbered receipts, and always **give a receipt** for money you are given. Keep either a carbon copy or a counterfoil, clearly filled in.

Always **write down** in a book you keep for this purpose and no other, **the money you have got in and paid out at the time**. If you are not too good at adding up, someone else can do that for you; or if you make a mistake it can be sorted out later provided it is all written down.

■ Hiring a hall for a public meeting costs £20. The collection raises £40. The treasurer therefore gives a receipt to the chair for the collection, and enters 'Collection £40' in the Income column of her little book. Then she gives £20 to the caretaker for hall hire, and is given a receipt for it. She enters 'Hall hire' in the book under Expenditure.

However rushed you are, **writing it down** is the best safeguard against people accusing others of bad faith.

If you are dealing with large sums of money, **open a bank**

account at an early stage, and get a cheque book. To do this, you need to pass a formal resolution at your meeting, and decide who is going to sign the cheques. If you go to a bank and ask to see the manager or assistant manager, they will be able to explain what has to be done (different banks have different systems). If yours is a fairly respectable campaign, it is worth asking if they would be willing to be treasurer, or to let one of their juniors do it.

Cheques for organisations usually need more than one person signing (each one is called a 'signatory') as a safeguard against someone going off to Bermuda with the proceeds of the last jumble sale. Have people who can be found easily as signatories, so that you do not have any delay about paying bills while you try to track the second person down. It is sensible for people who are related or married not to sign the same cheque, though.

For more details on how to do accounts and manage your finances, look at a book called *Accounting and Financial Management for Charities*, which is designed for non-experts. For straightforward book-keeping, try *Teach Yourself Book-keeping*, which goes into it very fully (details are under 'Useful books').

Paying for what you use

Some organisations can subsidise campaigning groups very easily. The regional office of a union, for instance, may not mind at all if their phone bill is pushed up by a group working for a cause they believe in. A Resource Centre, though, may be financed on the assumption that groups will be paying, even if at a reduced rate, for paper and printing and room space; other voluntary groups are probably just as badly off as yourselves.

So find out, before you get 5,000 leaflets run off, or make 20 phone calls to London, how much it is going to cost, and how soon they need the money. Some organisations have special 'hardship funds' or arrangements to help new groups with absolutely no money; or they might be able to delay asking for payment until after you have had a fund-raising event. An official or semi-official body might be able to disguise your spending in some other part of the budget. Or they might be able to lend you equipment you would otherwise have to hire.

Individuals' help

The group ought to reimburse individuals for money they spend out on its behalf. The person involved may feel too embarrassed to mention it, but the treasurer should check up. Booking a hall or arranging a coach, for instance, can easily use up a lot of bus fares, telephone calls, and stamps. The group should insist on sharing these costs, and not leave it to one or two people to foot the bill. If they refuse to take the money, suggest they can give it back as a donation if they want. You will be able to see much better what the campaign is costing you, and therefore if it is worthwhile, if these expenses are actually shown in the accounts, even if the money comes straight back. A person who absolutely refuses to take money could be bought a box of chocolates or a bunch of flowers.

If you use someone's house as a meeting place, and that person provides coffee and biscuits or a drink, then get everyone to put 10p or 20p in a plate at the end to cover costs, without making a fuss about it.

Volunteers

Your group may include unemployed or retired people who can work pretty well full-time for your event. What about expenses for them? Try at least to pay for their fares, but after that the rules get complicated, if you are not to create problems for them with Social Security. The ground rules are described below.

For **unemployment benefit** (UB), you must not earn more than £2 a day, after expenses, but before tax. You can have your travelling expenses and 15p a day for lunch. Payments in kind, like free pints of beer, are treated as earnings. If you earn more than £2, you lose all your UB for that day. You must be available to take up a suitable job, or go for an interview, at 24 hours' notice.

For **supplementary benefit** (SB) you must not earn more than £4 a week after tax, National Insurance contributions, travel, child care costs, and so on. If you earn more than this limit, your benefit is reduced pound for pound. However if you are a single parent, after the first £4 a week has been ignored, for every £1 of your net earnings between £4 and £20 only 50p is deducted; over £20 a week it is pound for pound.

If you are **on both UB and SB**, the UB rule is used first, to see what days you can still get benefit for. Then they look at your earnings to see what SB you can have for other days of the week.

For pensioners, under the age of 65 (70 for men) you can earn up to £65 net without having anything deducted from your retirement pension. Over that age, there is no limit. If you are on SB as well, the limits are the same as for younger people.

Widows can earn any amount without their benefit being affected.

For an unemployed person, there is a danger that Social Security may say that you are not available for work because you are helping a group full-time. So it is best to tell them first, and stress that you are not being paid and can drop out of it any time. They may then test you by sending you for a job. Make sure you go, and however busy you are, do not forget to sign on.

4.

Publicity

Working out your aims, as suggested in chapter 2, is especially important when you are thinking about publicity for the event. Who do you want to reach? What do you want them to know? What idea do they need to have of your event? Only when you have answered these questions will you know what sort of publicity you need, and who to aim at. Press publicity is covered in chapter 5. This chapter covers: **leaflets** to hand out in the street or put through doors; **posters**; **advertisements**. First of all, it looks at the law.

The law on printed materials

Anything printed must have **an imprint** – that is, the name and address of the printer and publisher – on every one, although the penalties for not doing so are not very great. The printer has to keep a copy, together with a record of who asked for the work, and can be prosecuted if s/he does not. In London, leaflets you hand out in the street must not be 'profane, indecent, or obscene'. You also have to be careful not to contravene the Race Relations Act (Black Power leaflets have been prosecuted for this).

Defamation

This is the most serious problem with anything you publish. It is a word that covers both slander and libel. Libel is defamation in writing, drawing, cartoons, photographs, broadcasting; slander is in speech. There is a law of criminal libel, but most cases are about 'civil' libel. This means that the police are not involved, and one individual brings a case against another. Not only the authors, but also the printers and publishers can be sued. This can cost a very large amount of money, especially since you cannot get legal aid, and if you are campaigning against, say, a bad landlord, he might find bringing a libel case a good way to get back at you. A printer can refuse to print what you have written, if s/he is afraid of the libel laws.

Equally, you might find yourself being libelled by opponents who might accuse you, for instance, of having a criminal record. You would then have to decide whether to follow it up or not.

You libel a person by publishing something untruthful that tends to **lower him/her in the estimation** of society; to make **him/her hated, ridiculed** or **disliked** by society; or to make people feel **contemptuous of him/her** or to avoid his/her presence. 'Society' means **conventional, 'right-thinking'** people. 'Publishing' means **communicating to anyone else** except the person concerned but, if a leaflet goes to very few people, and is then stopped because someone realises the dangers, this would be taken into account when the damages are worked out.

The person who claims to have been libelled is called the 'plaintiff'. S/he does not have to show that any actual harm has been done; the law assumes it. Plaintiffs have to show that the material refers to them, or could be taken as doing so. If you had actually been referring to someone else, but had, say, used a nick-name which could be taken to refer to that person, you could have unintentionally libelled them. So if you refer, for instance, to 'Nobby Clarke of X Street' when talking about a rotten landlord you have strong evidence against, you could find you have libelled *another* Nobby Clarke in X Street whose friends now thought he was a rotten landlord. If you make a **general comment, it is libellous** if you mention someone's name in conjunction with it: if for instance you said, 'Only criminals go to the XYZ Club. Mr P was seen there last Wednesday', or if someone **could deduce what you meant** by the implications of what you said it could be libellous. This is called 'innuendo'. An example is, 'A person not a million miles from Mr P was seen handing over money to a policeman on Friday.'

If **you libel an unnamed person** who is one of a small identifiable group, then each person in that group could take you to court. So if you said that the six members of a board of directors were stupid and dishonest, any or all of them could take action. You do not need to imply that the person is at fault for it to be libellous. So if you said someone had been mentally ill, it could be libellous, even though it is not their fault.

You can defend yourself in five possible ways:

- By showing that what you said was true (not just that you believed it was).

- By showing that the words were 'fair comment' – that it was an opinion, not malicious, about a matter of public concern. This cannot be used about a person's moral character.
- By privilege – some people, like MPs and judges, can say more or less what they like in parliament or in the courts.
- By qualified privilege – this covers people reporting fairly and accurately court cases, parliament, and public meetings. But for public meetings, if the person concerned asked the reporter or newspaper to publish a letter of explanation, and this was refused, this defence could not be used.
- By claiming innocent defamation. This is a very difficult defence to use. It means saying that you did not intend to be defamatory and took reasonable care to avoid making the mistake. You must make an offer of amends as soon as possible. This usually means publishing a correction and an apology.

Before the case gets to court, you can state that the libel was published without malice or gross negligence, and offer to publish a full apology, in the same newspaper or another one. You may also need to offer money. If the plaintiff accepts, the case would then not go to court.

Slander

It is convenient also to cover the law about this here, although it applies to the spoken rather than the written word.

To prove that you have been slandered, you usually have to prove that your reputation has been damaged. There are four things, however, that are slanderous simply by being said, even if there is no effect on reputation:

- that someone has committed a criminal offence serious enough to be punishable by death or imprisonment;
- allegations of 'unchastity or adultery', if made against a woman;
- imputing that at the time of the slander, someone has an infectious disease;
- alleging something calculated to disparage the person in their office, trade or profession at the time of saying it.

Slander cases are not very common, but you do need to take care.

The laws on defamation, especially on libel, are dangerous,

because rich people can use them to take ordinary people to the cleaners. You can avoid the straightforward libel by taking care over what you write, but if you are in any doubt, or if you have had a letter from someone threatening a libel action, don't try to manage on your own. **Get legal advice**. Libel is a fairly specialised area of the law; find the local expert by asking the local newspaper who checks their stories. Phone up and ask to speak to the editor, or the branch secretary of the NUJ, who is called the Father or Mother of the Chapel.

Leaflets

Printing methods

There are several possible methods of getting your leaflet printed. The main ones are: duplicating; photocopying; and printing.

Duplicating is cheap, can be done by amateurs, and need not involve any fancy layout. The equipment is fairly easily available. Each stencil costs money, especially if it is an **electrostencil** (see page 40) so it is not very economical for very small quantities. You can duplicate about 3,000 leaflets from the same stencil, or more if you are lucky.

Photocopying is expensive per copy, but does not involve a stencil, so it is useful for a small run of a large number of pages. A good photocopier can also produce very nice looking copies. Use it for up to 50 copies of each page – unless you are getting it for free, in which case you might as well get as many as you can make.

Printing is cheaper than duplicating for long runs, but you cannot so often get it subsidised. You can do more, and produce better quality work, but it cannot be done by amateurs, unless you know an organisation that owns an offset machine. It is the best method for producing a lot of copies of things where quality is important.

For all of these methods, it is important for the person actually doing the running off to be a perfectionist. It is no good producing something that is crooked, or with dirty marks all over it, and thinking 'Oh well, it will do'. **It won't**. People will not read it, so you have only created so much waste paper. Be tough about producing either **good** leaflets or **no** leaflets. Bad ones can put people off your campaign altogether.

The method you use cannot be separated from **the design** you want, and that in itself depends on **the reason** you want the leaflet. Is it for **giving out in the street** to busy people doing their shopping? If so, it needs to be well set out and eye catching with a **bold headline** so that people can see what it is as they come and can take a copy if they are interested.

It is very depressing when people pretend not to see you because they think you are a religious group or advertising a new hamburger place. You also need **only a few words**, so they can take them in. It can be duplicated if you can find a good duplicator, but otherwise will have to be printed.

Is the leaflet for **putting on chairs** at a meeting to explain the issues? You won't need many, and the leaflet can be longer, but it should still **set things out clearly**, and should not be so absorbing, or so difficult, that they lose the thread of what is going on while reading it.

Is it to **bring people you know already to a local meeting** about an issue they are all aware of? In that case, you probably only need **a short duplicated leaflet** saying, 'Come to a meeting on Friday night in the tenants' hall to discuss the damp' or something similar. However, for anything that goes through doors, you don't want it thrown away with the double glazing leaflets, so it needs **a clear message, in large letters**, that hits immediately. Then you can go into detail in the text.

Design

Use as **few words** as possible, and **do not fill the page** too full. Use simple words, and keep the sentences straightforward. Look at the *Sun*, or the *Daily Mirror*, and see the way their reporters write. Far more people read those papers than the *Guardian*. It may seem as if the ideas you have are too complicated to get across easily, but almost anything can be translated if you try hard enough. You are writing for people who don't know what you are trying to tell them, and you have got to interest them. Try to address people directly, and not to use abstract words.

■ The first leaflet about defending the South London Hospital for Women said, 'Your help is needed to prevent the closure of this hospital'. After people said this was not clear, it was changed to, 'Help us stop them closing this hospital' which was much better.

Don't split up stories, or use too many columns or little boxes, because it is irritating. Make it clear what you want people to do, and make it easy for them. If you want them **to write to their MP**, give the name and address; if you want them **to sign a petition**, say where they can do so. Put these 'action points' in a box, or clearly separated from the rest of the text at the bottom of the leaflet, with stars, arrows, pointing fingers, or anything you like to draw attention to them. Put an address where people can contact you, and preferably a phone number as well.

If your leaflet is going to be **one of a series**, (especially if it is a newsletter) then use a format that you can use next time as well, so that people can recognise it quickly. It is useful **to have a symbol** so that people know as soon as they see it what the organisation is. This is called a 'logo' by public relations people. You can see one by looking at the cover of this book, where the Pluto Press 'logo', which is 2 Ps back to back, is printed several times. Remember also **to date** your leaflet and **number it**. You need an imprint on any leaflet (see page 26).

If your organisation wants **new members, or money, or help**, put a form at the bottom for people to fill in, and an address for them to send it to, if they can offer anything. Even if it is the tenth leaflet you've done, it may be the first someone has read, so it's worth taking trouble.

Printing

There are two separate operations in printing. One is **getting the material ready** – called **typesetting** – and the other is **actually getting it run off**. Many, but not all, firms, do both operations. The next section assumes that they are separate, to make the explanation clearer.

For both operations you need firms who are not only cheap but also **reliable**. There is no point in getting dirt-cheap leaflets the day after the demonstration you want to advertise. For the sort of campaigns people who are reading this book are likely to run, you also need a printer who is **unionised**. Presumably you are convinced of the virtues of this anyway, but should you fall into temptation, remember that if you go to a non-union printer you will be criticised, and perhaps even boycotted, by the Labour Party and Trades Council.

The print union rules are, officially, that no one except a unionised printworker should do any typesetting, design, or printing work. In practice, they take the view that if, say the secretary of a community group lays out a leaflet in his/her spare time, without being paid for it, no one is going to worry much. But if you pay a non-unionised typesetting firm to do the job for you, you will not get a unionised print firm to run it off.

You can find a printer by:

- asking at the library or CAB for the addresses of any community print shops in your area. These are groups set up specifically to help community organisations. They will probably be keen to teach you how to use the equipment, rather than do it for you. The equipment is often quite good. If they cannot help with your specific project, they can probably tell you who can.
- asking the National Graphical Association (see 'Useful addresses') who are one of the main print unions, for their 'fair list' of unionised commercial printers in your area; or asking your local NGA branch, which you can find through the local Trades Council.
- talking to an organisation which has a lot of printing done – try the local Labour Party – about who they use. They will always be looking for speed and reliability, especially during election times.
- simply ringing up different printers and typesetters, or going to see them. Ask if they are unionised, and then ask for quotes. Tell them exactly what you want, and ask how much they will charge. If you don't know exactly, then ask for the most likely amount and size, so you can get an idea of comparative prices. Or ask for the cost of alternatives.

Avoid instant print shops – what they call in the trade 'Kentucky Fried Printing'. They are not unionised, pay their workers badly, and are little, if at all cheaper than reputable places.

Preparations for typesetting

Start off by talking to them about exactly what you want. They will know you are not a professional, and will be glad to advise you, as it will make the final job easier. There is usually a catalogue giving examples of different typefaces, sizes, linespacings, and layouts: or the typesetter may show you examples of other work to help you decide how you want yours set out. You can change your mind once you see a completed copy – but it will cost you money.

Agree a timetable with them, and then make sure both sides keep to it. The actual operations do not take very long, but your piece of work will have to take its place in a queue of jobs, and if you have booked a place and then do not take it up, you will go to the back of the queue. The most crucial time is getting the proofs back to the printer. Try and check them quickly. If there is a problem, say so, and they may be able to adjust the schedule. If you simply turn up late without apologising or explaining, they will not see why they should.

The words you want printed are called **the copy**. The main aim, in getting your copy ready, is to have it very clear. Try to find a typewriter with a carbon ribbon, or at least a new clean nylon ribbon. If no one in your group owns a typewriter, try to find someone who works in an office who can type it in the lunch hour. Type in black, on one side only of clean A4 sheets of strong white paper. Number your sheets, in the top right-hand corner. Make sure you keep a copy of the original.

Put wide margins round – at least two inches on all sides. Use double-line spacing on the typewriter, as this makes it much easier to follow the typescript, especially if there are alterations. But alter as little as you can on the typed copy. If you need to change words, cross out the original words and write the replacement words **legibly** above the crossing out. For other items try to follow the list of special marks that printers use, shown on pages 36–9. If you want to take some words out, score them through completely with a heavy black line. The more corrections there are on the copy, the more difficult it will be for the typesetters to follow. If it is very bad they will charge extra by adding on a 'bad copy surcharge' to the bill.

Start each article or section on a new sheet. Show clearly where new paragraphs start, preferably by **indenting** that is, moving the first word in by three spaces (as at the beginning of this paragraph). Do not break words by hyphens at the end of the line; type them whole on the next line.

Specification

This means giving exact instructions about how the copy is to be set out. The clearer and fuller your instructions are, the easier it is for the typesetter and therefore the quicker the job will be done. Write your instructions clearly and in a different colour from the typed copy – preferably in red. If it is a long job, it is easier and clearer to write out a separate specification sheet, so you do not have to mark everything throughout the copy.

The information the typesetter needs to know is **how long the**

lines should be, and **what size the margins** are; how **far apart** the lines are (called **linespacing**); and the **typeface** and **type size**. The typesetter will have a catalogue of different looking letters for you to choose from. The sort of typeface you choose can make a difference to the image you give. Tell the typesetter if you want some words or characters emphasised by being printed in *italic* or **bold**. Words underlined in the typescript will be set in *italic;* those with a wavy line in **bold**. If you are **quoting someone else's words**, do you want them in a smaller size, or in italic, or indented? Having several different typefaces will put the price up, but not by much. Do you want to put quotations in **single or double** quotation marks?

Do you want **gaps between the paragraphs**, and if so, how wide? Do you want the right-hand edge **justified**, that is, in a straight line (as it is in this book) or ragged, as it will be in your typescript? Do you want your **headlines and sub-headings in the same typeface** or a different one? What size are they to be? If you have several different sizes, mark the headings A, B and C to show the different sizes. How much **space** do you want before and after the headings? Do you want them on the left or right of the page, or in the middle (that is, being **centred**).

The person doing the layout also needs to know what **colour the print** is to be, or, if you're using more than one colour, which words are in which colour.

What **size is the leaflet** to be? Sizes go by numbers, and it is useful to know the measurements: this book is about A5 size; the telephone directory is A4; and A3 is twice the size of the telephone directory.

Style

You need to give clear instructions also about **punctuation**; when **capital letters** are to be used; the treatment of **abbreviation signs** and **figures** (for example are you using % or 'per cent', & or 'and', 6 or 'six'?); and about the treatment of **initials** (do you want WRUG or W.R.U.G?).

Most printers will have a 'house style' written out on a sheet, and will use it unless you tell them not to. Ask to see the style sheet when you are discussing the job with them. If you can use this style when you are getting the copy ready, it will help the typesetters.

When the copy has been typeset, they will do the layout and give you a 'proof' of the leaflet. On pages 41–3 there is a section on doing the layout yourself.

Proof reading

It is your responsibility to read through the proof and mark the mistakes. The chart on pages 36–9 gives the common marks, so try to use them, but if you are in any doubt, just make sure that what you want is clear. You can change the text at proof stage, but it will cost you money. Make clear which are your own alterations, and which are the typesetter's mistakes by using different coloured pens.

Proof-read copy looks a mess but don't worry too much about that. The typesetter's next job is to translate the corrections into a tidy piece of print. If there are a lot of mistakes or changes, the typesetter may offer to send you a second set of proofs. It is up to you whether you agree to this, or trust them to get it right without another check.

If you are using a separate typesetter and printer the typesetter will give you the corrected finished product to take away with you. This is called 'artwork' or 'camera-ready copy'. Treat it with great care. Keep it in an envelope or plastic folder and do not get dirty marks on it. Most modern printers use photographic methods, and you do not want your fingerprints on 5,000 leaflets.

Getting it printed

Let the printer know when you are coming in with your 'camera-ready copy'. Ring up if you are delayed for any reason, and explain.

Talk to the printer about the **sort of paper** you want. Thick, good quality paper is a lot more expensive than cheaper, ordinary paper. Think about what you want the leaflet for. If it's for handing out in the street, it will have to stand up to possible rain and rough handling, but for picking up at a meeting, strength matters less. Your design will also affect the paper. If you are printing both sides and have a lot of solid headlines, you will need fairly thick paper to ensure that the words do not show through on the other side. You may find the printer can help cut your costs, if you are not too fussy about the colour of the leaflets, by using offcuts – bits left over from other jobs.

If something goes wrong, and you do not get what you asked for, **complain there and then** – politely – and if it clearly is the printer's fault, it should be run off for you again free. But if your instructions were not clear, or if it is just that it doesn't look the way you thought it would, do not expect much sympathy. If you get it redone in those circumstances, you will have to pay.

Proof-correction marks

Instruction	Textual mark	Marginal mark
Substitute or insert comma	/ through character or ⋏ where required	̂ˀ/
Substitute or insert semi-colon	/ through character or ⋏ where required	;/
Substitute or insert full stop	/ through character or ⋏ where required	⊙/
Substitute or insert colon	/ through character or ⋏ where required	⊙/
Substitute or insert interrogation mark	/ through character or ⋏ where required	?/
Substitute or insert exclamation mark	/ through character or ⋏ where required	!/
Insert parentheses	⋏ or ⋏⋏	(//)
Insert (square) brackets	⋏ or ⋏⋏	[//]
Insert hyphen	⋏	/-/

Instruction	Textual mark	Marginal mark
Insert en (half-em) rule	⋏	*en* or *N*
Insert apostrophe	⋏	⸌
Insert single quotation marks	⋏ or ⋏⋏	⸌ ⸌
Insert double quotation marks	⋏ or ⋏⋏	66 99
Insert ellipsis	⋏	... /
Insert oblique stroke	⋏	Ø
Insert in text the matter indicated in margin	⋏	*New matter followed by* /
Delete	Strike through characters to be deleted	♂
Delete and close up	Strike through characters to be deleted and use close-up sign	⌒
Leave as printed	. . . . under characters to remain	(stet)
Change to italic	——— under characters to be altered	(ital.)

Instruction	Textual mark		Marginal mark
Change to capital letters	≡	under characters to be altered	(caps)
Change to bold type	〰	under characters to be altered	(bold)
Change to lower case	Encircle characters to be altered		(l.c.)
Change to roman type	Encircle characters to be altered		(rom)
Move matter to right	〔	at left side of group to be moved	〔
Move matter to left	〕	at right side of group to be moved	〕
Take over character(s) or line to next line, column or page	〔		(take over)
Take back character(s) or line to previous line, column or page	〕		(take back)
Raise lines	⤒	over lines to be moved	(raise)
	⎵	under lines to be moved	

Instruction	Textual mark	Marginal mark
Lower lines	⌐¬ over lines to be moved ↓ under lines to be moved	(lower)
Begin a new paragraph	[before first word of new paragraph	(n.p.)
No fresh paragraph here	⌐ between paragraphs	(r.o.)
Insert omitted portion of copy	⅄	(out see copy)
Close up – delete space between characters	⌒ linking characters	⌒
Insert space	⅄	#
Make space appear equal between words	/ between words	(eq. #)
Reduce space between words	/ between words	(less #)
Transpose	∿ between characters or words, numbered when necessary	(trs)
Place in centre of line	Indicate position with ⌐ ¬	(centre)
Indent one em	⌐	☐

Cost

It is very difficult to give an exact cost, because it will vary a lot in different parts of the country, and anyway figures quickly get out of date. But to give some idea, here are a few sample quotes given by printers in 1984 when this book was at proof stage:

	Printer	
	A	B
A5 leaflet, printed both sides one colour (5,000)	£72	£104
A4 leaflet, printed both sides two colours (5,000)	£140	£177
Tickets, postcard size, printed one side, one colour (500)	£27 (+ VAT)	£48 (+VAT)

Extras, such as having embossed letters or crinkled edges on tickets, folding and stapling leaflets, having things on glossy paper, using half-tones (see page 43) all cost money. Work out what you really need, what you can do without, and what you can do yourself, like folding leaflets.

Try to pay the printer quickly, especially if you want to use that firm again. Small printers work on very tight margins, and need the money.

Duplicating

For a small number of leaflets – say less than 500 – a duplicator is best, if you can find a good one. It can also be quicker, and less daunting if you are just starting off, so you may well want to use it even for larger quantities. It may be easier to find someone who will let you use their duplicator and only charge you the cost of the paper. To find one, try the sort of place listed in chapter 2. Your best bet is a **political party**; a **trade union office**; or **a school.**

If you are lucky, they will also have an **electrostencil machine**, which is a clever device which transfers your finished work to a wax stencil. This means you can use the same sort of layout as if you were getting something printed. Photographs, though, do not come out well. It is also best not to have too many solid black lines, since the ink tends to run. You can get electrostencils made commercially.

Without an electrostencil, you will be restricted to what you can type on the stencil, or draw on it with a sharp point (called **a stylus**). If you use a good typewriter and set out your words clearly, spacing them well apart, you can still produce a good-looking leaflet. Typewriters have a special setting, usually marked with a white blob, that you press when you start cutting a stencil. This stops the ribbon coming up when you press the keys. If you do not use this setting, the stencil will not be properly cut and the words will not come out.

Getting it ready

If you are duplicating or photocopying, or using a community group's printing machine, you will need to produce your own 'camera-ready copy' – that is, the material you want to produce, in the final form you want it to be.

Producing a layout is not difficult, but it does involve concentration, confidence, and neat fingers. If there is no one in your group with these qualities, pay a typesetting firm to produce a decent job which will make an impact.

To lay out properly you also need the right equipment. If you would have to buy it all, it is likely to be cheaper to go to a typesetter. But if you can find someone who will lend you the equipment, or somewhere you can use it, this will work out cheaper. Try a **community print-shop** or a **resource centre**; a local **community newspaper**; a well-established **local group who produce their own newsletter**, as well as groups like yours. What about the vicar, the Allotments Society, or the Residents' Association? The **art or design department** in your local secondary school, or Adult Education College may be able to help.

You are creating something that has to be photographed. You will need the following equipment:

- **Layout sheets**. These are sheets of plain paper with squares ruled on them in a very faint blue, which does not show up in the final printing, to help you keep your columns straight. You could rule your own with a **drop out pencil**. This is a light blue pencil (any one will do) so that you can draw faint blue lines on the paper for margins or working out spacing.
- **Clear plastic ruler and set square**. Pinch them from a child's geometry set.
- **A soft rubber** to clean the artwork. The best thing for rubbing off surplus glue, and other marks, is a ball of congealed Cow Gum (see below).
- **Black pens.** The professionals use drawing pens with different width nibs, but all you really need is a good clear felt tip or fibre tip.

- **A typewriter**, preferably electric, with a carbon ribbon. Someone who works in an office may be able to help you, if no one in the group has one. Get them to type out all the words you are going to need typed, and then you can cut them up and arrange them as you like. If you have only got a manual typewriter, clean the type with an old toothbrush, put in a new ribbon, and type as evenly as you can.

- **Dry transfer lettering**, like Letraset or Meccanorm. This comes in sheets and you rub over the letters to transfer them on to the paper. You have to buy a whole sheet at a time and are left with half the letters unused, which makes it expensive, so if you can find someone who already has a stock you will save money. Work out carefully what you will need before buying, and stick to one or two styles. If you buy a fancy style on impulse, remember you may get sick of it before you have finished the sheet. You can buy this at art suppliers or a good stationer's.

- **White correcting fluid**, so you can paint over mistakes and marks. Tippex is the most common one, but contains some rather nasty chemicals; there is a water-based one called Mistake Out.

- **Sharp scissors**, and a **Stanley knife, scalpel, or razor** to cut things out and paste them on your layout sheet. Take care of these, as they need to be very sharp. If only for this reason, keep children out of the way while laying out.

- **Glue**. The best sort is called Cow Gum, because it was invented by Henry Cow, not because it is made from dead ones. It lets you slide the bits of artwork around before finally sticking them down. You can use a bit of cardboard to spread it, or buy a special applicator. Cow Gum goes all over the back of the piece you are sticking, but leave a small border round the edges, and do not put on too much glue – it needs to stick flat without bubbles.

- **A layout board**, or a smooth hard surface – a piece of glass, a formica table top, a piece of hardboard – to work on. If you are cutting out with a scalpel or Stanley knife it will cut into wood, so don't use a valued piece of furniture.

Having assembled all your equipment, chucked the children out, and taken the phone off the hook, get all your items ready and arrange them as you want them to look. Do a rough drawing, so you can work out what is to be in large letters and what in smaller letters. Then you can start pasting down.

The text will have been produced on the typewriter, and you can cut it up to fill the space. **The headlines**, unless your have an expert designer in your group, are done with dry transfer lettering. Rub them on to a **separate piece of paper**, using a guideline to get them straight, and then cut them out and stick them on to the layout sheet. If there are cracks in the letters, touch them up with a black pen. You can also buy an amazing range of **other decorations**, from pointing fingers to flowers and all sorts of squiggles.

Leave spaces for any **pictures.** You might want a cartoon, or a picture, say of the hospital you are trying to save. You can use any drawing you like so long as it is in black and white, with no greys. This is because duplicators cannot usually cope with **photographs** at all. They *may* work, but the only sure way is by using a printer. The photograph is turned into **half-tones** which translates the photograph into a series of tiny black dots. A printer may be able to do this, or tell you a firm of plate-makers to go to, but it will cost money. Plate-makers will also be able to blow up or shrink a photograph for you to fit the space. You may be able to use a photograph that has already been printed somewhere else, but this does not always work; check before including the photograph in the layout. The clearer it is, the better it will come out.

Don't borrow cartoons, drawings, or photographs from commercial organisations or newspapers or famous people **without asking permission**. You are breaking their copyright and they can ask you to pay for it. Rather than risk it, find someone in your group who can draw, take a good photograph, or use a child's drawing.

Running it off

Duplicators come in all shapes and sizes, and they all have their little whims. **Check what the one you are borrowing is like** before you start your design.

Some duplicators will not print on **the second** side of a piece of paper at all. They just chew the paper up and spread it all over the room. A good modern machine can give nearly as good a job as printing; but work from an ancient machine on its last legs will look like it.

It is vital to be shown how to use the machine you are borrowing. If possible, get your instructor to put the stencil on the machine for you, get it straight, and make sure the ink is flowing before s/he goes away and leaves you to your fate. **Always try out on scrap paper first**.

When you have done the work, clean the machine properly – and probably yourself, too; it is a rare and enviable skill to be able to duplicate without getting covered in ink. So do not wear your best clothes while duplicating.

A common mistake when trying to run off leaflets is **discovering you have got the wrong sort of stencil**. Different makes of duplicator use stencils with different sets of holes at the top, where they hook into the machine. Check carefully what sort you need, or use a 'multi-head' which is supposed to fit all makes. If it is too late and you have got it wrong, fish around in the waste-paper basket for a stencil with the right top and cut this off neatly, then stick it to yours in place of the wrong one. Make sure it lies flat. This does, however, make it more difficult to get it straight on the machine, and it reduces the number of copies you can get from each stencil.

Another common mistake is **getting the words on the second side the wrong way up**. Check before you start on the second side that you have got all the paper in the machine the right way round, and go slowly until you are sure. If you make a mistake, there is nothing for it but to throw the paper away and start again. People get very irritated at upside-down leaflets.

Distribution

Where do you want your leaflets to get to? Look at the list of examples on pages 80–81.

- Helen's women's group wants them to get to members of other women's groups; so she needs to make sure that contacts in those groups have them to hand out.
- Abdul's anti-cuts campaign and Hugh's Labour Party both want to get to the general public. They will need to give them out in the street, and push them through doors. But they also want to get them to people in organisations like other Labour Parties and trade unions, to make sure someone comes to their meeting; so they can ask those organisations to put them in their mailings.
- Marie's Tenants' Association want them to get to tenants on the estate, so they will be putting the leaflet through letter boxes there.

■ Phil's Parent Teacher Association want them to go to parents, so they give them to the children to take home, and also hand them out at going-home time at the gate.

Using other organisations

Most secretaries of trades councils, unions, and political parties, will not mind being asked to put a leaflet about another sympathetic organisation with their routine mailing to members. To arrange this **contact the secretary in good time**, find out how many are needed, and when the mailing is going out. **Get the leaflets to him/her before the day the mailing is going out.** Do not expect them to come and collect your leaflets; *they* are doing *you* a favour, not the other way around. Provide a few extras, in case some turn out to have been messed up in the printing. **Offer to do the same for the other organisation** in the future.

It is important to send leaflets out a long time in advance of the event. They may well sit in the branch secretary's file for a while before being brought to the members' attention at the next meeting. At least a month is needed.

In the streets

The law on obstruction, which is the main offence you could find yourselves in trouble for, is covered in chapter 7. The police will usually start by asking you to move on. Go along the road a bit and try again: but they may end up arresting you if you don't stop. They can do this even if there are other people handing out leaflets whom they do not arrest.

■ In a 1963 court case, some students were prosecuted for selling *Peace News* in a place where there were other paper sellers. The judge said that he could not consider whether it was reasonable for the police to prosecute, only whether the alleged obstruction was reasonable.

There may be local by-laws against handing out leaflets; the library or the town hall should be able to tell you. The penalties for breaking by-laws are usually low, but if you argue with the police about them you may get arrested for obstruction instead. There have also been cases where people have been arrested on a charge of dropping litter!

You can also have difficulties with shopkeepers, who may object to you standing outside their shops handing out 'political' leaflets. They may call the police if you refuse to move on when asked. Covered shopping centres are usually private property, and if the manager objects to you handing out leaflets s/he can ask you to leave, or send security guards to do so. You are trespassing if you do not leave when asked.

These problems do not arise very often, though. The difficulty you are much more likely to come against is that leafletters will not do very much at a time, because they get bored, cold and wet (or too hot, if the sun is shining!). You need to be fairly thick-skinned to hand out leaflets in a shopping centre, because a lot of people are too busy thinking about what to buy to want to take a leaflet about anything, and it is easier to ignore you altogether than to say 'no thank you'. After about an hour of this, you tend to feel you are invisible. Before taking it personally, though, remember the number of times you have done just the same to other leafletters.

It works best if there is someone with a loudspeaker, either fixed on top of a car or hand-held, working with the people who are handing out leaflets. In this way, you can announce what the leaflet is about, and so people know whether they are interested, and take a leaflet if they are. If they have their hands too full of shopping and children, at least they will still know what is going on. See page 58 for more details about loudspeakers.

You can also hand out leaflets outside factories, railway stations, health clinics, unemployment benefit offices – anywhere that the group you want to attract might be. Important points to remember are:

- The **organiser must be there at the time** you have agreed. Most people will arrive anything up to half an hour late, but if there are one or two who come on time, they will get depressed and probably go away if there is nothing happening and no organiser.
- Make sure **you have enough leaflets**. It is annoying for helpers if they put themselves out and there is not enough to do. On a busy shopping street, for a popular cause, you can hand out 1,000 leaflets in an hour. Fewer people will take them if it is cold, wet or windy and they will not want to take their hands out of their pockets; or if the leaflet is not immediately appealing;
- Try not, as a leafletter, to get tangled up in long arguments with members of the public. You want people to come and

ask for more details, and to tell you their views, but if they are going on and on, after a while say something like, 'We're not going to convince each other, and I must get on with handing out my leaflets. Why not come to our meeting and put your point of view there?' More difficult to deal with are those who support you, but don't realise that by telling you at great length how wonderful the Health Service is they are stopping you convincing other people. With them, you just have to be very tactful.

Door-to-door

This is often a better idea than handing them out in the street, especially if you are trying to contact people from a particular patch.

You may be able to persuade children to help, but it is wise to have an adult in charge, as otherwise if they get bored they may shove all the leaflets in the bin and go to the park. The adult can walk along the street folding the leaflets and handing them to the children, who then run up and down the garden paths putting them through letter boxes. It is a good way of exhausting children, but they get wise to it after the first time and will probably need bribing.

You can organise a **mass delivery**. A lot of people go out together to an estate or area, with an organiser who hands out bundles of leaflets and sends each person off to a block or street, which s/he ticks off on a list. When they have done each bit people come back for more, until the whole area has been covered – when everyone goes to the pub. This method is useful if you are trying to create interest in a new area, and can get a well-disciplined group together. It also makes a bit of an impact, which is helpful during elections and big campaigns.

Alternatively, you can **give individuals responsibility for each doing a patch**. Bundle up the leaflets at home, label each with the name of a street, and either take them round to people who have agreed to deliver them or hand them out to volunteers at a meeting. This means trusting people to do what they say they will, and there is usually someone who forgets about the leaflet until the night before your meeting and then rushes round at midnight putting them out. Don't give any one person too much – it won't get done. A hundred terrace houses take about 20 minutes to deliver. Try to give people patches they know, and compensate

for difficult patches – with long driveways or steep steps – by
giving them fewer houses.

Other useful points are:

- If they are going through letter boxes, **don't make them too
  big** – A5 (the size of this book) is best.
- **Fold them up** before you go out into the street, especially if
  it is cold or wet, to save time once you are there;
- Push the leaflets **right through the letter box** (unless there is
  a dog on the other side waiting to eat your fingers). People
  do not like having leaflets hanging out of the letter box, as it
  can be a sign to burglars that the house is empty.
- Shut gates behind you and do not go over people's flower
  beds, even if it is a short cut to the next house, because it
  annoys people.

A group like a Tenants' Association, trying to get people to a
meeting to report back on their campaign, may not want simply to
put the leaflet through the door, but to knock and give it to the
person, and to say what it's about. This is well worth doing, but it
takes a lot longer, and you need to be sure that every helper
understands the issues properly. See pages 160–3 about organising 'canvassing'.

Other ideas for distribution

- Send a leaflet home with children from school. You can
  reduce the chances of it being used as a paper dart on the
  way home if you put it in an envelope and address it.
- Leave piles of leaflets in places where interested people are
  likely to be, like the launderette, an old people's club room,
  or a post office. Put them on chairs, or hand them out at the
  door, before another meeting.

It is difficult to tell how effective leaflets are. One experienced
Labour Party activist calculates on one person coming to a
meeting for every hundred distributed, so if you distribute 10,000
leaflets you get 100 people to the meeting. This is only guesswork
and it may sound depressing, but if you look at it the other way
round, that for every one person who comes to your meeting
there are probably a dozen who read the leaflets, find out what is
going on, and perhaps show their support in other ways, it is less
so.

Posters

People do not stand in front of posters for long to absorb a mass of detail, so you need to put **essential information** on the poster, and no more. The basics are:

- the date of the event;
- where it is happening;
- what time;
- what it is about;
- who is speaking;
- who is organising it.

A picture or cartoon to illustrate the point you are making can be useful. It needs to be clear and unfussy, and the connections with the event should be obvious. If you cannot get a suitable drawing or a photograph, manage without. Be careful about using copyrighted pictures without permission. Disney will sue you for a fee if you use Mickey Mouse to illustrate your views of the local council.

Use large plain print, especially if your poster is going up in supporters' windows. A lot of people have poor eyesight, and will not want to press their faces up against windows to read the poster.

Making and printing posters is time-consuming and expensive, so work out first what you need them for, so you don't get too many. Look at the examples of different sorts of meetings on pages 79–80.

- Helen's women's group doesn't need any posters at all.
- Abdul's anti-cuts campaign needs a lot to put up in public places, to flypost, to ask supporters to put in their windows, and to try to get put up in shops and launderettes. They decide on 300.
- Marie's Tenants' Association committee need about eight to go in the TA clubroom, the lifts, and the entrances to the blocks.
- Hugh's Labour Party canot risk being taken to court by breaking the law flyposting, so they need fewer posters than Abdul; they decide on 100.
- Phil's Parent/Teachers only need two, one for the school entrance and one for the staff room.

The people who need a lot of posters, Hugh and Abdul, will

need to operate differently from Marie and Phil, who only need a few. Marie and Phil can do theirs by hand, and need spend no time worrying about putting them up. Hugh and Abdul need to get posters printed, and to make sure someone distributes them. Hugh, with a 'political' meeting, will find it difficult to get people to put posters up; whereas if there is widespread opposition to the closure Abdul is fighting, it will be quite easy to find willing people.

Producing posters

There are four ways of producing posters: writing them out **by hand**; getting them **printed**; **enlarging** a small original **on a photo-copier**; and **silk screening.**

You can do a combination of these; if your group is having a series of meetings which all need to be advertised in just a few places, such as a workplace union branch, you could spend some money getting posters printed or silk screened to give the name of the organisation, and the place where the meetings are held, but leaving blank spaces for you to fill in the date and the subject of the particular meeting.

By Hand

This is cheap, since it only costs the price of a large sheet of paper and a couple of thick felt-tip pens. But it takes a long time. You also need to be able to letter neatly. It is more interesting if a group get together one evening and do them all at once, rather than let one person slog away alone.

Getting posters printed

This involves finding a printer who can do large sizes. Phone around printers in Yellow Pages, or look on posters locally to see who did them. Find out if they want you to get it ready for printing, or if they will do this (see chapter 4 about this). A printer can usually enlarge something you have already done – perhaps the leaflet you are using to hand out in the street, so long as the proportions are right. You can have your poster in colour on white paper, or in black or another colour on coloured paper. 'Dayglo' – brilliant coloured paper – is expensive but eye-catching. Having more than one colour ink also costs extra, because the paper has to go through the presses twice, but it can be worthwhile. Whatever the final colours will be, all the original work should be done in black, as this makes the printing process easier.

Silk screening

Although you can do this yourself, it needs a certain amount of special equipment. For people who may have this, and know how to use it, try the local Art or Further Education College, Adult Education Institute, the art department of a secondary school, or a resource centre or community printshop. The *Alternative Print Handbook* (see under 'Useful books') explains silk screening.

Enlarging a leaflet

Many modern photocopiers can enlarge to A3 size (four times the size of this book). If you can find an organisation with the right supplies, you can use coloured paper, but you will only be able to print in black ink. Drawings enlarge successfully, photographs less so. It is cheap, and not difficult to produce a reasonable result, but you need someone really skilled in design to make it eye-catching. You can produce as many or as few as you want. Someone in your group may be able to borrow a good photocopier at work – with or without permission – or there may be a commercial photocopying firm in your town, if there is no community group with the right facilities.

Distribution

The law

Posters count as advertisements, and are covered by the Town and Country Planning (Control of Advertisements) Regulations. The local council has power to refuse or agree to the display of advertisements in their area. They cannot usually object to the design or content of a poster, but only to where it is put. If a commercial firm has got agreement to posters going up on a particular site, there is no need for anyone who hires part of that site to apply for permission as well.

Posters advertising local, non-commercial events of a 'religious, political, social, educational, cultural or recreational character', and posters about parliamentary or local elections, do not need planning permission so long as:

- you have the permission of the site owner;
- the poster does not block or obscure the view of the road;
- it is no bigger than 0.6 metre (about 2 feet) (election posters can be bigger). This means that hanging a large banner in front of a hospital or block of flats is against the law, but people are very rarely prosecuted;

- it is not put up more than 28 days before the event, and is taken down within a fortnight afterwards.

Tenants do not need the permission of their landlords to put up posters by law, but there are other ways in which the landlord can make life difficult. If tenants nail or glue something to a wall, they may be breaking the terms of the tenancy, if it says they need the landlord's permission to make a 'material change'.

Flyposting

This means sticking up posters without permission from the owner or the local authority. It is illegal. It is not often prosecuted unless the council or police are feeling nasty, or you are caught red-handed. The law punishes the person or organisation benefiting by the poster, as well as the person sticking it up. You can be fined £100, plus £5 for each day a poster stays up after the court has ordered it to be taken down.

To go out flyposting, you need the posters, wallpaper paste, and a large brush. A few sensible precautions are:

- Put your paste bucket in a large carrier bag so it is not too conspicuous.
- Put your posters in a bag too, not in a roll under your arm.
- Choose a time when not too many police are about, like early evening or Sunday morning.
- Have one person acting as lookout; if the police approach, or someone else asks what you are doing in a tone of authority, don't argue, just clear off, and come back later to finish the job.

However, do not be in so much of a hurry when you are actually sticking up the poster that you don't do it properly. Cover it all over with a lot of paste. Otherwise it will simply be torn down, and your efforts wasted.

Flypost on corrugated iron, or derelict buildings, rather than places in use. The police are less likely to prosecute if no one is interested enough to complain.

When you are making a poster to flypost, put the basic information – date, time and place of meeting – in the middle, because that is the bit least likely to be torn down.

People's windows

Ask all your supporters to put posters up. They will not want them too big – no larger than A3 – otherwise they will block out too much light. If your cause is controversial, like Troops Out of Ireland or Gay Rights, people may not be happy about taking posters, because they might get their windows broken.

Shops
Get some people to go round the local shops, post offices and launderettes, asking them to put posters up. This is hard work, and it can be depressing if you get a lot of refusals. Allocate the job to two or three thick-skinned but nice people, each of whom takes on a specific street or part of one. Shops will not usually take a poster for anything political, or for unpopular or controversial causes. They are afraid that customers who disagree with that particular cause will stop using the shop. You will get more put up if they are small – A4 size at most – as people will not want to fill up too much space in their windows.

Public places
Try the library, community centres, clubroms. Libraries almost always have a notice-board, although they may restrict it to 'non-political' events. Ask whoever is in charge to put your poster up. Some areas also have a system of public notice-boards in the streets, on which people can advertise. Ask at the library or the town hall about this.

Also try putting up posters in the lifts and entrance halls of blocks of flats. They get torn down, so be ready to replace them.

If your event has an appeal to a particular group, think hard about where they will be going, and try to get the poster put up there.

- Bill is organising a meeting about employment law. He distributes copies to union branch secretaries via the Trades Council and asks them to put them up in the workplace.
- Rosie takes round a poster announcing a march about the nationality laws to the Sikh and Hindu temples, and the mosque.

Advertising

Some groups will not want to advertise, and in some cases, like a small group just setting up, it might be actually harmful. Think, before you spend the money, whether the ads will be read by the people you want to come to your event.

Local papers

Which papers actually cover the area? Often there are two or three 'local' papers, but only one will circulate widely in the patch you are interested in. Advertising in them is fairly cheap, and quite a lot of people read them. Much of the profit for local papers comes from ads, so they will be keen to sell you space and help you get the best results.

There are three main sorts of advertisement: **classified, semi-display** and **display**.

Display is the most expensive; these are the bold advertisements in boxes. Semi-display look rather the same, but do not have lines round them, so they don't stand out so much, and are much cheaper. If you can, go into the newspaper office with the wording you want, and ask to discuss it with someone, or talk over the phone. If you have the words written out, and make clear which ones you want bigger, the paper will usually lay them out for you, but sometimes you may have to take in the artwork (see page 41). Other points to remember are:

- If you want **to put in a picture**, or your organisation's symbol, you will have to pay to have a 'block' made, and this will be **much more expensive**. It might be worth it if you can use the block for other things, like a leaflet also advertising the event.
- It is often a good idea to have your ad **'run of column'** which means that it appears on the news pages, rather than at the back among all the others. In many local papers the ads are not read by many people, whereas the news pages are.
- If you have only a small amount of money, use it for a 'double column' ad. This means it is wide, spreading across two columns, which is more eye-catching than a long thin one going down a column.

Put your ad in the edition that is coming out a few days before your event. If this is, say, on the Wednesday, get it in the paper for the previous Friday. This may mean getting it to them on the Monday or Tuesday before, or even earlier. Ring up well in advance and find out.

Other places

Other possible places to advertise, to reach the people you're interested in, are:

- **free advertising papers** – so long as they use union printers and journalists, and are not therefore being boycotted by the labour movement locally. Find out by ringing up a local newspaper and speaking to an NUJ or print union representative;
- local **'community' newspapers**;
- the **free 'listings' services** run by national magazines like *New Statesman* and, at least in London and a few other big cities, specialist publications like *City Limits*;
- **magazines** that your particular interest group is likely to read, like *Spare Rib* for feminists or *Sanity* for peace campaigners;
- tenants' association **newsletters**;
- or even the **parish magazine**, if it is delivered to everyone, not just regular church-goers. They probably will not take 'political' ads, though.

You will need to phone each of these to find out how much they cost, what they need from you, and when the ad has got to be in. Do this in good time, particularly for monthly magazines which have long deadlines.

Other ideas for publicity

There are other, more imaginative things you can use to publicise your cause. For instance there are **stickers**, **badges**, **balloons**, and **T-shirts**. You can sell any of these to raise money, or give them away, and use them before, during, and after a particular event to gather support for your cause. On page 14 there are suggestions for finding suppliers.

Stickers

These need to be printed by specialist firms. Look in Yellow Pages or the Thomson Local Directory under 'Label makers' or 'Label printers', or ask other campaigning groups who they use.

You can use up vast numbers very quickly. Children love them, and if you are handing them out in a school playground you can get rid of a whole roll at a time. They can be put anywhere – on doors, lamp posts or policemen – but they tend to leave a mark on paintwork when peeled off, and the owners of, for instance, parked cars, tend not to take too kindly to them. A good idea is to get a large number of eye-catching stickers printed to advertise the date of an event, and give sheets or rolls out to as many people as possible to distribute.

Badges

These also usually need a specialist firm, but it is possible to buy a hand-operated badge maker, and one of the organisations listed on page 17 might have one. Making your own badges takes time, and is quite hard work, so allow for this. The design of badges or stickers can usually be done by the firm chosen, for a price, but you usually need to give them an idea of size, shape, words, and colour. Phone first, and get a quote, not only on the price, but also on the time it will take, and then do a sketch to send them.

Badges are longer-lasting than stickers, and more expensive to produce, so use them for a general slogan rather than to publicise a particular event. You will have to pay 10–15p per badge, but the larger the number you order, the lower the cost of each one. You can sell them for perhaps double what you have paid, so they can be a useful source of money. Keeping track of this will be an extra job for the treasurer.

Balloons

These also go down very well with children. Again you need a specialist firm. Look in Yellow Pages or your Thomson Local, not just under 'Balloons', but also 'Carnival supplies' or 'Novelties'. Get lots printed, with a good slogan – one Labour Party said 'Lift Off with Labour' – and hand them out to children at the same time as giving leaflets to their parents. Remember that you need some way of inflating them. This involves either **a balloon pump –** from a toyshop; or **a helium cylinder**. You can probably hire this from the balloon shop. It makes the balloons lighter than air so they float away. The extra expense, though, means you will probably need to sell the balloons rather than handing them out.

T-shirts

An effective way of drawing attention to your event is to have the people handing out leaflets, or loudspeaking, to wear identical T-shirts advertising it. Most main shopping centres have places where you can get a few T-shirts printed fairly easily. Alternatively, you could write or paint on plain T-shirts – most people have the odd one – with Dylon fabric paint, which you can get from a craft shop.

If you want larger numbers, you could either get them made, or screen-print your own. The *Alternative Print Handbook* (see under 'Useful books') tells you how to screen-print. It also tells you how to make your own screen. The problem is that if this goes wrong, you can waste a lot of T-shirts, which is expensive. A compromise is to get the screen made professionally, and then do the printing yourself, getting the T-shirts from a wholesaler. Some Technical or Further Education Colleges have the equipment to produce screens photographically, and might help you. If you do not have a contact, ring up and ask for the department that runs courses on printing, and try to speak to a technician there. See pages 17–19 for other ideas on finding help.

Getting the whole job done professionally would have cost, in 1983, about £2 a shirt. There would also be the cost of the artwork and the screen, which would be another £30–£50. So the more you get, the cheaper each one will be.

When you have found a printer, ring up and find out **prices**, not only per T-shirt, but also for getting the design ready, the screen, carriage, and VAT. **What form** do they want the design in? If you can only supply a sketch, can they get it 'camera ready' and how much will this cost? **How long** will this take? What are their **delivery arrangements**?

Remember:

- The **amount you spend initially will be quite large**, and it may take a long time to get your money back.
- It gives **the treasurer a heavy job to do**; you could make someone else responsible for organising it.
- You will need **somewhere to store** at least one large box, probably for quite a while.

All these ideas cost money, and are only worth doing if you are sure you can use them effectively. Plan your distribution **before you spend the money**, not afterwards. And allow yourselves **plenty of time**. It would be disastrous to get the stickers in the post the day of the demonstration they were supposed to be advertising!

Slogan painting

Unlike the ideas above this is cheap, but it is illegal; the police are more likely to prosecute, and the owners to take a dim view of your artwork, than with flyposting. Water-based paint soaks into brickwork, so if you are taken to court you may have to pay for the cost of cleaning it, which could be high. On the other hand, so long as you are not caught in the act, it is very difficult to trace the actual person who painted a particular slogan.

Incidentally, painting *out* slogans, for instance racist graffiti, is also illegal, but not often prosecuted. If you are planning this, try asking the owner's permission first, because many owners will be glad to see it done.

Loudspeakers

One other activity which is useful for publicity is to send out a car with a loudspeaker fixed on it. Do this either **on the Saturday before your event**, when people are out shopping; or **in the early evening**, before your meeting starts.

The law is that loudspeakers are forbidden everywhere, between 9 o'clock at night and 9 o'clock in the morning, and sometimes for longer than that according to local by-laws. These sometimes say that you have to give written notice 48 hours in advance to the police station in the area where you intend to use loudspeakers. Check at the town hall or at the library. In London there are special regulations about what you can say; you are not allowed to call people to a meeting, simply to announce that the meeting exists. In practice if the police are not bothered they will not take any notice of you anyway. If they get complaints, even if you're following the rules, they will say you are disturbing the peace. Do not worry about the law too much; but remember that using loudspeakers may put people off, if they are too loud or it is too late at night.

If you have not done it before, **practise**. Find a large open space, and ask a critical friend to stand some way away and tell you how you sound. You will be surprised how slowly you have to speak, and how careful you have to be to finish every word, for it to come over clearly.

Use your loudspeaker to **repeat a short, simple message** over and over again. Different people will be hearing it each time, as you drive along. It gets really difficult to keep the message straight after a while, and you start mixing up your words, **so get people to take it in turns**, changing over fairly frequently. You can put a message on tape, but this tends to sound a bit stilted. Alternatively, put some music on tape (especially if it is relevant to the cause) and play that when your voice gets tired.

Another idea is to **ask an important person** to do some loud-speaking for you, and use their name as an additional draw. For instance, the local MP could say 'This is Charlotte Despard MP and I am calling on you to support the St Mary's Hospital campaign.'

For people to hear what is being said over a loudspeaker, the car needs **to go very slowly**, which does not do the engine much good; be sure the owner realises this. Also make sure car, driver, and any passengers are insured (see page 238).

5.

Getting the press to your event

This chapter goes very briefly into the basics of getting press coverage for your event. Most of the information in it is taken from *Using the Media* (see 'Useful books'). This is comprehensive, and you will find it useful to get a copy from the library, or consult it in the reference section.

It is sensible for a group to appoint a press officer – or more than one if necessary. **Decide before they start the job how much freedom they have**. Is every press release to be checked with the group? Or with the chair? Have they authority to act on their own judgement? Having decided, **stand by** that person if press releases get distorted or messed about by the media.

Local reporters

The Thomson Local Directory (see page 13) will give you the addresses of your local papers, and also the local radio stations and television. If you want to contact a national paper, look at a copy to find the address and phone number.

Many towns also have a freelance 'agency', that is, independent journalists who work on their own or in small groups, covering different stories, and then sell them to newsrooms in different papers, radio and TV. A short-cut to contacting all the different newsrooms in an area is to get in touch with such an agency. If they think there is a story in it, they will sell it for you. Find their address in the Yellow Pages (look under 'Journalists'); alternatively, your local library may have the Freelance Directory published by the NUJ.

You could also, if you think your story is big enough, send or phone through a release to the Press Association (see 'Useful addresses'). They will then send it to any national or regional newspaper they think will be interested, through their own system.

Do not forget **local radio stations**; send them anything you send to the local papers, and ring them up and offer assistance. They are usually run on a shoe-string, with very few journalists. However, the number of people who listen is very small. **Local television** has more of an impact, and warning people that you are going to bring in the cameras often gets action.

Making contact

Having decided who you want to tell about your event, issue a press release. This should be short – the shorter the better – and clearly set out. **You really must type it**, double spaced and on one side of the paper, preferably headed notepaper, saying PRESS RE-LEASE in capitals at the top.

Journalists are busy, and are interested in easy stories that they do not have to work at understanding. Journalist training schools teach a set of rules called the five Ws, on what should go in. These are:

- **what** is happening;
- **who** is doing it;
- **why** is it happening;
- **where** is it happening;
- **when** is it happening?

Check you have included all these facts needed by a journalist. Get all the basic facts in at the beginning. The first paragraph should be a complete story in itself, with the extra detail following because the paper might print only the first paragraph; even if it prints the whole lot, many readers skim and only read the first paragraph anyway.

At the end, put 'for further details, contact . . .' and then a name, with work and home telephone numbers. The journalist may want to check if the story is genuine, and may not use it if queries cannot be followed up easily.

Address the press release to the newsdesk. If you know particular journalists, or if you think from the way they write stories in your local paper that particular people might be sympathetic, send them a copy as well.

If you think there is a particular national radio or television programme that might be interested in your event, send your press release to the producer. Find out the name by looking in *Radio Times* or *TV Times*, or by ringing up the TV station and asking the switchboard. If you send something in without addressing it to a particular person, or to the newsdesk, it will probably get lost.

Most events give you the chance to get into the local papers **three times**: when you first announce it is happening; when it is about to happen; and when it has happened. If you use these chances, people who do not come to the meeting will still get to know what it is about. Taking Abdul's anti-cuts meeting in chapter 8 as an example, his three press releases can develop the story.

■ Abdul issues the first press release when he has got a date, a speaker, and a place; it is brief, just these facts plus a summary of the issues.

The second goes out to catch the paper that comes out just before the meeting. It repeats the details and expands on the issues a bit. As he has an important speaker coming, Abdul adds a 'Note to Editors' saying when and where s/he can be contacted on the day of the meeting. If it were a theatre group, or something else that would make a good photo, he would add a 'Note to Picture Editor' too.

Abdul then phones up the people he has sent the information to, or the newsdesk, a day or two before, and asks, 'Are you coming to the meeting? Do you need any more details?' He offers any help he can, including arranging to meet reporters at a specific point in the proceedings, to introduce them to the chairperson and speakers, for instance.

He sends out the third and final press release, immediately after the meeting, saying what went on. The draft can be written before the meeting, and the details filled in afterwards.

If a big announcement is going to be made, or a major speaker is coming and lets you know what s/he is going to say, put it in a press release before the meeting, and hand this out to journalists who come along. Mark it 'Check against delivery'. This then puts the responsibility on them for listening and making sure nothing has changed.

If you think journalists will not come along, you can send out a report of what is going to be said in advance, and **embargo** it until after the meeting. This means that you type on the top 'Not for use before 8 p.m. Saturday 20 Jan.' They will then not publish it before then. You can also do this if your event is supposed to be a surprise. The journalists' code of conduct is supposed to stop them tipping off the opposition.

For any national event, arrange for press releases to go to the national newspapers, and to the television and the radio newsrooms. If people are coming from all over the country, you should also get publicity in *their* local papers, which the local MPs and councillors will certainly read. Send a draft press release to any organisation that you know is sending people, whether one or a coachload, and ask them to turn this into their own press release, stressing that local people are involved, and send it to their local papers. Also suggest they try their local radio and television.

Deadlines

When does your local paper go to the printer? The time to think about this is when you are planning your event. Find out by phoning up a reporter and asking – it will usually be two or three days before it appears in the shops. If you want to catch that week's paper, you will have to time your event to fit. If your demonstration is on a Thursday when the local paper goes to the printer on Wednesday, you will have to wait for publication till next week's paper. You will probably still get coverage, but it will not have the same impact. If you want to get on local radio news, though, the deadline may be as little as an hour before it goes out, or a bit longer for an interview. National dailies have deadlines of about mid-afternoon, or rather earlier for the northern editions.

Pictures

There are two main types of picture that illustrate stories in newspapers. Journalists call them **mugshots** – pictures of the main people involved in a story – and **wallpaper** – pictures that explain the story, possibly dramatically.

In local papers there is a third type that could be called the **event picture**, where the paper sends a photographer along to take a whole series of pictures of a carnival or fete and uses these, with very few words attached, as a complete story in themselves.

If your event is intended to be spectacular you need to make sure a picture is taken, for it to be much use. You can do this by **putting a 'Note to Picture Editor'** at the bottom of your press release, saying where, when, and what photographs can be taken; then ring up and find out if they are coming.

■ Your note might say, 'The youth group with their petition of 4,000 signatures can be photographed with Councillor Bill Brand at 4 p.m. on Friday on the waste ground, where they want a youth club built.'

If *they* are not interested, there are **freelance photographers** who might be. There is an agency called Report (see 'Useful addresses') which has links with photographers all over the country. If they agree with you that the story is important, they may be willing to send someone to take a picture and sell it to as many journalists as they can.

If these ideas fail, **find a good amateur**, with a good camera, and get him/her to agree in advance, to take pictures, develop them quickly – that day if possible – and take them to the local paper as soon as s/he can, together with a note about the event. Offer to pay for the cost of films and printing. Pictures should be printed on glossy paper, 6 ins by 4 ins. This may not succeed, though, as many local papers are suspicious of amateurs.

If your story is not very spectacular, but includes one or two named people, **send in a few mugshots of them**, together with your press release. This makes the sub-editor's job of putting the paper together much easier, so s/he is more likely to use the story. The only time when you should hesitate about doing this is where it might mean someone would be harassed – like a gay person who could be recognised by his/her neighbours – or where it might get someone into trouble at work, perhaps because s/he has been taking time off without permission. So never use a mugshot **without asking the person concerned**. To get one, again you could use an amateur, or send the person to a High Street photographer – but this will cost money.

If a professional photographer comes to take a picture of the event, expect him or her to shift you around and even to ask you to do things twice, like handing in a petition, to get a good picture. This is understandable, but make sure you are not being used to provide a picture that will give a different story from what you want. Denis MacShane describes in *Using the Media* how in 1979 a group of picketing lorry drivers had their pictures taken silhouetted against the sun, so that they looked sinister and threatening, and this was then used in a very anti-union story.

If you are deliberately trying to get picture coverage, try to plan your event to use **children**, **animals**, or people **dressed up in funny costumes**, or **something a bit odd** which gives an easily understood image of your campaign. See page 55 for ideas on how to create an image.

If your campaign appears in the paper, make sure you get some copies of the press cuttings and also any photographs. This is not only to satisfy your personal vanity; you will be able to use them for publicity again in the future.

Complaints

If you think you have been treated unfairly by the press, then don't just let it go by; **complain**. Denis MacShane says:

> If a single reporter produces a story, then no other journalist is in a position to judge its accuracy and fairness.
>
> That is why it is so important, if a story is wrong . . . that the journalists be told so. If they are not told, they will believe they got it right . . . [they] will consider that s/he has told the truth and will base future stories on the assumption that the account is correct.

Even if your complaint does not seem to have any effect, it will make the journalist, and perhaps the editor, more careful in future. **Phone up, speak to the editor, ask for a full retraction**. But make sure you are absolutely accurate in your facts before complaining. If you think that you **might** have said what you are reported as saying, or that someone else said or did something they are not admitting, tread carefully – you could discredit the group.

6.

Transport by coach

Coach operators will be in the telephone book, but you also need to know if they are on the 'fair list' that is, if they recognise trade unions. The TGWU keeps this list up to date, so if you telephone the local or regional office they should be able to tell you which operators to contact.

Then **phone two or three to get the best quotes**. A number of public transport companies also hire out coaches or buses, so contact them too. Having found the cheapest, **confirm it in writing**, with all the details of pick-up points and destination. They will probably ask you to pay a deposit. Hiring a 50-seater coach costs about £150 for a day, or more if it is a long distance.

Since you have to pay out the money, you need to be sure of getting it back from the people who are going. Alternatively, you might be able to get someone to sponsor you for part of the cost. Try a **trade union**, the **Trades Council**, the local **Labour Party**, the political organiser of the **co-op which covers your area.**

Write them a letter explaining what your lobby is about, why it is important (see pages 21–2 for ideas of what to put in this sort of letter). If you get this money, you will need to raise less from the participants. Then work out how much you still need, and divide it by the number of seats to find out how much to charge.

Allow a safety margin – say, dividing the sum by 45 seats instead of 40 – in case you do not fill every seat. Do you want to charge less for the 'unwaged' – children, pensioners, people out of work? If so, to cover your costs, you will either need to charge more to other people (and guess how many reduced cost seats you will sell); or get sponsors to agree to make up the difference on those tickets.

Next, write a leaflet giving all the details:

- **where** the coach is leaving from;
- **what** time it leaves;

- **how much** it will cost;
- **where** it will leave from in London;
- **what time** it will get back.

Put a form at the bottom for people to send back, like this:

Name...
Address ....
I want to book .... seats on the coach for £3.50, and
.... seats for £1 (unwaged) and I enclose £ ....
in payment. Cheques should be made payable to ....

Include an address to send it back to. Get people's money **in advance**. Otherwise, if it is raining, you will end up with empty seats and too little money. Don't trust your friends any more than anyone else. Send out receipts as the money comes in; these then act as tickets when people get on the bus. Make a list of all those who are coming, as you need to check people off as they arrive. Don't forget to allocate a seat for yourself!

A day or so before the event, phone up the coach firm to check things over. Then, on the day, the organiser should be at the pick-up point **at least 15 minutes before the coach is due** – however horribly early that is. Check that the coach driver knows **exactly** where to drop you – provide a map with the spot marked on it. S/he may well not know the area you are going to. You need a **list of the people** who have booked, and a note of anyone who has not yet paid, so you can tick them off like a schoolteacher as they get on. Check that everyone intends to come back with you as well. Someone might be staying the night, and you could wait an awfully long time for them. Expect to wait a few minutes for stragglers, but not so long that it throws your whole programme out.

On the way, if it is a long distance, the driver will probably stop at a cafe so people can go to the toilet and buy a coffee. **Before anyone gets off,** tell them what time they have got to be back, and count them as they get back on. If someone is missing, you will *have* to wait for them this time – or possibly send a reliable person to look for them. **Don't let anyone else off the bus** while you are waiting, or you will lose someone else! **When you arrive**, tell people **where** and **when** the coach is picking up again, and remind them to look at the coach closely as they leave, so they can identify it. Put a poster in one window with the name of your group on it.

Count people again when they get back on the bus to go home. It is a matter for your own judgement how long you want to wait for anyone who is not on time. It is usual to collect a small amount of money from each person for a tip to the driver, and the organiser gives him/her this at the end. If you have not made as much money on the tickets as you need, you could have a raffle on the bus. Have this on the way there, in case people have spent all their money before coming back.

7.

The police

This chapter is intended to cover general points of the law, as it applies to a number of activities that can take place on the streets or indoors. A number of points on the law have been dealt with elsewhere, the specific issues are covered. For instance, the law on **advertising, flyposting**, and **libel and slander** are all in chapter 4 on publicity. Look in the index for other places where the law is covered.

This chapter also covers general points on dealing with the police, although particular issues about them are covered in other places.

The best books covering the law as it touches on campaigning activities are *Trouble with the Law*, and *Civil Liberty: the NCCL Guide* (see 'Useful books' for details). These are now rather out of date because of the new Police and Criminal Evidence Bill 1984, which will take away a lot of rights we used to have, especially on arrest.

Stop and search powers

The police have already got powers to stop and search you for drugs and offensive weapons. Under the new Police and Criminal Evidence Bill their powers to stop and search you in the street and in your car will be much increased. They can arrest you if you do not co-operate. They are also now able to set up road blocks almost anywhere, for as long as they like. This power could well be used to prevent people getting to a demonstration, for instance.

Offences

Breach of the peace

The commonest thing to be charged with, arising out of a meeting or demonstration, would be **insulting, threatening, or abusive words or behaviour likely to cause a breach of the peace**; or **distributing or displaying any 'writing, signs, or visible representation'** which is threatening, abusive, or insulting, intending to provoke a breach of the peace. This would include a leaflet or a placard.

'Threatening' the NCCL say, is defined as 'any behaviour which causes people of ordinary firmness or maturity to fear physical harm to themselves or their property'. 'Abusive' is vaguer, but generally means some verbal hostility which is likely to provoke disorder. The words you use, or your behaviour, need not be abusive to everyone, but can be to a particular group in your audience.

■ In 1963 there was a court case in which a group of Fascists had insulted Jewish people at a public meeting. The judge said that even if the speaker had not expected Jews to be present, he must 'take the audience as he found them' and he was therefore found guilty.

A 'breach of the peace' means that someone intentionally uses, or threatens to use, violence against someone else. But to be charged with this, all you need to be doing is acting in a way that gives a police officer a reasonable suspicion that you (or someone else because of your actions) might provoke a breach of the peace.

■ A judge said in 1960, 'There must exist proved facts from which a constable could reasonably have anticipated such a breach . . . it is not enough that he believes there was a remote possibility, but there must be a real possibility of a breach of the peace.'

Obstruction

Anything you do which is intended to stop the police doing their job is **obstruction**, and you can be fined or sent to prison for it. If you hit or in any way hurt a police officer, however slightly, the offence would be **assault in the execution of their duty**. The penalties for this offence are tougher than for obstruction.

You can defend yourself by saying that you did not intend to assault the officer, but it would still be an offence if you were hitting someone else. You can be arrested for this without being warned by the police.

The phrase 'in the execution of their duty' means when the police are acting lawfully within their powers, even if they are only directing the traffic. However, this does **exclude times when they are clearly acting unlawfully**, for instance by assaulting someone. If you were prosecuted for trying to stop someone being arrested, and showed that you had **a mistaken belief** that the police were acting outside their powers, you would probably still be found guilty.

The judges have said that it is not the police's job **to interfere with people who are peacefully and lawfully exercising their rights**. For example, if the police said you were obstructing them by continuing a meeting after they had told you that you were obstructing the highway, you could defend yourself against **both** charges by proving that you were not obstructing the highway.

Involvement in law breaking

There are offences that people can commit if they help someone else break the law. These are:

- **helping**, at the scene of the crime, the person who is committing it;
- **counselling**, which means giving advice about a crime;
- **procuring**, which is bringing it about by finding someone to do it; and
- **assisting** an offender to impede apprehension, which means sheltering or actively helping someone you know has committed an offence.

Inciting – that is, persuading – someone to commit a crime is also illegal, even if the crime does not in fact take place. It is a more serious offence to incite soldiers or police to a crime, or to disobey their officers.

Next, in this catalogue of misery, is **conspiracy**. If a person agrees with anyone else to do something unlawful, s/he has theoretically committed the crime of conspiracy, even if s/he does not then do anything about it. A conspiracy is an agreement between two or more people either to do something illegal, or to do something legal, but in an illegal way.

Unlawful assembly and riot

An **unlawful assembly** happens when three or more people get together to commit a crime, or to do something, whether legal or not, in a way which 'endangers public peace' or makes reasonably sensible people afraid that there is going to be a breach of the peace.

A **riot** is defined as a 'tumultuous disturbance' by three or more people who have come together to carry out a common purpose, and to help each other, by force if necessary, against people who oppose them, using enough force and violence to alarm reasonable people. In recent cases, this has been stretched to mean you are guilty even if you did not know the assembly was likely to be 'riotous'. It can carry heavy penalties.

A person involved in a fight could also be charged with **affray** which means a fight in the presence of other people, some of whom become afraid. You can also be charged with this if you were encouraging the fight. The prosecution would have to show that this was what you intended to do, that is, that you were deliberately egging people on.

Picketing

The law is now very restrictive about picketing, and especially about sympathisers helping to picket. A union that organises what the law calls 'secondary picketing' lays itself open to civil court injunctions to stop the action and massive fines. So ask the union concerned whether they want you involved. They might prefer you to organise something elsewhere, like a public meeting or a lobby, to support them. For more information on this area see John McIlroy *Strike! How to fight. How to win* (in 'Useful books').

Arrests

The Police and Criminal Evidence Bill will widen the powers of arrest. Given here is only a very brief summary of the position.

In effect, the police will be able to **arrest anyone without a warrant** for any offence, including the most minor, **if they doubt the name and address** given by a suspect, or if they think it necessary to **prevent a suspect** from causing an 'obstruction of the highway' or an 'affront to public decency'. The power is unclear, and discretionary.

You can also be arrested **for carrying an 'offensive weapon'**. This must actually be on you at the time of arrest, but almost anything, even a steel comb or coin, can be treated as an offensive weapon if the police want a reason to arrest you. They have to show that you intended to use it, but the judges have considered carrying something in self-defence to be an 'intention'.

The police officer is bound to tell you why you have been arrested; make sure you ask. If s/he does not arrest you, but just asks you to come to the police station, you do not have to go – but you will probably be arrested if you refuse.

Don't automatically assume the worst when you get to the police station; a lot of people are released without being charged. If it looks as if you may be in trouble, and the police are intending to question you, **ask to speak to a solicitor** for advice, and **to inform a friend or relative of your arrest.** Later, if you are charged, **ask for bail and legal aid.**

If you are suspected of a 'serious offence' the Police and Criminal Evidence Bill will allow them to detain you for up to four days before charging you with that offence, and to deny you access to a solicitor for the first day and a half. They can also delay for up to 36 hours your right to have someone informed of your arrest, or 48 hours if you are arrested under the Prevention of Terrorism Act. They can also take the fingerprints of suspects (including children over the age of 10) before a charge is brought, using 'reasonable force' of necessary. There is a similar power to obtain samples of hair, and nail scrapings. Intimate searches of body orifices can also be carried out in certain circumstances. The police may take photographs without consent whenever three or more people are arrested together.

However, this is what happens in the worst case. Make sure, if it happens to you, that **you follow it up** with your MP or through the police committee (see page 75). More usually, you can expect to sit in the police cells for a few hours and then either be **given bail** by the police, or **brought before a magistrate.** Bail does not mean handing over money. You will be asked to find a 'surety'. This is someone who promises to the police or to the court that s/he will be responsible for making sure that the accused person returns to the police station or court on another day. To be a surety, you have to be over 18, have a job, a fixed address (not a squat) and no criminal record. Once someone acceptable has appeared, the police or the magistrate then decide how much money s/he will have to pay if you do not turn up. See *Trouble with the Law* ('Useful books') for more details. Try your relatives; they may not approve of you, but they will not want you to spend a night in the cells, which is what happens if you are remanded.

Make sure you have **legal advice and help** before you get to court. Try the CAB or other local advice agency, for the names of lawyers.

Co-operation or confrontation

There are so many offences you could commit when you are campaigning, it is practically impossible not to do something the police might object to.

The problem of whether or not to co-operate with them in planning an event has to be looked at in that context. In practice, you will often have to work with them, either by law, or because they could make it too difficult for you otherwise. For instance, if you wanted to organise a street festival but did not tell the police, they would not stop the traffic and could arrest participants for obstructing the highway.

After you have worked out the main purpose of your event (chapter 2), then decide whether a confrontation with the police, which will make the news rather than the event itself, will work for or against that aim. You may not want to co-operate if, for instance, you are trying to show how bad the law is on a particular question: or you may accept the risks if you know that what you want to do is illegal – so co-operating with the police is not an option. **Think it through first**.

If you decide to work with the police, contact the local station first. They may put you on to someone higher up. Get the name of the officer in charge and keep a note of your conversations.

You may be able to do everything by telephone, or letter, but for a big event it is helpful to meet the police at the early stages of planning and just before the day.

If you need to go and see them:

- **dress 'respectably' and be polite**, at least while they are being polite to you. If you cannot bring yourself to do this, get someone else to go;
- **always have more than one person at any meeting.** If you know how many the police are sending, try to equal that number.
- **keep a note of your meeting**. If there are two of you, one can talk and the other can take notes.
- **get the names of the people involved clear.** Ask them a second time, if they mumble when introducing themselves.

Try to establish links with one or two of them when you are

planning your event, so that you know their names and have a contact point if their colleagues start being obstructive.

Problems you might run into include very heavy pressure **to change your plans or date**, an outright **threat to ban** a march (see page 102) or hints that they will **search everyone** for offensive weapons, or put **huge numbers of police** in. Stay polite if you can, since police are human enough to react against you if you are rude. Try getting someone they will see as important involved, like an MP or Justice of the Peace. Quite a few Labour Party or trade union people are JPs – ask around. Failing them, a solicitor, cleric, or doctor might be useful. Don't start threatening injunctions, court orders, or the like too soon, as the police usually win. Going to court will give you publicity, which could be useful for your cause, especially if you are not going to be allowed to hold your event, but it will cost money.

The best people to advise on whether you have a good case or not are the NCCL. If they think you will be establishing an important point of principle, they may find you a lawyer, and perhaps appeal for funds for your case. There may be a local NCCL group in your area, or a law centre, and you could ask either of these for advice.

The police are very conscious about rank, so if you can find a senior person who is reasonable, this will help outweigh hostility from juniors. Police ranks though are very confusing, as they all sound important. The order is: constable, sergeant, inspector, chief inspector, superintendant and chief superintendant. Outside London, the top brass are the assistant chief constable and chief constable. The equivalent ranks in the Metropolitan Police are assistant commissioner and commissioner. The Metropolitan Police have two additional ranks below these: commander and deputy assistant commissioner.

Who controls the police?

In London, the Metropolitan police come directly under the control of the **Home Secretary**. The City of London, and the Royal Parks have their own independent police forces. Outside London, there are **police committees**, often joint bodies between several counties, who are nominally in charge of the police. A sympathetic member of a police committee can be useful to help you make a fuss if the police push you around.

There are also various **liaison and consultative committees** in different places, which again may be able to help. They have very little power, but could get publicity and make sure your case is heard.

In London, several boroughs have set up their own **Police Campaigns** and **police monitoring groups**. To find any of these organisations, start off by asking the library or the CAB for names of members, or phone up the office town clerk or chief executive at the council.

Part 2
The events

8.

Public meetings

Aims

Read chapter 2, and then ask yourselves why you are holding a meeting? They are often pretty poorly attended these days. Listening to speakers in a draughty hall is not everyone's cup of tea. The impact of television and fear of going out at night means that it is not easy to get people to come to public meetings today. They will only come in large numbers if there is a really **big name speaker**, or the meeting is **about something happening locally** which is important to them.

If a local school or hospital is going to be closed, you can probably get a packed hall. But a local MP, talking about education or health in general, will probably only preach to the converted and the party members who turn up because they think they ought.

Even so, having a public meeting can be very useful if you can get:

- committed people together to plan the next stage;
- press publicity for your cause;
- the opportunity to hand out a lot of leaflets and talk to people about your campaign.

Here are some reasons particular groups had for holding a public meeting. Find out what your own reasons are.

- Helen's group wanted to get sympathetic interested people together to talk about forming a Women's Committee covering the whole borough, but they did not feel ready to talk to people who were not already convinced.
- Abdul's anti-cuts committee wanted to get a lot of publicity for their campaign against a hospital closure.
- Hugh's Labour Party wanted their MP to report back to the electors on what s/he had been up to in the last year. So they

wanted a lot of publicity, even if it meant opponents came along to argue.

■ Marie's Tenants' Association wanted to tell the members about the result of their meeting with the councillors about dampness.

■ Phil's Parent/Teachers Association wanted to persuade more parents to become involved in the activities.

Is a straightforward meeting the right thing for all these groups? Phil's for instance, might do better with a film show or a dance. Decide on this before moving to the next point.

Priorities

What is **important** for your meeting, if it is to succeed in its aims? What **don't** you need to do?

■ The women's group need to make contact with sympathetic people, and they need to arrange the meeting so that at the end people will know each other and can decide if they want to carry on working together. They want a room that is comfortable, and allows informal discussion. Too much publicity would be actually harmful to their aims, so they don't want posters or advertisements in newspapers, but they do need to be sure that they have got in touch with every women's group in the area. They need someone to lead the discussion, but not a formal speaker.

■ The anti-cuts campaign needs to convince lots of people using their own publicity and also the press, television, and radio. They need good leaflets, posters, and press releases, which will get their message across even to those who do not come. They want someone well-known to speak to bring in the crowds. So they want someone in the chair who can keep order and encourage constructive discussion. They must have a person who can get a response when asking for money. The date doesn't matter very much, but it is important to have their meeting near the threatened hospital, so that the local people most affected will come.

■ The Labour Party need to build their meeting round the MP; so they have to find a date that fits his/her diary. They also need a leaflet that briefly says what the MP has been doing. They want press coverage, but as they know it will not be front page news, they have to work on making press contacts before their meeting, so that the MP can write or feature in an article that also carries his/her report. They know there is a possibility of heckling, so they need to ensure that they have a reasonably tough chairperson, and some good stewards.

■ The Tenants' Association do not want press coverage, but they do have to make sure their meeting is on a night and in a place convenient for people from the estate. They need a leaflet that persuades people the issue is important for them, and they need people to go and knock on the doors before the meeting and talk about it. They will want to arrange for younger people to call on any of the older residents who are afraid to go out on their own.

■ The PTA does not need publicity across the town. Their most important contacts are going to be the letter that goes home with the children, and the discussion at the school gate while waiting for them. As the problem is that people are not coming to meetings, they need to persuade them that this one *is* worth coming to – which means serving refreshments, and making it a social occasion, with a lot of friendly discussion rather than speeches from a platform. They don't need to worry about a hall, as they have the school, but they do need to concentrate on making it attractive.

Having worked all this out, you have the main points to concentrate on: **date, hall, speakers, publicity**. Later sections go through these points in detail. First, here is a note of the law affecting public meetings.

The law

The owner of a hall can refuse to let you hire it without giving a reason, so long as s/he is not discriminating on grounds of race or sex. Local authorities have to allow any candidate to hold a public meeting in a school, during an election campaign.

The organisers of a meeting have the right to refuse admission, without giving a reason, whether there is an entry fee or not. If people force their way in, they are trespassing; under the Public Order Act 1936 (see page 101) the organisers are entitled to remove them using 'reasonable force'. Once someone has paid an entry fee they can be lawfully thrown out only if they misbehave and refuse to leave when asked to do so. If you don't charge, they can be removed without warning at any time. If they are actually trying to break up the meeting, the Public Meeting Act 1908 entitles you to remove them and request police help.

This Act makes it an offence to break up meetings or to take them over. The Act is not often used; usually a more common offence, like a breach of the peace, will have been committed as well. (See Part 3 of this book for ideas about what to do if there is trouble.)

In legal terms, a person who lets a room to you is licensing you to use it on certain conditions. If you break the conditions, you lose the license and can be asked to leave. You may be trespassing if you don't go. The owner could have you removed, or call in the police to clear the room. The sort of conditions that might be imposed are:

- **no alcohol**; this is quite common with church premises;
- **the time** the meeting must finish;
- **the numbers allowed**. This is often laid down under fire regulations.

If you are caught overcrowding, you may be asked to leave. You can offer to reduce the number of people in the room, but legally that does not change the fact that you have already broken your licence.

Dates and times
When should you hold your meeting?

If your meeting is not a success you can always blame the date or the time, but in fact it is more likely to be that your publicity was not good enough, or people just weren't interested. There are though, a few particularly bad times:

- the fortnight before and the fortnight after Christmas;
- the whole of August;
- any time over a Bank Holiday weekend, or the Friday before it;
- clashing with a major national or local event, like the Cup Final or a match between two local teams.

Royal weddings and the like are not recommended either. If you have booked a meeting for a particular day, and someone else very inconsiderately fixes something like that for the same day, it is better to cut your losses and cancel, rather than persevere when you know no one will come.

Check before setting a date that there is not another meeting which will attract the same people as yours, going on at the same time, or any television programme that those people would want to watch.

■ Helen's meeting is going to be 6 May; they then discover that the Women's Aid Support Committee are having a social that night, so they change their date and go along to that.

In some areas and with some groups, a Saturday or Sunday afternoon may be a good time. If so, **you must provide a creche**. Generally though, an evening will be better, starting about 7.30 or 8 o'clock, finishing about 10 o'clock. People will start to drift away if your meeting goes on longer than that, so that it tails off, rather than finishing on a rousing note. If you start earlier than 7.30, people will not be able to come because they will be still eating, putting the children to bed, and so on. The very worst time for people with children is 5–7 p.m. when they are fully occupied.

Booking a hall

- **How many** people do you expect to come?
- **How much** can you afford to pay?
- **What time** do you want the meeting to begin and end?
- **Where** are you expecting the people to come from?

Ask yourselves all these questions before you start looking for a hall, because they affect what hall you can use. Size is important. If you have 200 people in a hall that should hold 800, it will look disastrous and people will feel cold and isolated. If you have the same number, with standing room only, in a hall with 170 seats, it will look like a very good turnout. Don't be over-ambitious.

Before you book, find out how much they want you to pay, and when they want the money. If it is more than you can afford, can you cover it by having a collection? Pubs are probably the cheapest places, but they have **disadvantages**:

- young people and children will not be able to come;
- a lot of people, especially women, do not like going into pubs on their own, and so will not come;
- there will be a lot of disturbance from people going out to buy drinks and clattering glasses;
- people who have had a drink or two may talk too much, or get argumentative, as the meeting goes on.

In some areas, council-owned buildings and schools will be cheap, but not always, as many Tory councils have put up hiring rates hugely. Other possibilities are church halls, trade union or Labour Party premises, or a youth club or old people's clubroom on a night when they are not meeting.

Will it be easy to reach for the people you want to come? If it is a particular estate you are interested in, you will need something on or close to it, not across two busy roads and through a subway. If you want an audience from all over the area, you need somewhere near bus routes or a station. If it is a place people will not know, or might be afraid to go to, perhaps because it's down a dark alleyway, you will have to make a special effort like printing maps on your leaflet and offering lifts. Make sure that disabled people – and elderly people, and people with prams – can get into the hall.

To find out what is available:

- ask in the local library for a list of halls for hire;
- ask a school secretary or head teacher who you should contact about using a local school;
- ask a vicar about using the church hall.

Having got a list of possibilities, phone up the people who actually have the authority to let the hall. Tell them about the **date**, the **time**, **what** the meeting is for, the **numbers** you expect, **how long** the meeting will last, and whether there will be **any other activities** like dancing. Make sure they tell you, not only whether the hall is free, but also:

- what time the organisers would be allowed in the hall before the meeting;
- where you get the keys before the meeting, or if there is a caretaker, where to find him/her to let you in;
- when you must leave by;
- any special restrictions like not drinking or smoking;
- whether there is a power point, if you are planning to use microphones;
- how much it will cost, and where to send the money;
- whether they want a deposit.

Make a note of all these, and try to go and see the hall. If there is a caretaker, introduce yourself; having him/her as a friend will make a lot of difference. Check the hall, looking especially at **the lighting**, **the heating**, **the toilets**, and **the chairs**. If it is a primary school or playgroup hall, it might only have baby-size chairs, which would mean the audience would not be able to sit still for more than half an hour. Ask if there are any ordinary chairs tucked away in a store. If not, you will have to borrow them from somewhere.

If your group is planning to serve tea or other refreshments, you will need to find out about a kettle and cups. In the winter, you will also want to check on the heating arrangements. You might have to pay extra for heating, or to arrange for someone to come in early to switch a fire on.

Having found a hall that will do, write to the people letting it – even if they have said you don't need to – and set out all the details agreed on the phone. Enclose a cheque for the deposit or letting fee. Keep a copy and send a stamped addressed envelope with the letter; ask the person to reply confirming the arrangements.

If you are hiring a place from the council, or another organisation that does a lot of letting, you may be given a standard form. Read it through carefully, and keep a copy after filling it in and signing it. (If necessary, get a photocopy from a print shop or the library). You may find that signing the form makes you personally liable for the cost of damage or cancellation. The group as a whole should agree to cover this, and put this in the minutes of the next committee meeting.

Speakers

Don't have **too many speakers**. People get bored easily, and they want to put their own point of view. Three people each speaking for quarter of an hour, with the chairperson opening and summing up, is quite enough; the rest of the time is for questions and discussion. If you want more speakers cut down on the time allowed to each of them. If you think someone needs more than 15 minutes have fewer speakers. If that leaves you with people you think ought to speak but cannot fit in, either ask them to say something briefly during question time, or hold another meeting.

If you are inviting a 'big name' put him or her on **last**, so people who have come specially will listen to the others as well.

Who to ask

Having decided what the meeting is for, you will have an idea of who is most suitable. Celebrities such as national politicians or television stars will probably make the same speech as they make everywhere, and not know much about your local issues. So you also need someone who does know the details to explain them. Try not to have an all male, all female, or all white platform. Try to find one person who can be fairly light-hearted, to persuade people's money out of their pockets during the collection. Take this just **before** your main speakers, so that people do not leave to avoid it.

If you have decided you need outside speakers, but don't know who:

- ask other local groups if they know who is sympathetic and a big draw;
- look back through the local papers, especially those around Christmas (try the library for back numbers) to see if there are useful names of people who opened local bazaars or fetes;
- look at the magazine or publication of your group, or a similar one, for reports of famous people doing things for the cause. For instance, it was reported in *Sanity*, CND's magazine, that a famous guitarist had opened a peace shop in Cardiff for CND, so he might be worth approaching for another CND event.

If you want to ask the mayor, write to his or her secretary – the library will tell you the address. If you want, say, the chairperson of the Housing Committee, again the library, or the town hall, will have a name and address.

You might want to ask the person you are trying to convince (say, the leader of the council or the local MP) to speak, in order to put him or her on the spot. Make sure you have someone recording what s/he says, or taking notes.

Finding people

The suggestions in chapter 2 should help you to get hold of a local person. National personalities are more dificult, but some possibilities are given here.

The local library should have the address of the local MP. For others, there is a book called *Vacher's Parliamentary Companion*, which the library should have, and this has most of the addresses. Or you can write to, or phone, the House of Commons (see 'Useful addresses'). If you cannot get an answer from the MP, you can leave a message, or ask the switchboard if they have another contact number. If you don't know who the MP for an area is, the Information Service at the House of Commons can tell you.

If you know someone is connected with **a particular organisation**, phone them and ask for an address. Check before sending letters marked 'Please Forward' that you've got the right organisation, and that they will do it. If it is urgent, say so; otherwise it may be days before anyone gets around to looking up the address and sending it on.

Who's Who should be in the local library. It gives the address of many famous people, and sometimes the phone numbers as well.

If someone is appearing in a particular radio or television show, or a play, **ask the producer for the address**, or ask their union to help. **Equity** is the union that organises actors, and the **Musicians' Union** for musicians. For a writer, try their **publisher**.

If someone has recently been on a platform for **another group**, try the group for an address. So for instance you could try CND's head office to get in touch with people they have recently used.

Sorting it out

Decide on a list of possible speakers, with first and second preferences (not that you tell them that's what they are). Then give one person the major responsibility for arranging them. If one member of the group knows a particular person you want to invite, s/he could talk to them, but make sure s/he reports back as soon as possible, so there is no muddle about who has been invited.

Having found the addresses, phone anyone you can; write to the others. Follow up each phone call with a letter giving all the details, and ask them to confirm by letter that they are coming. A stamped addressed envelope will encourage them. It is best to write even to people who live locally and who you know, so that they have something to refer to when they are sorting out their diaries.

If one speaker you hoped for cannot do the night you want, s/he might suggest other people. If they are not already on your list, check with the chair and secretary whether they are worthwhile substitutes or not.

Once you have got replies from the speakers saying they can come, write again giving them full details of:

- **the time and place** of the meeting;
- **how to get there**, by car or public transport;

- **how long** they are expected to speak, and whether there will be **questions**;
- **who else** is speaking;
- **who to contact** if there are any problems; give them a phone number to contact if there is a last minute crisis.

Enclose a leaflet for the meeting, so that they can see what the publicity says. Ring them a day or two after the letter has gone, to check that they have got it, and find out if they **need to be met**, for instance off a train; and whether they would **like a meal before or after** the meeting.

On the day before the meeting, phone the speakers again, to make sure they are still coming. Even experienced people who should know better, let audiences down sometimes, either by not putting the right date in their diaries, or by forgetting or thinking it does not matter. They have got much less excuse if you have checked things several times with them. See Part 3 for what to do if a speaker does not turn up.

At the end of the meeting, offer the speakers **travelling expenses**. Get them to write the cost down and sign the note, and then the treasurer can pay out of the collection, getting a receipt.

Next day, write them all thank-you letters. Even if they were boring and went on too long, they still need thanking – they might be in a position to influence things, now or later.

Media publicity

Look at chapter 5 for ideas on writing a press release, and getting the media to your event. Some meetings do not want or need publicising; think of your objectives before you decide what action to take.

Chairperson and stewards

If yours is a small informal discussion between like-minded people, like Helen's meeting of women's groups you will not need anyone formally in charge of it, although if someone will take responsibility for starting it off, it does prevent that awkward silence at the beginning while everyone feels embarrassed about volunteering. For a public meeting of any size, you need a chairperson. The best ones are reasonably **tough**; people who **do not lose their tempers** too easily; and who **don't hog the meeting**

themselves. The job of a chairperson is to allow **other people** to talk.

It is best to give the job to someone who knows what they are doing, rather than a big name, and use the big name as a speaker. Nor should you give the job to someone just because they will be offended if they do not get it. It is too important for that. Better to offend them, if they are not up to it, than turn your meeting into a fiasco.

Organise your chairperson well in advance, at the same time as the speakers, and remind him/her in the same way. Offer expenses as well. Make sure s/he knows all the plans. Arrange for the organiser, the chair, and the speakers, to meet up for quarter of an hour before the meeting starts to go over everything. If the arrangements are at all complicated, write out a timetable for the chairperson. This should cover;

- **the times** things happen;
- **the order** people are speaking in;
- **details** about those people;
- **any announcements** to be made;
- **any other points.**

Here, for example, are the notes from Abdul's meeting:

- 7.45: If enough people in the room (otherwise wait a few minutes) announce meeting is open; spend 5 mins explaining what it is about: <u>to start a campaign to save the local hospital</u>. REMINDER. Please ask people not to smoke, or the fire sprinklers will go off.
Introduce platform, who are:
1. Mr E. Moore, Chair of District Health Authority, Borough Councillor for last 29 years, ex-mayor;
2. Ms F. Finlay, nurse at hospital, to tell us what's happening in the campaign there;
3. Mr K. Watson MP, Shadow Minister of Health, to talk about the national campaign;
4. Abdul Choudry, campaign organiser.
Speaking order; please try to keep them to time!
7.50 Mr Moore
8.05 Ms Finlay
8.20 Abdul Choudry, who will explain what the committee are planning over the next few weeks, ask for volunteers, and take a collection. Stewards have got buckets to pass round.

8.40 Mr K. Watson.
8.55 Questions and discussion; please ask people to be brief.
9.35 Ms F. Fanon thanks speakers.
9.40 Meeting ends. Please ask people to leave quickly and continue if necessary in the pub next door, as we only have the hall till 10 p.m. and we have to clear up.

Sometimes a councillor or MP who is hostile or uncommitted may turn up and sit quietly in the audience. If you know enough about him or her, work out whether it would be useful, or act against you, to pass a note up to the chair suggesting that s/he is asked to speak, and put on the spot. Some people would react very badly against this, feeling that you have not played fair with them.

Stewards

These are the people who sort out the room, as well as dealing with any trouble. Their jobs include:

- helping **to set up the hall** in advance;
- **taking entrance money**, or **handing out leaflets** at the door;
- **answering queries**;
- getting people **to leave quickly** afterwards;
- **clearing up**;
- **handing the buckets** round during a collection;
- **dealing with trouble**.

Pass a list around at your planning meetings, and any other suitable places, to get people to sign. Both men and women can steward; if you are expecting trouble you will want to be sure you have a few large tough people in the hall.

Stewards need to be reliable people who do not panic. Ask them to come to the hall half an hour or so before the meeting, so the organiser can brief them before they go off to do the different jobs.

Taking a collection

If entrance was free, or not very much, then a collection is usually sensible, and people who come to a meeting tend to expect it. However, if it is a meeting of members who have already paid a subscription, or if you are charging a lot for entrance, it is not reasonable to take a collection as well.

For the collection you need:

- a person who is not shy about standing up and asking for money; preferably someone who can tell a few non-sexist, non-racist jokes while doing so;
- bowls or buckets for the stewards to pass round;
- someone to count the money and take responsibility for banking it;
- a place to count in, where the clink of coins will not disturb the meeting.

Work out the amount you need to cover the cost of the hall, leaflets, and other expenses, and announce that as your target. If you get more, it can go towards the cost of your next meeting.

It makes people feel good if you announce the amount received at the end of the meeting – pass a note up to the chairperson. If it is an odd amount, like £99, this gives a chance to say, 'Who's going to give us the extra £1?'

Some fund-raisers like to start off with a sort of auction, calling for volunteers to give £20, £10, £5, and so on. This can persuade people to produce more cash than they intended, but it is very embarrassing if the call for a £20-note meets a stony silence and no volunteers. Start off at a realistic level – £10 rather than £20 – and make sure someone is ready to start the ball rolling with a note, even if it comes out of your organisation's funds and goes back there.

See page 242 for what to do with a large sum of money overnight.

Stalls

Someone who knows enough about the organisation to answer queries should sit behind a table with leaflets about your organisation, membership forms, posters, copies of past newsletters, and anything else you have.

If there are unions involved in your campaign, ask them also to provide a stall with literature and badges, especially stuff to give away.

If there is a radical or alternative bookshop in your area, they might be willing to provide a stall at a public meeting. Some Labour Parties also do this. They should get hold of copies of pamphlets and magazines that are relevant to your organisation; ask them to give you a share of any profits. Delegate someone to look after them, and to check on transport; have they got a van, or do they need someone to pick up a box of books?

If your group is part of a national organisation, they probably have pamphlets and newsletters which they will send on a 'sale or return' basis. This means you get them on credit, and what you do not sell you send back, with the money you have made. Again, it is best to put one person in charge of this.

Setting up the hall

Sorting out the chairs may be done by the caretaker, or you may have to do it – check when you first book the hall. Decide in advance how you want it arranged. Do you want **straight rows** of chairs or the chairs **round in a circle** (which is better for a small meeting)? Will you need a table and chairs **at the front** for the chairperson and speakers, or a table and chairs **on a platform**? The latter should only be used for very big meetings, as it is intimidating.

If you have arranged for the hall to be set up, and when you get there it is all wrong, ask the caretaker if s/he minds if you rearrange it, and put it back the way you found it afterwards.

Try to get a jug of water and glasses for the speakers' table, and ashtrays, both there and in the hall, if you are allowing people to smoke.

If you want people to sign a list or a petition, or if you are charging for entry and want to take their money off them, put a table right by the door, possibly half-way across it so that only one or two people can get in at a time, and have stewards sitting behind it.

Public address systems

In a big hall, or if you have a band or theatre group playing, you may want to have microphones or a public address (PA) system. Check when hiring the hall that this is all right with the owners, and that there are **electric points**; and that the electrics **are sound, and will not blow a fuse**.

See pages 111–12 for more details about PA systems. If you are having microphones in the centre of the hall, for people from the floor to use, make sure you **tape down any trailing wires**. The organisers are liable if someone breaks a leg. See page 238 for insurance on this.

Decorating the hall

Check whether you can put things on the walls, using Blu-tack, which does not mark. If you are not allowed to, can you tie things to the blackboard, or pin them to the front of the speakers' table? To create a good atmosphere, get together some posters, trade union banners, if possible a few pictures that relate to the reason for the meeting, and put them round.

Get together a 'kit' in advance, of large pieces of **plain paper, drawing pins, string, Blu-tack, scissors, sellotape,** large **felt-tip pen, hammer, first aid box**.

Put them all in a large box so that you can grab it as you set off for the meeting, together with your banners and posters.

Making a good display is especially important if a press photographer or TV crew are coming. It will make your group look much more impressive, whatever the size of the meeting.

If you have banners or posters you have used before, unroll them and **look at them in advance of the meeting**. They could have faded, stuck together, or be torn and tatty looking – so ruining the image you are trying to create.

Put up signs directing people to the meeting outside the hall, especially if it is difficult to find, or if there is more than one entrance. If you are not allowed to do this, put stewards at the entrances to direct people. Do not forget to take your posters and signs down afterwards.

Leaflets

If you have got literature about the issues involved, or membership forms, or ads for another event, put them on chairs before the meeting starts, or hand them out on the door. Often people from other groups will want to hand out their literature as well. Be cautious about allowing this; if it is quite a different cause from yours you risk confusing people. Be especially careful about political groups, as people may think the meeting is being run by that group. If necessary, say they can only hand out their leaflets outside the door.

You may want to pass round a list asking for volunteers to help, or for people to sign up as members. Bring along a clipboard, or make one from cardboard, and attach a pen to it with string. The chair should ask for it back when the meeting closes.

At the end of the meeting

The caretaker probably will not be able to go home until everyone is out, so try and persuade people to leave and carry on their conversations elsewhere.

Check that you have got everything you came with, such as posters and signs, your hall-decorating kit, leaflets and papers, collecting tins.

Who is responsible for cleaning up? If it is the caretaker, ask him/her if s/he would like you to help. If it is you, then however tired out you are after the meeting, make sure the hall is left in a decent state. If you do not do this, you will be landing the caretaker next day with an extra job s/he is not paid for, which is anti-social. You are also making it less likely that the hall will be hired out again, which may not matter to you, but it might to other people who want to run similar campaigns in the future.

If you have been left to lock up yourselves, someone should go round and check that:

● all the lights are off;
● electric fires, or other heaters, are switched off;
● windows are shut;
● no one has left taps running in the toilet.

Afterwards

If the meeting has gone well, you will feel very happy; if badly, fed up. Either way, try and go over it afterwards as a group: decide what went well and where you made mistakes, and learn from it. Was it worthwhile? What are the pluses and the minuses? And what is your next step?

Remember also to:

● write your thank-you letters;
● pay your bills;
● follow up useful contacts you made, like people who filled in membership forms, or said they would be interested in helping.

Checklist for public meetings

Why bother?

(1) Why are you having the meeting?
(2) What are your priorities?

People

See page(s) Date done

Have people been given the jobs of:

- booking the hall?   83
- finding speakers and chairperson?   85
- contacting the press?   60–5
- doing leaflets, posters, and other publicity?   26–59
- taking along material on the night?   90–3
- organising the stewards?   90
- taking and banking the collection?   90–1, 242

Things to do

Book speakers and chairperson: 87–8
- Letters written confirming
- Reply received
- Phone call to check
- Expenses offered
- Thank-you letter

Book hall: 83–4
- Phone call to book provisionally
- Visit to hall, check:
    chairs
    access for disabled
    you can put things on the wall
    heating
    toilets
    what time you can get in
    arrangements for clearing up
- Deposit sent
- Letter confirming, or booking form
- Paid bill

Press contact: 60–5
- 1st press release sent
- 2nd press release sent

- Phone to see if they are coming
- 3rd press release, after meeting

Publicity: 26–59
  - Ad in local paper:
      paid for
  - Leaflets: how many?
      printed
      delivered
      paid for
  - Posters: how many?
      printed
      put up
      paid for
  - Any other publicity ideas?

Loudspeaking: 58
  - Car organised?
  - Loudspeaker
  - Insurance
  - Someone to do it

For the night

Stewards: People available to   90
      set up the hall in advance
      take entrance money
      hand out leaflets
      take the collection
      clear up afterwards
      get people to leave
      staff information table

The hall: check you have   91–3
      posters for decoration
      toolkit to take along
      material for information desk
      leaflets to hand out
      clipboard for addresses/petition
      buckets for collection
      cups/saucers, etc. for
          refreshments
      PA system – does it work?
      signs to direct people

Afterwards

- Thank-you letters sent?   94
- Bills paid?
- Borrowed equipment returned?
- Was it worthwhile?
- What is the next step?

9.

Marches and demonstrations

The first part of this chapter covers the fairly straightforward marches and demonstrations where people come together to show how strongly they feel about something, and then go away. There are separate sections at the end about events that you plan in ad vance, but **keep secret** until they happen; **spontaneous demonstrations**; and **direct action**. This last expression covers those demonstrations where you come with a purpose and intend to carry on until you have achieved it. A group of parents might decide decide to walk back and forth across a busy road until they get a promise of a pelican crossing. It also covers actions where you know you are breaking the law – like sitting down in Trafalgar Square.

This chapter deals with local demonstrations and big national ones - usually held in central London. Transporting people by coach to a national demonstration elsewhere is covered in chapter 6.

Aims

Why have a demonstration? Often it simply seems to be the next thing to do after you have been running your campaign for a while, but unless you have a goal it is unlikely to be a success.

In fact, as was said in chapter 2, it can actually do your cause harm. It can alienate the people to whom it is a nuisance, and it can tie up a great deal of energy without converting anyone. Five hundred people marching through the streets on a dark, rainy Wednesday evening before picketing a council meeting will upset people trying to get on buses held up by the march, and may well not make even the local papers, but will take a lot of sweat that could be better used elsewhere. It can also make supporters feel they have done their bit, when they haven't done anything useful. Would you have more impact handing out leaflets and a petition on a council estate, or in the shopping streets on Saturday morning?

However, there *are* good reasons for having a march. For instance:

- as a counter-demonstration – not letting someone get away with something unopposed;
- publicising an issue, and giving ordinary people the chance to show their support;
- boosting the morale of your supporters, and showing them they are not alone;
- commemorating a particular event.

Here are some examples of the different reasons:

- The Tory Employment Minister is coming to Victor's factory, and the shop stewards want to make sure he gets to know about the opposition. It will work best with a small easily controllable group, so they don't want to recruit large numbers.
- Mary's group need to make maximum impact, to get a lot of people along, to draw attention and to get the message across. So they will need to think hard about the route, about press publicity, banners, placards, leaflets and hand-outs. They want a gimmick to get the press and TV along.

  They have to think about where the march should assemble, where it should end, and what to do when it gets there. They need a lot of advance publicity, and they do not want trouble, as it would reflect badly on the cause, so they need to co-operate with the police.
- Jim's Trades Council needs a lot of publicity among committed activists, who are probably the only ones who will be interested enough to come along. He must persuade them that even though the demonstration has happened every year for as long as they can remember it is still worth coming. So he needs to concentrate on good publicity material and on getting a celebrity or two – major trade union or political figures – to speak at the rally. He also needs to make sure the marchers put up a good show, even if the numbers are fairly small, for instance by bringing along a lot of historic banners.

Timing

Do not underestimate the length of time it takes to organise a big march. You have got to:

- let people know about it;
- persuade them it is worth giving up time for;

- allow them to put it in their diaries;
- give time to book buses, or make other arrangements to get there.

If the issue is one that people know about already and feel very strongly about, they will give the event priority. The TUC demonstration in support of the health workers in September 1982 took less than a month to organise. But if you have to build support by showing that the issue is important, or that it is worth going on yet another demonstration about cruise missiles, you need longer. CND start advertising the date of their national demonstrations three or four months in advance.

There is a risk that your plans may be upset by other events. For example, at least one planned national demonstration had to be cancelled when the 1983 general election was announced. But the work that has gone into publicity will not be wasted, as it draws the issue to the attention of a lot of people.

Scale

It is impossible to guess accurately the numbers coming to a demonstration. One rule of thumb is that for every person coming on a specially booked train or coach, at least one more will be coming under his/her own steam. The important thing is not to announce that you are expecting too high a figure, because then if fewer come the event will be written off as a failure when in fact it was successful. If you have told the press 1,000 people are going to turn up, and 50 do, you have egg on your face and they will make the most of it. So be realistic about your objectives and what you can hope for.

Lay your plans to fit your resources. If you know you cannot expect huge numbers to turn up, perhaps a march is not the right thing. Banners and street theatre outside the town hall with 50 people, if well organised, will get much more attention than 50 or even 100 people marching to the town hall through rather empty streets.

The law

There is **no right to demonstrate** in this country; any march, demonstration, or rally, can be broken up or banned, if the police think public order is in danger or some other offence is being committed. Walking along the street by yourself is not illegal, but as soon as you stop in the road or pavement, or start walking with a group, you could theoretically be committing the offence of obstructing the highway. If you do not move on or disperse when asked to by the police, you could be arrested for obstructing them in the course of their duty. However, the police probably will not arrest large numbers of people unless they feel the event is a nuisance, or too 'political' for them.

The NCCL publish a very useful, brief fact sheet called 'Organising a March' which summarises the legal powers of the police and your legal rights. Information in the next few paragraphs is based on this.

In general, you do not *have* to tell the police in advance if you are going to have a march. There are, though, specific local Acts or by-laws, mainly in large towns, which do require this. It is a criminal offence in Greater Manchester, the West Midlands, and Merseyside, not to give to the police 72 hours' notice of a march. Find out your own local position by ringing the chief executive's or town clerk's department at the town hall. Ask them specifically **what Act or by-law** covers the point, and **the length of notice required**. This can be between 36 hours and five days. It is not usually laid down whether the notice should be verbal or in writing. Also find out **who you have to tell**. In most cases this is the police station in the district affected by your march. If you are going through more than one police district, you will need to tell a police station in each one. Check on **what you have to tell them**. In most cases you will need to give them the route, the date, and the time. You do not have to let them know the subject, the speakers, or how many people you expect. The police do not have to agree the route; simply to know about it.

In areas with special laws, organisers can be fined up to £200 for failing to give notice. An offence is also committed if the march takes a different route from the one notified to the police. The organisers, not the people taking part, should be summonsed for any offence rather than being arrested on the spot. The Director of Public Prosecutions (a senior government lawyer) must approve any court case.

Public Order Act

This statute was originally passed in 1936 because of fascist and anti-fascist activities; it can be used against marches anywhere in the country, if the police believe 'serious public disorder' will occur if they go ahead as planned.

The Chief Constable (or the Metropolitan Police Commissioner in London) can reroute a march under this Act, or impose conditions on the organisers and the people taking part. If the police decide this is insufficient, they can then apply to the local council for a ban, and consult the Home Secretary. In London, the council is not involved; the Commissioner goes straight to the Home Secretary. The ban can be on specific marches, or all marches over a period of time in an area. The area can be as wide as the whole of London or Manchester, or it could be a specific borough or district. In recent years, it has been used mainly against National Front marches but has also been used against left-wing ones. The police often use blanket bans, which mean that any other march in the area, however peaceful it was intended to be, is also caught, including events like carnival processions. 'Traditional' events are usually exempt, so a Guy Fawkes procession that has been going on for 300 years could take place, but an anti-nuclear rally that had been happening for only two years could not. If you try to march where there is a ban, the organisers may be prosecuted.

The Act also allows the police to prohibit banners; and makes it an offence to wear a uniform in any public place, in order to show that you are 'associated with any political organisation or to promote any political object'. Wearing IRA uniform, or simply their black berets, is also an offence under the Prevention of Terrorism Act.

Special powers in London

In London the special Metropolitan Police Act 1839 is used occasionally to ban specific arches and meetings. The police need only say they are concerned about traffic congestion.

There are also extra regulations about marching in central London, and there is always a ban on open-air meetings and processions on the north side of the Thames, within a mile of parliament, when it is sitting (rougly, Monday to Friday, November to July). You are not allowed to display banners or placards in the area, or to hand out leaflets. (Pages 144–9 deal specifically with organising a parliamentary lobby).

Trespass

This means entering and staying on someone else's land or building without their permission. It is not usually a crime except in an occupation, (which is covered briefly on pages 126–7). If, for instance, you used an NCP car park as your starting or finishing point without permission, it would be a civil wrong and if any damage or inconvenience is caused, the owner could sue for compensation. If the owner knew your plans in advance s/he could also get a court order to remove or to stop you.

Co-operating with the police

See pages 74–6 for suggestions on this. Most organisers of marches, even in areas where they do not have to give notice legally, do contact the police and work closely with them but it is a matter for your own group to decide. If your march or demonstration is intended to be large and peaceful, you will probably need to work with them in planning a route, going over assembly and rallying points, and so on. They may even have some sensible ideas, for instance about how to avoid hazards like steep hills or traffic islands.

In some areas, the police issue a code of practice for march organisers, covering arrangements for stewarding and agreeing the route with them. This is guidance which you do not have to follow if you don't want to; it is not legally binding.

If you decide to work with the police, **start early on**. Ring up the local police station and explain; let them tell you if they want you to go higher. Where the march is intended to be large, and is likely to stop the traffic, for instance by going through a city centre, you may be asked to contact the police headquarters.

In central London, the first point of contact is the Ceremonial Office, at Cannon Row Police Station (see page 257) but they may ask you to contact Scotland Yard if you are planning something big.

Give one person the responsibility for contacting them. Before going to a meeting, this person should acquire a map, and have a clear idea of the assembly and finishing points, and the route, that you want. **Go and walk along** your preferred route, looking out for:

- places where there might be **traffic problems**, such as roundabouts, or awkward junctions;

- **bottlenecks, sharp turnings, steep hills**.

These are the sort of things police will worry about. You will need to counter their objections or, if you think they are fair, to find an alternative route. Your assembly and dispersal points might be obvious (outside a hospital or the town hall, for instance) or there might be several different parks or commons you could use. If there is a traditional place that marches always leave from or end up at, sticking to that means the police cannot object on the grounds that it is not practical. If you are planning to use council or private land (a car park, for instance) you will need permission from the owners.

In some areas, there are local laws or directions about where a march can go. For instance, the Metropolitan police have issued a direction that prohibits marches going down Oxford Street except on Sundays. If the police tell you there is a by-law or direction that stops you taking a certain route, ask them to send you a copy of it, so you can check. The direction will usually mention specific streets, so you should be able to go down any other streets that are not mentioned.

Especially in London, the police often send organisers a 'notice of route' form and ask them to sign it. Legally you do not have to, but if you have agreed the route and there is no problem with it, you may as well sign and avoid any argument later. You could also write to them setting out what was agreed.

Central London police, and those in big city centres, are quite experienced at dealing with marches; those in smaller towns and rural areas are not. The **traffic control police** will probably be involved, and will chiefly be interested in getting large numbers of people from A to B without disruption, rather than in what you are marching about. Other, more public-order-conscious police will be interested in the issue, and will be more or less sympathetic or helpful depending on what they think of your cause. If you are campaigning about a local school or hospital closure, you may find them quite friendly; but they will be less so if the march is about a death in a police station. If they see you as a troublesome group – for instance if yours is a counter-demonstration against the local fascists – they may be difficult from the beginning, and it could be sensible to take a lawyer along to any meeting. Unless there is a reason for wanting your march to be protected – for instance, against the National Front – try to negotiate for as small a police escort as possible. Stress that you intend to have plenty of stewards, and they will be taking care of the march.

Give them the name of a 'chief steward' and ask them to co-ordinate all the arrangements about stewarding with him/her. The police cannot really cope with non-hierarchical collective groups, and you will probably have enough to do without trying to educate them. (See pages 74–6 for what to do when you run into problems with the police.)

Where to take a march

Large towns often have a fairly standard marching route, and a place where open-air public meetings are frequently held. In Newcastle-on-Tyne, for instance, marches assemble in the car park by the railway station, and then finish in the main park. You can find out about these routes by asking other groups like the Labour Party or the Trades Council, or possibly ringing up the Council Recreation Department. It will be easier to get police agreement to this than to any other route, so if it suits you in other ways, you may as well use it. If it does not suit you then say so, and aim to get another route that does. The police will probably try hard to dissuade you from some routes, and may threaten to ban you if you insist on going ahead. They may well mean it – this is a gamble you will have to take.

In central London, the only Royal Park you will get permission to use is Hyde Park (for telephone number see 'Useful addresses'), which has a number of restrictions on its use. You cannot put up structures there (like a display), play music, or carry banners – you are supposed to leave these at the gate. Restrictions like these are particularly annoying because they are not enforced equally on everyone. The London Marathon gets away with a great deal more than the People's March for Jobs. But the problem of fighting this is the usual one that taking matters to court costs money, takes time, and may well not succeed. Again, it is a matter for your judgement how far you want to push the issue.

To use Trafalgar Square, you need specific permission from the Department of the Environment (see 'Useful addresses').

It is illegal to make a speech or distribute a leaflet in the Square without their permission. They are unlikely to allow it to be used except on Sundays. They have the power to make whatever rules they like about the use of the Square; for instance, they have banned all meetings that have anything to do with Ireland.

Alternative places to use are; **the Embankment** which is a public highway and needs police permission; **Jubilee Gardens** next to County Hall, which is booked with the Recreation Department of the GLC; **Clerkenwell Green** in Islington which needs council permission. You are only allowed to march down Oxford Street on Sundays.

Assembly point

When your march is forming up, you want a large flat open space, preferably without trees, bollards, or traffic islands to get in the way. Look for **a car park**; **a recreation ground**; or **a quiet street** just off the road you are going to march down.

Try to be near public transport routes; if you are expecting coachloads of people, you will also need to organise a place where they can drop people off.

The route

What is your march for? Who do you most want to see it? Mary's group are trying to get the general public to support them, so they will want to go down busy shopping streets and through the town centre. A group that is looking for help from other workers in industrial action, would want to go past the maximum number of workplaces – perhaps through an industrial estate. If yours is a small march about a local issue you will want to go past the houses of people most affected. If you are trying to make a point about bad press coverage of your campaign, you might want to go past the local newspaper office.

The route should be about an hour's walk at most. Remember that a large group moves more slowly than a small one. If you are marching over private land, like the roads on an industrial estate, you will need to decide whether to ask permission, or risk being accused of trespassing. Try to avoid steep hills and sudden bottlenecks.

Finishing point

Make sure your march does finish somewhere definite, rather than just petering out. You might want to finish at the town hall and present a petition or lobby councillors (see chapters 10 and 11 for these). You could have a speaker or two very briefly thanking the marchers, or a full-blown rally with bands and celebrities, or something in between. Find a place where passers-by can see and hear you. If it is in a park, for instance, try to be near a road.

If you are marching in the autumn or winter, though, try to plan for an indoor finish, or you will not have an audience for very long. In a city centre, there is usually a hall you can use, perhaps attached to the town hall or the public baths, though it may well be expensive to hire. A political group or union might sponsor your march, and pay for the hire of the hall as their contribution. (See chapter 8 for booking a hall, and chapter 13 for booking an open space).

Dates and times

Your date may be set for you by some other event – a meeting, May Day, a national demonstration – or you may have a choice. Weekends are best if you can choose, because people are free then. Saturdays are better than Sundays if you are trying to make a point to the general public, because that is when they will be around in the shopping streets. The usual time for marches to assemble is about 11 or 11.30 a.m. moving off about 12 midday and finishing by 2 or 3 p.m. This is not very convenient for the marchers, but it is when the maximum number of people are doing their shopping.

Check if anything else is going on at the same time which might interfere with your activity, especially a home football match; a college 'rag'; another demonstration; a festival or carnival procession.

Your local library will probably know about these; if they don't, ring up the people who are likely to organise things, like the football club secretary, or the students' union. You could also ask the local newspaper.

Marching in the early evening, perhaps before demonstrating outside a council meeting, can create problems if it coincides with the rush hour. A lot of people will see the march but they may well not come from the local area. People with child-care responsibilities will find this time particularly difficult, so do not plan for large numbers. You might do better to arrange something like street theatre (see chapter 11) which will work even with small numbers.

Advance publicity

Read chapters 4 and 5 which cover publicity and contacts with the press. Double-check that every bit of paper you send out about your march has, in large print, **the date, the time** of setting off, the **assembly point**.

If you are part of a national campaign, and are having a local march because you are too far away from the main one, then you will not need to worry about publicity for the cause, as it will be done elsewhere, but you will need to make sure people know that something is going on in your town as well as in Hyde Park.

A march should give you the chance to send out at least three press releases (see pages 60–5). Many people are automatically hostile to marchers, so you have got to convince them. **Try to get on local radio and TV** to explain the issues (see chapter 5). If you are going to hand out leaflets in the street, concentrate on the area covered by the march. Saturday shoppers tend to go to the same places each week, so if you tell them about the march one week, they will know what it is about when they see you marching the next. Many of them may not come from the area, so they will need an explanation if it is a local issue. You could also do some loud-speaking beforehand (see pages 58–9).

Things to organise

At the starting and finishing points, you need to think about **speakers**, **entertainment** (and also on the march itself), **loud-speaking equipment**, **creche facilities**, **information points**, and **transporting your equipment**.

For **the starting point**, you also need to think about getting people formed up ready to move off, and who is going to do this.

Finding **speakers** is covered in chapter 8. Make sure that **you confirm** that they are coming just before the day. It is crucial **to keep the speeches short** – ten minutes at most. Out of doors, people can drift off without being disruptive or feeling embarrassed.

Whether you need **entertainment** as well depends on the size and type of march. A march that is happening just 'because it always has', like Jim's May Day March in the examples, will need a few attractions to get people to come along. A march that is going to take a long time to form up or move off needs a band to keep people happy while waiting.

Booking entertainment

Think carefully about booking a band or theatre group. You need one that is used to playing in the open air, before an inattentive audience, and possibly being interrupted by announcements about lost children. If they have not done it before make sure they know about the problems. Possible people to ask about a theatre group are:

- another group that has had a festival or event recently;
- a local arts centre;
- the Regional Arts Association which covers your area; get their address from the local library;
- the drama department at a local school or college.

The type you want will usually be called a **community theatre group,** as opposed to the sort who do Noel Coward revivals in the church hall.

Sources for a band might be:

- the Musicians' Union (try their London office first, for a local contact);
- a music teacher in a school or college;
- a local youth club (most areas have a section of the Education Department dealing with youth groups, so contact them first, and they should be able to point you in the right direction);
- in mining areas, you could also try the NUM.

Entertainers need a stage – although this could be the back of a lorry – and adequate sound equipment. They will also usually need their expenses paid, and if there are 20 or 30 of them, this will be quite a lot. They probably won't be able to play musical instruments at all if it rains.

Marching bands

These are a special type, as it is much more difficult to play walking along than it is standing still. If you are in an area where juvenile jazz bands are popular, try to get one of those. If your band cannot march, you could put them on a flat-bed lorry at the front. With any music on a march, though, remember the following:

- The people marching just behind are going to hear the music a lot, and so you will get complaints if it is too way-out.
- The musicians will need somewhere to leave their instrument cases. On a long march, you may need to arrange

transport back to where they started from. If they come in a coach, the best thing will be for them to leave their cases on the coach and for the driver to wait for them at the other end. You may need to arrange this with the police.

At the front of the march

You could have people marching in a group at the front dressed in a way that makes your point, or put them in a lorry with a display as well. (See page 5 for creating an image.)

Also, keep an eye out on the day for good images. Often people turn up out of the blue in good costumes or with really witty banners. Try to get them to march at the front, or at least to let themselves be photographed by the press.

Lorries

The police usually say that vehicles on a march must go at the front. Otherwise, if the brakes fail or the driver's foot slips, there might be a serious accident.

You can hire or borrow flat-bed lorries, but you ought to tell the owner what you are using it for, as it does not do the gears any good for it to crawl along for hours at walking pace. You can drive a lorry of up to 3 tons weight with an ordinary driving licence; for anything heavier, the driver needs an HGV licence. Anyone who drives a large lorry for a living will have this; many bus drivers also have them, so if there is no one in your group, contact the local TGWU branch, or the convenor at the local bus garage or council transport depot, and see if they can find you a volunteer.

Make sure the **lorry**, the **driver** and **anyone riding on it**, are all **adequately insured**. If your lorry is 3 tons or less, having an HGV or PSV licensee driving it may mean you get the hire and insurance charges reduced.

Creche

Any large demonstration ought to have a creche, although if the weather is fine and the march not too long it may not be used by many (or any) children as their parents will take them along. Creches in general are covered in chapter 12, but the particular problem with a creche for a march is that the parents have to collect the children afterwards, and this will be difficult if they are at the wrong end of a route choked with marchers and traffic.

The ideal creche is a **playbus**, a double-decker specially adapted to run playgroups in. This is parked at the assembly point, the children collect together there, and then just before the march starts the bus is driven off to the finishing point. The children then play happily until the parents turn up with sore feet to collect them. However, playbuses do not exist in large numbers, and some of them belong to councils that will not lend them out to radical causes.

The next best thing is **a large Transit van** or similar vehicle, that can be filled up with children plus suitable equipment and again, driven off in advance of the march. Try a youth group, a union or a friendly supporter for a vehicle.

As a last resort, find **a church hall** or someone who lives near the starting point and is good enough to volunteer **his/her house** for the purpose. See pages 189–90 about equipment.

Advertise the creche on any leaflets you put out, so that people with children know they can come. **Arrange for lost children to be taken to the creche.**

Loudspeakers

The more people you think will turn up, the bigger the loudspeakers or PA (public address) system you need, especially when the march is assembling, and you have to get the people in order so that they can move off in line and not in a messy crowd. A really large march needs a person in a 'cherry picker' (the sort of lift-truck council workers mend lamp posts with), with a microphone for the PA, so s/he can see what is going on, and a system powerful enough to be heard all over the assembly area. A smaller march needs loudspeakers on the top of a car or lorry, while a simple local demonstration may only need a hand-held megaphone.

You can hire all this equipment – look in Yellow Pages for hire shops. Cost depends on size, but for smaller items, it is not exorbitant – unless you lose or break it. So treat it with care, and especially look after things that can walk off, like hand-held megaphones. Make sure **it is all insured**.

You may be able to borrow PA equipment – try a trade union office, the Labour Party or other left groups – and you will need to treat that with equal care. With any borrowed or hired equipment, it is important to make sure **the arrangements for picking it up are foolproof**. Is your volunteer reliable, does s/he know the way to the pick-up and is the person lending or hiring it definitely going to be there at the agreed time? Double-check all these arrangements, even at the risk of irritating people.

Allow plenty of time for setting up the equipment – it always takes longer than you think, and **check that it works before you need it**. It is infuriating if the first speaker at a meeting or rally starts and things go wrong. **For a small demonstration**, if having set it up and checked it, it starts to behave badly, you may do better to cut your losses and switch it off, and ask the speaker to talk more loudly. **For a larger one**, you will be stuck. Is there any back-up equipment you can use? If not, you will have to use the stewards as 'runners' to instruct marchers where they should be, and scrap any speeches.

If you do not have a band or a display at the front of the march, put a loudspeaker van there instead, with someone announcing what the march is about and asking people to join in. This **should not be the same van that you are using to get people in order** at the assembly point; for a march of any size, you will still need that to marshall the later groups of marchers.

At the finishing point, especially if you are having a rally, you will also need loudspeaking equipment of some sort for the speeches. The car at the front of the march will do if necessary, but try if possible to arrange some sort of platform – even if only the traditional soapbox – so that your speakers can be seen as well as heard. If the rally is in a public park, there may be a bandstand or something similar you can use, though it is best to ask permission first. Or there might be steps at the front of the public building you are converging on. At Blackpool it used to be traditional to hold rallies on the beach, with the speakers standing on an upturned boat. You can also hire staging, including a canopy to keep off the rain, and if the rally is an important part of your event this may well be worthwhile. (See chapter 13 on festivals, for more information about this.)

You may also need crash barriers to keep people from getting too close to the platform. Ask the police if they can supply these, or can tell you where to hire them.

Refreshments

There is always some food around when a march of any size is assembling or finishing, because the ice-cream and hamburger vans from miles around home in. For those who do not like, or cannot afford, a diet of coke and choc-ices, you may want to arrange for people to provide more interesting food. (Chapter 13 covers this, and arrangements for toilet facilities, in more detail. Also, see chapter 13 for first aid information points).

Stewarding

You need stewards while the march **is assembling**, while it **is on the move**, and when **it reaches the other end**. The jobs they need to do are covered below. You may not need all of them depending on how big your march is and how fully you have organised it.

At the beginning you need them for:

- controlling entry to the assembly area;
- marshalling people into marching order;
- dealing with queries by the loudspeaker van or platform;
- meeting up with speakers or entertainers;
- liaising with the press;
- meeting coaches to check pick-up points;
- helping set up the platform, PA equipment and so on;
- if necessary, staying behind afterwards to clear up rubbish.

On the march you need them for:

- marching with each column or group of people;
- acting as 'runners' between each steward;
- handing out leaflets to passers-by and shaking collecting tins.

At the other end you need them for:

- getting people to move up nearer the platform so there is room for late arrivals;
- staying near the platform to deal with speakers/entertainers/press/requests for announcements;
- going round with rubbish bags to clear up the mess, if necessary.

If you don't have many stewards, you will have to give each of them two or three jobs – at the beginning, on the march, and at the end. The more you have, the less hard each need work. Try to get each organisation involved to provide some stewards, and aim to **get their names and addresses** (they might be needed as witnesses); and **have a meeting of stewards beforehand** – preferably a few days before. If this is not possible, then ask them to come to your assembly point early, to sort out the different jobs.

Even if they have met beforehand, they should still come early so that you can sort out any gaps. Give each one **an armband** or other identification, and hand out **briefing information**, preferably as a leaflet, about the march. There is an example of one on page 117. Try to cover:

- the route
- the speakers at the rally
- where to take lost children
- where the toilets are (or that there are not any).

You will also need to tell them how you are communicating between stewards, and what to do in case of trouble.

If there is any chance of **a confrontation with the police**, stewards should also be given a leaflet explaining people's legal rights, and the phone number of a solicitor or law centre (see below). Tell them what tactics to apply if there is trouble, and ask them to make a note of any arrests they see, and report on them to the organisers.

If you are asking stewards to work for all or most of the day, it is only fair to give them a packed lunch and a can of beer. It also reduces the chances that they will abandon their posts and disappear to the pub.

For setting up the site, see chapter 13 under festivals.

Getting people in order

For a big demonstration, draw up in advance a plan showing **where the groups should assemble, and the order in which they should march off.** Send this out to the organisations you expect to be sending groups.

If there are vehicles at the assembly point – loudspeaker van, creche, first aid or whatever – mark their parking spaces on the plan too, and give copies of it to the drivers so they know where to go. If you are assembling somewhere with restricted entry for motor vehicles, like a public park, you will also need to give them letters or permits, and arrange in advance with the authorities that people with such identification should be let in. You might anyway want to restrict entry yourselves, to avoid being cluttered up with coaches and private cars. You will need to put people on the gate to control this.

Marshalling

An important person among the stewards is **the marshal for the assembly point**. The marshal is the one who gets on the loudspeaker, asking people to get into line, telling those with the banners where to go, and generally getting the demonstrators ready to move off. It is a job that appeals to aggressive people, especially at large demonstrations where they will be on a platform above the crowds. You need someone tough and with **a voice that people will listen to**, as it can be difficult getting trendy lefties into line. But **avoid aggressive people who will lose their tempers**, and people who will make sexist remarks or tell dirty jokes to pass the time. The marshal will need help from stewards on the ground, asking people to move to the right places.

A big march takes a very long time to move off. A hundred thousand people will take three hours – even 20,000 can take about three quarters of an hour.

The marshal needs to be given **a timetable**, setting out what is going on, in the same way as a chairperson at a meeting. Also give him/her all the other information the stewards are getting, as there may be odd queries.

You also need at least one **'platform steward'**. This is because a particular problem for speakers and entertainers at a demonstration, is that of finding the organiser, who will be rushing around from place to place sorting out last minute problems. Even wearing an armband, s/he will not be visible, because s/he will be in among crowds of people. So give someone else, **with no other responsibilities**, the job of staying near the loudspeaking equipment or stage – and refusing to move even in the face of urgent appeals to do something elsewhere – to make contact with the people you are expecting. S/he can then brief them on what is going on, and answer any last minute questions or problems they have.

The same person, with extra help for a big event, can **deal with the press**, who can be told on the press release who to look for and where; and **deal with any messages** about people needing a doctor, lost children, meetings people want others to know about, and so on.

This person needs the power to decide whether or not to pass up a message to the speaker to interrupt what is going on and make an announcement, and should not let anyone else speak directly to the people on the platform. It is distracting and can cause muddle and confusion.

Stewarding the march

Even on a small march or demonstration it is important **to have more than one person who knows what is happening**, can direct people to different points, and to shepherd the marchers along. These are the basic jobs of stewards. They need to make sure that the march does not get strung out with large gaps and so becomes fragmented. Stewards should be able to deal with minor trouble – disputes between marchers, marchers trying to change the route – without calling on the police to intervene. The stewards should be told that **the police** are responsible for **the control of the public**; **the stewards** are responsible for **the control of the marchers**; and the two should be kept separate. In London, the police issue 'guidance notes' for stewards.

The stewards may also need to see that placards at the front of the march are **only about the demonstration**, not about any political group; and to ask people selling newspapers to do so behind the head of the march so that they do not distract the marchers. Allocate as many people as possible as marching stewards. About 1 per 100 marchers is about right. If you can persuade the police you have enough stewards, they should be willing to reduce their own numbers.

Each steward should be allocated a section of the marchers, preferably people they know. Work out a way of passing information between stewards, for instance why there is a delay, or changes in the arrangements for coach pick-up afterwards, so that they can tell people.

On a big march people sometimes use walkie-talkies between senior stewards, although their use is often over-rated. For them to be worthwhile, you need **someone who really knows about them** who can work out a system of call numbers and points for people, and then to brief thoroughly those who are going to use them. It is a skill people can pick up in organisations like St John's Ambulance or the Sea Cadets, and so you may well have someone in your group who knows what they are talking about.

There are problems, though. Many people (especially men) start playing out their Starsky and Hutch fantasies as soon as they get a walkie-talkie in their hands, and will not listen to the instructions. The systems are expensive to hire, and if you lose one item you have messed up the set and will be charged a fortune. Also, you may get a lot of interference from other groups of users, including abusive remarks if you are cutting into their conversations.

Alternatively, now that Citizens' Band radio is legal, it should be possible to arrange for a communications system based on that, at least between the assembly point and the finishing point.

Less high-tech, but much more reliable, are a couple of people on bicycles, who can move up and down the march passing on messages. If you are short of stewards, you could also give them hand-held megaphones and ask them to make announcements to the marchers direct (they need to be good cyclists though).

Here is an example of a briefing for stewards before a big demonstration in London.

■ **To all stewards on the 10 July Demonstration**
Assembly
At Hyde Park; March assembles 11.30 a.m., moves off 1.00 p.m. and goes to Trafalgar Square via:
  Park Lane
  Hyde Park Corner
  Piccadilly
  Lower Regent Street
  Pall Mall
  Cockspur Street
  Trafalgar Square South Side.
Nicholas Bryanson will be Chief Marshal in Hyde Park, with five stewards to assist.
Creche
Will be provided in a double-decker playbus, which will be parked from 12.00 to 1 p.m. opposite Speakers' Corner in Park Lane. Immediately before the march starts, the bus will move off to Northumberland Avenue near the Embankment and stay parked there until the end of the demonstration. Parents should be asked to hand their children over at Park Lane and collect them at Northumberland Avenue. A leaflet will be given to them explaining where the bus will be parked.
Police
Commander Frame and Inspector Williams will be in charge at Hyde Park. Inspector Hugh Scarman, tel. 000-000 will be responsible for transport arrangements.

Lorries

There will be two lorries on this demonstration. One in Hyde Park to act as a speakers' platform, parked at Reformer's Tree. The other to lead the march off, carrying a steel band. It will be parked ready at the gate in North Carriage Drive in Hyde Park.

Public Address

The PA system is going to be delivered by Sound Developments Ltd at 10.30 a.m. Three people are needed to help set it up in Hyde Park. It is being collected by the contractors at 4.30 p.m. and those same people are asked to help with this.

Stewarding

There will be 40 stewards for the event, with 4 senior stewards who are:

T. Freeman

W. Stevens

P. Hince

J. Kane

In Hyde Park stewards will be needed for the following:

(1) coach stewards in Park Lane, at the dropping-off point, to give out maps and information where to pick up (4 needed);

(2) stewarding the platform to ensure it is protected, and also to make contact with speakers and press (2 needed);

(3) column stewards to ensure that the march forms up in the correct order (8 needed);

(4) all these stewards are requested to clear up the Park after the demonstration has left, and then catch up with the marchers;

(5) all the other stewards are asked to take up position with the march as it moves off. Please keep the march together, without large gaps between groups.

Music

The following bands will be performing on the day:

(1) Musicians' Union band;

(2) Gill Peterson and her Trinidad Steel band (mounted on lorry) which will lead the demonstration.

A bus will be provided for the Musicians' Union band and it will park in Northumberland Avenue after it has dropped off at Hyde Park.

Trafalgar Square

On arrival it is intended to have the bands playing in the Square, directly in front of the plinth of Nelson's Column. There will then be speakers, who will be:

(1) The Chairperson of the Committee;

(2) Jimmy Conway, MP;
(3) Sarah Coote;
(4) The Bishop of Nowhere;
(5) A health worker (to be found by health service unions).

Sylvia Jamieson will be chairperson on the platform. She will be assisted by two stewards within the platform enclosure. Any messages for the platform must be passed through these stewards. Speakers and entertainers should make contact with these stewards in the first instance. Press contact should be with Fred Bassett, who will also be in the platform enclosure wearing a press badge. No one else should be allowed in the enclosure.

All stewards are requested to stay in the Square after the end of the demonstration to help clear up.

If there is trouble

Please read the guidance notes issued by the police. We would like to emphasise that this is a peaceful demonstration, and stewards are asked to help ensure that it is so. Contact a senior steward with any queries. If there are difficulties or arrests, please observe carefully what goes on and make a note of it as soon as possible afterwards. You may be needed as a witness. Please report incidents to the senior stewards.

Thank you for your help

Publicity

Leaflets

You will need leaflets **beforehand**, to advertise your demonstration, unless you want to keep it a surprise. (See chapter 4 for ideas about printing and distribution of leaflets.) But you will also need them **at the time**, to hand out to passers-by, so that they know the reasons for the demonstration. It will be important for the leaflets to be easy to read, and eye catching. In writing them, **assume the readers do not know anything about the issue**. People often shop a long way from home, and even local people may not read the local papers. Unless the issue has made the national press, it will have to be explained. If there is a rally at the end, use your leaflets to invite people to that; they might not want to walk with you, but could be willing to come to a park and listen to the speakers.

Have some of the marchers going along the pavement beside the march, handing out the leaflet as they go, especially to people standing in bus queues, and anyone who comes to a shop door to watch – they may actually have time to read it.

People can walk along the pavement selling badges or giving away stickers (see pages 55–6 for details on these). You can also take along buckets for people to put money in, to help pay your expenses. Put some cash in each one from your own funds, to start it off – no one likes being first. Put someone in charge and make sure:

- all your sellers and collectors are wearing stewards' armbands;
- all your buckets are properly labelled;
- the chief collector knows how many have been given out, and ensures s/he gets the same number back;
- that you have an arrangement for counting and checking the money; and
- that someone is going to pay it in, or hang on to it over the weekend afterwards.

You do not need a licence to collect money in the street if it is connected with a public meeting or demonstration, so long as you stay clearly close to, and connected with it. There may be local by-laws though about collecting in a particular park or public open space, so check with the town hall or local library.

Placards and banners

These are important – you have got to catch the eye of passers-by, and tell them what it is all about. Otherwise all your effort will be wasted. Try and get commitments from people in advance to bring banners, especially large trade union banners that will photograph well. Set aside some time before the march when people can make placards. This is a tedious job, so it is more fun to get together as a group rather than leave it to individuals soldiering on by themselves. Work out a few slogans – short and easy for people going past to understand.

If yours is a small demonstration, write them with thick felt-tip pens on large sheets of cardboard, which then need nailing, or stapling if you can get hold of a giant stapler, to poles or pieces of 2 ins by 4 ins wood. If you have already got posters about the issue, use them instead or as well.

- Mary's group, campaigning against the hospital closure, can use the big posters they had for a public meeting, with the bottom section that advertises the meeting cut off.

If you are getting help from a union, political party, or individuals who have been politically active for a while, they might have some old placards, in which case you need only glue your poster, or a large sheet of paper, over the previous slogan. This will save time and money. If you have not got a ready supply of wood, then ask around among DIY enthusiasts because they rarely throw anything away.

Once you have made your placards, try to hang on to them at the end of the demonstration, and do not let people just chuck them away as you may need them again, or you might want to pass them on to the next group.

For a large demonstration, it may be best to get a lot of posters printed (see chapter 4). Printing on heavy cardboard is expensive; it is cheaper to get the posters printed on ordinary paper and stick them on card yourself.

Banners are easy enough to make. You need a large piece of material and some paint, and someone who is reasonably good at lettering. Or you can cut the letters out of material and sew them on with a machine. You can also make very elaborate and beautiful designs. The important points are:

- don't make it too heavy – someone's got to carry it;
- make sure it is waterproof;
- cut holes in it to let the wind through – it is always windy on demonstrations; cutting out the centre of an O is the easiest way to do this;
- first write or draw what you want to say on a piece of paper and then chalk or mark it on the banner. Follow it carefully. It is very easy to leave letters out, and the banner then looks like a joke.

Once you have got your banners and placards, you need to get people **to bring them**, and **to take them away**. Get people to agree in advance to do this, and if they are taking them back to their houses, make sure you know where they are afterwards. You do not want to waste all that work.

At the end of the march, arrange for the big banners and good placards to be grouped behind the speakers' platform, and along the front, to make a good show for press photographers.

As the march sets off, the stewards need to hand out placards to people without one. During the march, ask them to keep an eye out for people who are getting fed up with carrying placards and are about to abandon them, and try to persuade someone else to take a turn instead. If you are rallying somewhere that placards are not allowed (Hyde Park is an example of this) you will need someone at the gate collecting them.

At the end of the march

You need here **an anchorperson**, to do much the same job as the chief marshal at the other end (see page 115). S/he should have a loudspeaker, and welcome the demonstrators and tell them they are wonderful, and that the demonstration is the biggest since the last one. S/he should also tell them where to put their banners and announce the speakers or entertainment. S/he needs to be able to jolly things along, especially if it is cold and miserable, and to be a person who does not panic when a speaker does not turn up.

As people reach the assembly point, there is a natural tendency to drop the banner and sit down, or at least stop marching, as soon as possible. This can mean that the entrances get clogged up with the first arrivals, so that later arrivals cannot get in, and your march may then grind to a halt, with frustration all round. So you need the anchorperson, with help from the stewards, to persuade people to move on, closer to the platform, and to keep the entrances clear. They often combine this with rattling collecting tins or buckets to persuade the marchers to give their last few pennies to pay for the organisation.

Clearing up

The arrangements for this vary enormously. In some places the park keepers or street sweepers may be expected to do the extra work without any extra pay; in others they will be given overtime. There are also places where the organisation concerned has to pay for clearing up, possibly to a private contractor. So you need to **find out in advance** what the official position is; ask the council's Recreation Department if it is a park, or the Cleaning Department if it is a street. Also find out what **the manual workers would prefer you to do**. Try ringing up the convenor or senior steward at the town hall – s/he should be able to put you on to the right person. If they want you to clear up, then do, but otherwise leave it. If you have not got the money to pay the council for doing it, explain that to the union and they are likely to accept that you will have to do it with volunteer labour.

If clearing up *is* needed, then people need to stay behind both at the assembly point and at the rallying point. Give them each a large plastic bag, and ask them to put in all the rubbish, and stack them at a convenient point. They should hand any lost property to the organisers. You will also need help in dismantling any staging or other fixed equipment, and if necessary transporting it away.

Trouble on the day

The law, and what to do if people are arrested, is covered in chapter 7. There are precautions you can take in advance:

- Find **a law centre**, or a **friendly solicitor**, who will agree to be available on the phone throughout the day, so that the number can be given to the stewards and the marchers to contact if anyone is arrested. Try one of the sources of advice on page 16 for the name of a solicitor.
- Try and find out **which police station has been allocated** for any arrests on the march – the police always allocate one in advance, and often now choose a station well away from the march so that there is no demonstration outside it. See if your local police station will tell you.

Trouble with the Law (see 'Useful books') goes into detail about preparing for a march when you expect trouble, so consult this if necessary.

After the march

Your first priority must be to see that any equipment you have hired gets back to its right place as fast as possible, as you are probably paying for it by the day. Borrowed equipment also has to go back. If you have lost any, you will have to sort this out, and probably pay for it.

Write to thank, not only your speakers, but everyone else who helped you. Do not forget the **park or hall staff**, if they were co-operative; and **the police**, unless they behaved really badly. This may feel a bit hypocritical but it will help to smooth your path next time.

Unpublicised demonstrations

The principles of organising surprise demonstrations are the same as those given above, but since you do not want anyone to know about them beforehand, the organisation has got to be kept within a tight group of people, and recruiting people to come along can only be done by word of mouth among those you trust.

No one really knows how good the police are about picking up information about things you do not want them to know, and therefore how careful you have to be. They are probably better in London than elsewhere, and will be more on the lookout if something where they can expect trouble is happening in their area – a visit by the Prime Minister or a fascist demonstration.

Assume that phone calls from the convenor's office or the union district office phone are not private; it is better to be too cautious than too confident. Use the home telephones of people not usually involved in politics or union activities, or use call boxes. Post letters in boxes well away from work or home, but keep them to a minimum. Avoid hiring things, but if you do, use the name of someone unconnected with your activity. You will need leaflets to tell the world what you are doing once the demonstration has started, but do not go to a commercial printer; instead, go to a community print shop or an organisation that prints left-wing magazines, or rely on good quality duplicating or photocopying. Check that you have not left dud copies lying around by the duplicator, or the original in the photocopier.

You will need stewards, who must be briefed carefully about what the tactics are, and who is to give them instructions. Decide on a spokesperson, both with the police and with the press, and get everyone else to direct them to him/her. Remember, though, that if your demonstration breaks the law, it is the spokesperson who is likely to be prosecuted, so be prepared to give him/her your support. Arrange for a lawyer to be available at the end of a phone, if you know a trustworthy one.

If your demonstration is to have any impact, you must not keep it a secret from the press once it has started. There are two ways you can deal with letting the press know:

- **Issue a press release**, but with an embargo on it (see page 62). This is best if your demonstration is not going to make front page headlines.
- Give someone the job of **phoning up the local papers, radio and TV** as the demonstration starts, and telling them the details. Make notes in advance so that you are sure of getting everything across. If it is a big story, they may send a reporter down. You can also phone up the Press Association direct; *Using the Media* (see 'Useful books') tells you how to do this.

Make sure you have a photographer (see page 63) so that

afterwards you can send photographs to the newspapers who do not send anyone.

In some cases, for instance if you are opposing a visit by a government minister to your factory, the press and TV cameras will already be there. This gives you the opportunity to put your case over to a wider public.

Having arranged a spokesperson, s/he should make the approach directly, saying, 'I am speaking for this group – do you want to know what we are up to and why?' **Make sure you are prepared** for both newspaper and television interviews that arise out of this approach. *Using the Media* explains how to get your point across and how to avoid being caught by the tricks of the trade. If you cannot get your case across, your demonstration could back-fire very badly.

Direct action

This is only a short section since each activity of this sort is a bit different and most of the organisational points have already been covered earlier in this chapter.

Direct action includes demonstrations where you go beyond simply marching and speech-making to *doing* something, whether it be occupying the council chambers, or cutting down the fence at Greenham Common.

This book is not intended to make a judgement on whether these activities are good or bad; that is up to your group to decide. But when thinking what to do, **consider why you are doing it**, and whether it will be effective in achieving your aims. Some direct action will alienate the public; some will alienate those who should be your supporters. For example, after Brent Council was twice stopped from carrying out its business by demonstrators, the Labour chairman of one of the committees resigned because he objected so strongly to the tactics. Would you mind this? Is it a risk you are prepared to take? Alternatively, is there action you can take that will be effective but not alienating?

There are several possible reasons for taking direct action: **because you feel morally bound to oppose in any way you can**, whatever the repercussions.

■ Sonie's group, for instance, plan to lie down in front of cruise missile carriers because they object so strongly to their installation.

Or you want **to dramatise your grievance**, and either cannot find another way of getting it to the attention of the decision-makers, or have tried and been ignored.

■ Errol's group protesting about hospital closures invade the Health Authority meeting for this reason.

Or maybe the cause is nearly lost and it is **your last possible chance to create a change**, or at least to show how strongly you feel.

■ Annette and her friends occupied a day nursery for the day before it was due to close, and tried to run it themselves, as a last resort.

The key points on all of these are:

● you are bound to break the law at some point; so **you need to know your rights**;
● **you need to trust each other** if your plans are to work; so you should be a fairly small group who know each other, and have beforehand had some discussion of your tactics, or possibly some training. This is particularly important if you are determined to be non-violent whatever the provocation;
● **be imaginative**; the Greenham Common women have kept up public interest by creating a whole series of worthwhile images.

Plan in advance how you are going to tell the press what is going on and why you are doing it. Otherwise it is pointless. See the section on demonstrations you don't publicise in advance, pages 123–5, for ideas on this.

Breaking the law

Chapter 7 gives details of the law in a number of areas. *Trouble with the Law* (see 'Useful books') gives you a lot more information on this. Get someone in your group to read it and explain to the rest of you. There are particular points to bear in mind.

If you **force your way** into a public meeting, the organisers can throw you out; see page 81 for the organisers' rights. **Occupations are not themselves illegal**; but under the Criminal Damage Act 1971 **forcing locks or breaking windows to get in** are. So is **entering premises violently** if there is someone opposing your entry (under the Criminal Law Act 1977). Choose a time during the day when the building is open, but there are few people around, to do this. If the owners say things are damaged or missing after an occupation, you could be charged with criminal damage or theft. One group occupying a day nursery got their MP to come in early in the occupation, and then again at the end, to be an independent witness to the state of the building and furniture. They were wise, because the council did in fact try to prosecute.

A sit-down will usually count as **obstruction of the highway**. If you do not move along when the police tell you to, you will be **obstructing the police** as well. If you are going to make them carry you away, **try to get some practice.** It is not as easy as it might seem to go limp and not thrash out when you are being manhandled. Each person should be instructed **to observe what is happening to others**; so if someone is being dragged away by his/her hair, another person should try to get a note of the number of the police officer who is doing it.

Sticking it out

If you are planning to go on until you have got a result or a promise of action, you need some long-term planning. How long can you sustain an occupation of the nursery, or walking back and forth across the road? How soon will your supporters get bored and start drifting off?

Decide in advance if you really do mean to stick it out. You might want **to plan on a time limit** – better to have a really good piece of action that goes on for 24 hours and then stops, rather than one that is planned to go on much longer and fizzles out.

Alternatively, **pitch your demand at a level where it can be met fairly quickly** – that is, saying, 'We'll go on until you agree to reconsider the closure of the nursery', rather than, 'We're going on until you agree the nursery won't close'.

If you might be going on for a long time, people, particularly those with children, need to think **about arrangements if they cannot get home**. At the least, each person should warn a spouse, friend or neighbour what might happen; and someone should slip off and ring these contacts once it becomes apparent that you are going to be there all night. You need to think about arrangements for getting blankets, thermos flasks of tea, etc. The same friends and neighbours may be able to help.

Spontaneous demonstrations

If your demonstration really is on the spur of the moment, you certainly will not have time to read this book. But just in case you are reading it afterwards, or if the idea of having a demonstration has occurred to you if to no one else, several points may be useful.

How are the press going to know? You could get someone **to ring them up** as the demonstration starts. If it is too late for this, send out **a press release** as soon as possible afterwards, saying the demonstration happened, how many people were involved, and what it was about.

It may well not be used, but it's worth a try. Also **try to provide photographs** – send someone home for a camera, if necessary.

The law on demonstrations is given on pages 100–3 . There are usually loopholes for genuinely spontaneous demonstrations. If your local by-laws have none, the organiser could be prosecuted, but this is unlikely to happen if the demonstration was **an understandable reaction** to a dramatic event. Council tenants marching on the town hall after a fire in a tower-block for instance, would attract too much sympathy for the police to bring a prosecution.

If you do get taken to court, it will give you extra publicity.

Checklist for marches and demonstrations

See page(s) Date done

Why bother?   98

(1) Why are you having the march?
(2) What are your priorities?

People

Have people been given the jobs of:

- finding the assembly and finishing points?   106
- sorting out route with police?   103
- organising vehicles?   110
- finding speakers?   108
- contacting the press?   108
- organising creche?   110
- doing leaflets, posters, and other publicity?   119
- taking along banners and equipment on the day?   120
- organising the stewards?   113
- taking and banking the collection?   120

Things to do

Book speakers and entertainers: 108
- Letters written confirming
- Reply received
- Phone call to check
- Expenses offered
- Thank you letter

Book assembly and finishing points: 106
- Letter confirming
- Deposit paid
- Check:
  - electricity supply   216
  - toilets
- Lorries: organised   110
  - driver found
  - insured
- Arrangements for vehicle access   114
- Arrangements for clearing up   122
- Paid bill   123

See page(s) Date done

Press contact:
- 1st press release sent   60–5
- 2nd press release sent
- Phone to see if they are coming
- 3rd press release, after meeting

Publicity:
- Mailing to local groups   26–59
- Ad in local paper:
    paid for
- Leaflets: how many?
    printed
    delivered
    paid for
- Posters: how many?
    printed
    put up
    paid for
- Banners and placards:
  Who is making them?
  How are they getting there?
  How are they getting back?
- Any other publicity ideas?

Loudspeaking: 58
- Car organised?
- Loudspeaker
- Insurance
- Someone to do it

Coach parks: 66–8
- Where?
- Maps?
- Info sent out

On the day

Stewards: people available to   113
- set up the site in advance
- be chief marshal
- look after the platform
- march with each group
- hand out leaflets
- take the collection

- steward at the other end
- clear up afterwards
- staff information table

Equipment: Check you have
- toolkit   92
- first aid box   237
- material for information point
- leaflets to hand out   29–48
- clipboard for addresses/petition   154–172
- buckets for collection   120
- rubbish bags   122
- PA system – does it work?   111
- briefing sheets for stewards   117

Have you:
- organised first aid?   237
- found a solicitor to go on standby?   16
- found out what police station
  people would be sent to?   123

Afterwards

- Thank you letters sent?   123
- Bills paid?
- Borrowed/hired equipment
  returned?
- Was it worthwhile?
- What is your next step?

10.

Lobbies

'Lobbying' is what you do when you put your case directly to the decision-makers, and listen and respond to their objections. You can do it face to face or by letter; you can do it in a small group (or a series of them) or as a 'mass lobby'. In some cases there is hardly any difference between mass lobby and a demonstration. The distinction, so far as there is one, is that in a lobby your particular targets are the individuals who are going to decide about the point that matters to you, rather than the world in general.

You could lobby:

- MPs at the House of Commons;
- the local council at a meeting;
- individual MPs or councillors at their surgeries;
- other bodies such as the Health Authority or school governors.

Aims

The aim of any lobby is to reach the people who are actually going to make the decisions. But within this there can be different priorities. Are you trying to;

- inform people about an issue which might seem rather obscure and unimportant to them, so that they will actually turn up to the meeting and come to the right decision?
- convince people of your support for, or opposition to, a particular measure which is going through in the near future?
- persuade people of the need to take more interest in, and give more priority to, a particular group?

Here are some examples of the different sorts of aim:

■ Anthony's youth group have applied to the council for an

increased grant so they can build an extension to the youth club. They are afraid their application will get lost among all the others, and that the Finance Department will cast doubt on it because it is not very professional. So they want to see all the members of the Grants Committee before the meeting to explain what they really want and why.

- Sylvia's group are worried that MPs are going to vote to tighten up on the 1967 Abortion Act, especially since the papers are saying that they are getting six times as many letters against abortion as in support of it. So they want to show that there are a lot of people who feel very strongly the other way.
- Olly's pensioners' group feel that pensioners are being given a raw deal because it's assumed they will not make a fuss. So they are going to see their newly elected MP to tell him that he and his party have got to give more priority to pensioners.

Priorities

These three groups need to approach their lobbying in rather different ways:

- Anthony and his youth group have got to impress the councillors with how sincere and responsible they are, and convince them they will make good use of the money. They need to send along a small group who must know exactly what they are talking about. They also need to put a lot in writing so that the councillors can refer to it afterwards.
- Sylvia's group want to stress the level of support for their case. So they must get as many people as they can on a lobby of parliament and also organise the people who cannot get to the Houses of Parliament to write letters. They believe they will convince MPs best by telling them about personal experiences, and so they do not need to concentrate too much on facts and figures (though they will need enough to be able to counter MPs' arguments) but they must make sure they are not too nervous to speak out. They must also think about press publicity, to counter all the columns the anti-abortion lobby has been getting.
- Olly's group want to show their MP that they will make a fuss if there is a threat to their interests. They can do this by turning up in numbers, and can risk being mildly disruptive – such as sitting-in until he listens to them – because they know the police will not want to arrest them, and that the worst they will

get from the press are patronising remarks about 'battling grannies'. They want to get over to him the strength of their general claim, so they need to do quite a lot of research in advance and have information about all the aspects of pensioners' lives at their fingertips. They also need to keep a record of any commitments the MP makes and to publicise them so that he cannot go back on them later.

Who, where and when

For all these groups, the first action is the same. This is to find out:

Who actually makes the decision? You must find out who you have to argue your case with. Often the real power does not lie with the people who carry through the procedure. For instance, on many local councils all the controversial decisions are made in the party groups, and the politicians come to the committee meetings having already made up their minds.

When is the decision to be taken? You want to get in before it is made, but not too far in advance, as people will have forgotten what you said by the time the meeting comes round. So you need to time it carefully, just a few days before the crucial meeting, or even on the day itself, as people are going in to the meeting.

Where will you find the people you are going to lobby? Some organisations hold their meetings in rotation in different places – health authorities often move round the hospitals, for instance. MPs hold their surgeries in different parts of the constituency, and if you are lobbying parliament, very few MPs are there on Fridays. So you need to be sure you are there at the right place and the right time to catch the people you want to see.

Finding out who takes the decision

This can be difficult and it may not always be possible to get it right. Find a sympathiser who understands the system, and can tell you how it really works. Some of the groups listed on pages 257–258 may be useful here. There are other places or people to look for.

Is there a **councillor**, or a **local politician**, on your group's management committee, or that of another group that you know? Even if they do not come to the meetings very often, and have only been put there to fill up a space, they are likely to have developed some loyalty to the group and should be willing to give some advice.

Is there **a national campaign** with whom you are linking up, who asked you to lobby on the subject? If they have not sent the information out in their mailing, phone them and ask – and suggest they put their facts in their next mailing so that no one else has to waste time doing the same.

Is there a **local reporter** on newspaper, television or radio, who has taken an interest in your story or in similar cases before. S/he may understand the system already, or may be willing to use contacts to help with finding out. Don't bother, though, to try this source if the newspaper generally is hostile to your sort of cause. Even if reporters themselves are sympathetic, they will not be able to use up the time on stories they know the editor will not print.

If none of these work, then it may be necessary to go to the official channels, in which case you will be told where the decision is **officially** made. This would be: the town clerk's office for the council; the district administrator, for a health authority; the government department involved for a decision being made by parliament.

The local library should be able to help with names and addresses for these and other official bodies. If you can only get an official answer on this, stay flexible. Once you make contact, you may find out the information you are really after.

- Anthony is told by the town clerk that the Finance Committee decides on all grants. So he rings up the chairperson to make an appointment to come and discuss their application. 'Oh no,' says the chairperson over the phone, 'we only rubber stamp the decisions of the Grants Committee. The person you want to see is Jo Bellotti.'

Finding out when and where

Once you know **who** is making the decision, it should be fairly easy to find out **when**, from the same source. But double-check and if there is any uncertainty, follow it up a bit later with the same person, or a different one who knows more. If in doubt, plan to lobby **before the earliest meeting** that the issue could come up at, and if necessary to do it a second time as well.

- Jo Bellotti says to Anthony that he is not sure whether the

Grants Committee are going to discuss the youth club at next month's meeting or the one after. He suggests Anthony ring the town clerk a week before the next meeting, just to check. Anthony does this and meanwhile, just to be sure, he and his group prepare their case for this month's meeting. When they ring the town clerk, they find the youth club is not on the agenda till the following month – which gives them extra time to get ready.

It is always worth **checking again** just before the meeting, in case there has been a sudden change of plan and something urgent means your item has been postponed. If you turn up on the wrong day you will look foolish, however understandable your mistake. Also check carefully on **the time** of your meeting – it could easily have been brought forward half an hour.

Double-check **where** you've got to go to. If you turn up at the wrong place, all your effort is simply wasted. You must not assume that just because the health authority met at Springfield Hospital last month, it is going to the same place this month.

The following sections look at different types of lobbies, and the different points you have to remember.

Arranging a meeting

You have decided you are going to try to meet, say, three local councillors, to give them all the facts and figures to back up your case. Decide **who is going to meet them**. You want a careful discussion of your points – but you don't want them to feel over-whelmed and therefore threatened, because it will not help your case if they do. So you need to **select a small group**. Aim for no more than twice the number of people you are going to meet, and perhaps fewer, and appoint a spokesperson. S/he will take charge of the meeting from your side, give everyone the chance to speak – but make sure you don't all speak at once – and check that all the points you needed to make are covered. You may want to split up different parts of your subject among the group.

- In Anthony's group they decided on Anthony to talk about the demand among teenagers for a bigger club, and the current waiting list; Sharon to talk about how long it will take to build; and Kevin to talk about how they arrived at the cost.

Once you get there, **don't argue among yourselves;** present a united front. Decide in advance what to do **if someone gets a fact wrong.** For instance if someone else notices, s/he could pass a note up to the person chairing your side who can then, without making a great fuss about it, say something like, 'Perhaps I can just make the point that . . .' and put things right. Make sure the people on your delegation get on reasonably well, or at least are prepared to swear friendship for the evening.

Appoint someone who will **take notes and write them up afterwards.** This is important if you are trying to get a specific agreement. If Jo Bellotti says, 'Yes, I will support your project and tell the officers they must recommend it at the committee meeting on Tuesday,' you want a record of this. You could also write to him after the meeting saying, 'We are so glad that last week you agreed to support our project,' so that you have got him even more firmly pinned down.

Getting in touch

Make an appointment with the people you want to see. **Write a letter** explaining who you are and why you want to meet them, and then **ring up a day or two later** and ask for a specific date and time. If you are trying to meet two or three people – say, councillors or MPs – it may be very difficult to find a time when they can all be there at once. Be prepared for a lot of phone calls to and fro, as you will need to suggest several alternative dates and check them with all the different people. If there are people in your group who have to organise meetings like this in their jobs, ask if they would mind doing it this time, as they will be used to the frustrations.

If you simply cannot find a time they can all make, decide whether you want more than one meeting, or to do without one or two of the people. Obviously you need the leader of the group of people you have planned to meet, but you could, if necessary, say apologetically to others 'We're terribly sorry, but it's proving impossible to find a date when all three of you are available, would you mind if we went ahead without you?' Be careful though not to give the impression that you think that person does not matter – **you are in the business of trying to win them over.**

It will probably be most convenient for them to meet on their own territory – in the council offices, or the Tory party rooms for instance – **but is this best for you?** If you want to convince them that the estate is damp, you could invite them to meet you in a damp flat, and this would make your point better than a lot of words. You will then need to find somewhere suitable for the meeting – a family who do not mind their flat being invaded – and to be sure that it is clean and tidy, and that there are enough chairs.

Having arranged a date, **write a letter confirming** – and tell everybody on your side as well. You might want to send the people you are lobbying a 'briefing', that is, an outline of the points you want to make, to give them a chance to study it before they come.

There is a story that when people start writing reports in the Civil Service, they are instructed, 'First tell them what you are going to say, then say it, then tell them what you've said'. That is, you need an **introduction**, which summarises the problem and the solution, the **briefing itself** which sets out the details, and the **conclusion** that says what you want the councillors/MPs/ whoever, to do. Work on the assumption that they will only read the introduction and the conclusion closely. Here, as an example is the group's briefing on the youth club:

■ *Introduction*
   This report outlines the history of the Bassett Youth Club, and the activities that go on each week. It gives figures of the number of young people aged 13 to 18 in the area around the club, and on the waiting lists for different activities. It then gives details of how much the proposed extension will cost, how the money will be spent, how the club will cope during the building work, and finally how the extension will be used.
   (Then there are paragraphs on each of these points, and finally there is a conclusion which says:)
   In this document we have presented the reasons why the youth club extension is needed, and how it can be done. We are asking you to:
   (a) give us a grant of £ . . . . to build it;
   (b) grant outline planning permission for it;
   (c) arrange for the youth club to move out temporarily and use X school while the building is going on.

It will be useful to make your notes in this order anyway when you are doing your homework in advance. This means that, if you talk from your notes, you will be able to get the main points across, and to remind them of everything you want at the end. Putting something in writing is sensible, however short it is, so that they can take it away from the meeting. Councillors or politicians might have a dozen meetings that week, and if they are going to remember what you have said, they will need something to jog their memories.

Keep your briefing simple – do not bury the issue in jargon and long words. If you have a lot of figures, decide which are the important ones, and only put them in. Since a lot of people skip tables and figures, try and include the main point you are making in the heading to the table, or in the paragraph before or after the table. You could say, for instance, 'This table shows that 43 per cent of the houses on the estate are very damp, while only 6 per cent have no damp problem at all.'

Writing a document like this is not difficult. You will know the facts, having lived with them for a while, But it does take time, so you need to allow for that. Try to get it nicely produced, preferably typed, without mistakes, and well spaced so it is not a strain on the eyes, and then duplicated or photocopied clearly.

Although this is great deal of work, once it is done you can use it for other things as well: as the basis of **a press release**; to **give to anyone else** who enquires; to **turn into a report** to circulate more widely.

Other exhibits

There may be other things you want to get ready as well:

- photographs of the damp conditions, or of the bit of land you want to build on, or of the Christmas party at the club;
- maps and plans of what you want to see;
- charts that illustrate the points you want to make;
- perhaps even samples of what you are complaining about, like clothes with mould on.

Everything you provide needs to add to your case, and be clear and easy to understand. Use someone who does not know much about the question as a guinea-pig. If s/he doesn't get the point, the councillors probably will not either.

At the meeting

Arrange to meet up **half an hour before you are due**, to check up that everyone is there, to calm your nerves and talk over any last minute points.

If anyone is going to have difficulty getting to the meeting, try to arrange lifts rather than depending on unreliable public transport; if you have got things to bring, you will need a volunteer with a reasonably foolproof method of transport.

Dress to suit the occasion – again, you are in the business of winning them over. If you are offering hospitality, stick to cups of tea and biscuits or sandwiches, rather than anything fancy, especially if you are asking for money.

You want to be sure of getting your points across, so if they interrupt and raise different issues, lead them gently but firmly back to the point. **Try to keep control of the meetings yourselves**, rather then handing it over to one of them. You may find one of them talking so much you cannot get a word in – a lot of politicians like the sound of their own voices more than they do other people's – but at least try to get the last word by winding up with your prepared points.

You may find that someone really hostile comes along, but it is more likely that the hostile people will simply stay away and those who do come will be indifferent or friendly. Try to get them to tell you the reasons that people might have for opposing your project and think of answers to them. **Aim to arm your supporters with arguments they themselves can use**. Ask them if they would like any other facts and figures, and if they say there is some information that would be useful, **make sure you get it to them**.

Afterwards

You may want to **issue a press release** about your meeting – see chapter 5 for this – but it is wise to tell those you have lobbied you are planning to do this. Otherwise they may feel you have double-crossed them, and be offended, which could spoil what you have achieved. Or, as suggested on page 137, you may want to **send them a letter** reminding them of any commitments they have made.

The person who has been keeping notes should **write or type them out afterwards**, so that all of you have a record of what happened, for when you have to report back, or if there is any argument about what was said later.

Send thankyou letters to the people you have lobbied – it reminds them of your existence as well – and also to anyone who has taken trouble for you, like the family whose flat you used, or the person who drew the charts for you.

The next thing is **to follow up and find out what happened.** If possible, some of you should attend the meeting where your problem is being discussed, and take notes. If the people you met know you are there, they are more likely to speak up for you and make points you asked them to.

If you lose, and you can show that your views were not properly put forward or the information given was wrong, you might have a chance of another go.

If the meeting is private, as most party meetings of councillors are – then ring up a contact afterwards and find out what happened. This may be the moment for press publicity. Give credit to the people who helped you, even if they did not manage to win for you – you may need them again.

Lobbying to show the level of support

The important thing here is to show **how many people feel strongly about the issue**. You can have a 'mass lobby' at the Houses of Parliament, or at a meeting, or at some other place like an advice session being run by the MP. Finding out **who, when and where** will be important for this as well, so look at pages 134–6 for this.

The next thing will be to work out how to get your supporters to the right place. If you want people to go under their own steam, how will you tell them about it? It will be easy if it is just members of your own group who want to go, but if you want people to join in, you will need to **get in the papers,** you will need **leaflets** and other publicity, and you will need to **distribute your leaflets.** (Turn to chapters 4 and 5 about this.)

Arm people with information about the issue. Prepare a leaflet which gives brief but clear details, no longer than both sides of one page, that people can read before they go in to lobby. Write it bearing in mind that people must take it in quickly. You might also want to prepare a separate, large briefing. (See page 138 for how to do this.)

Are you going to let the person you are lobbying know you are coming? If you think you might meet hostility, you may not want to, in case s/he finds a reason for not being there. But if you are telling the press you are going, you must also tell the person concerned, or it will give them a chance to score a point by saying that you are rude.

Deputations

If 50 people turn up at, say, an MP's advice session, you will probably find s/he will say s/he will see a deputation, but not all of you. You may want to dig your heels in and insist on being seen. But if there is no large meeting room and you are holding up other people, doing that will be seen as unreasonable and you will lose part of your case. So you should plan in advance **who is going to make up your deputation.** Ten people is probably the maximum. Try to get a representative group – not all white, or all middle class, or all men. It should be the ones most affected who do most of the talking. So if you are a group of tenants complaining about the damp, and a social worker has been helping you, the tenants should do the talking and the social worker remain in the background.

You will not have very long for your deputation, so plan what you want to say in advance. Think also what you are going to take with you. (See page 139 for some suggestions.)

You may also want to organise banners (see chapter 9). Those left outside should make a good showing with the banners, especially if the press are around. Ask people not to drift away once the deputation has gone in. It will be more impressive if they wait, and hear a report of what has been said, and possibly shout a few slogans before leaving in an orderly way. You might want to organise a speaker for those left outside. Do you need loudspeaking equipment? (See chapter 9 for ideas on this.)

If you are interrupting an advice session or a meeting, the people you are interrupting will probably be pretty hostile. So be prepared to be apologetic and not lose your tempers. Explain what the issue is and why you needed to do this. It will help if you say you are not planning to stay any longer than you need.

The person you are lobbying may also be hostile. Don't be thrown by this, but give as good as you get, without being abusive. The leaflet you have prepared should give you lots of counter-arguments to use. Don't worry about having to take a fairly tough line. Politicians decide on a lot of issues, like hanging for instance, more by emotion than by reasoned argument, so although you will need to put the reasons, it is your strength of feeling and the numbers you have been able to muster that really count. If you can affect the person's career, perhaps because s/he will need your votes next time to be re-elected, point this out – but be realistic. Fifty people are not going to affect the result in the safest

Tory constituency on the south coast, and the MP will know it.

Decide your tactics in advance, if the police are called to throw you out. Are you going to leave quietly, or sit down and make them carry you out? (See chapter 7 for details of the law on this, and also chapter 9 under 'Direct action'.)

As well as the people who can be at the lobby, how about giving those who cannot get there a chance to show their feelings too? You could present a petition (see chapter 11) or bring along a lot of letters from different people, or get supporters to post them separately to arrive at about the same time.

If people are writing letters, provide a 'model' – an example which they can use. But ask them not to follow it too closely, and especially to write or type it out themselves, not to send in your printed version. Politicians tend to ignore a lot of identical printed letters, because they know there is an organised campaign behind it. If the letters are hand-written, they have at least got to start reading them to be sure of that. If they are all different, they are much more likely to feel they are individual expressions of opinion and therefore should be taken notice of. Give people paragraphs to include in their letters, rather than the complete letter, so that they have to copy it out, and encourage them to add their own amendments while doing so.

Stewarding

If a large group are lobbying, **you need stewards who know what the plan is**, and can keep things under control. Look at page 113 where there is a list of the jobs stewards have to do on a demonstration, and decide which are relevant to your lobby.

There is a lot of standing around in mass lobbies, so it is important that the stewards know what is going on and can tell everyone else why they are hanging about. Try to have a meeting of stewards in advance, to talk about organisation.

The police

Look at pages 74–75 on the question, before deciding how far you want to co-operate with the police. A crowd standing outside a building is usually breaking the law anyway, by obstructing the highway. The police may ask you to move on, and arrest you if you don't, or they may be willing to let you stay so long as you do not obstruct the road or stop vehicles going in and out. It really depends on how they feel. Decide in advance whether the stewards should be asking people to keep the road clear, or whether to leave the police to get on with it.

Mass lobbies of the House of Commons

There are some special points about these lobbies, so this section goes through them in detail. What arguments to put, and how to organise a deputation, has been covered in this chapter already, so turn back for those items.

If you go on a mass lobby you **arrive** at the House of Commons and **join** a queue. You may be **collected** from the queue by your MP and taken inside, if you are lucky; or else be **let in** by dribs and drabs to the Central Lobby. You then **hand over a card** saying you want to see the MP to a flunkey in morning coat and **wait** while he finds the MP and s/he comes to see you. At last you **put your point** to the MP; then **go away** again.

You are not allowed to have marches within a mile of the Houses of Parliament, and people must not carry placards or banners (see chapter 7 for details on this). People arrive as individuals or in small groups. The most the police will allow is for people to walk in a body from a coach, parked just along the Embankment; if you are having a rally in central London, or marching from elsewhere, you will be made to break up into small groups as you approach the Commons.

Setting it up

You need first of all to set a date for your lobby. It must be when parliament is sitting, which means **not between the end of July and the end of October;** and **not near any of the big public holidays,** when they usually have a week or a fortnight's break.

Your local library may be able to tell you the dates, otherwise you local MP would be able to, or you could ring the Houses of Parliament Information Service to find out.

The best days to lobby are Tuesdays and Thursdays, when Prime Minister's questions are on, as many MPs are there then. Budget Day is a Tuesday in March or April, and is only announced a few weeks beforehand, so steer clear of Tuesdays in those months to make sure you do not clash. Friday is a very bad day because the MPs from outside London will have gone home.

There is no way to guarantee that you will not clash with something important, as the programme of debates each week is not announced until the Thursday before. The police at the

Ceremonial Office (see 'Useful addresses) will be able to tell you, though, if another lobby has been booked for that day.

Lobbies start at 2.15 p.m. You are allowed to queue up before then, but not let into the building. They usually finish about 5 o'clock, and during that time a maximum of about 700 people can go through. If you expect more than that, try to arrange a meeting as well. The usual place for this is the Grand Committee Room, just off Westminster Hall, which is at the side of the House of Commons. It holds about 200 people. It can be booked only by an MP, and there also needs to be an MP there before the meeting can start.

Have an MP as chairperson, if possible, and some speakers from your organisation. A number of MPs will drop in for short periods, listening to the speeches or the questions being put from the floor, and perhaps saying a few words themselves about their support for you. Hostile MPs usually stay away. If there are a lot of people, the police will suggest you run a shift system: after about three quarters of an hour, the meeting stops, the people in the room leave, and the police let in another batch for a repeat performance. You could get particular MPs to arrange smaller meetings in other rooms. For instance, a Scottish MP could organise a meeting for all the Scottish lobbyists, and invite the rest of the Scottish MPs along.

All this does involve the co-operation of at least one MP. You can go to any MP for this. There may well be one obvious one who takes a leading part in your campaign. If not, try phoning the Labour Party, ask to speak to the person in the Research Department who deals with your subject, and ask him/her for ideas.

The co-operation of the police does help a lot here – although it is perfectly legal to organise a lobby without telling them. For a large group of people, they can make life difficult if you do not work with them. Contact the Ceremonial Office at Cannon Row Police Station which deals with lobbies of Parliament. You will also need to write to the **Inspector in Charge** there; **the Coaches branch** (see 'Useful addresses') if you are expecting a lot of coaches full of supporters; and **the Seargent at Arms** at the Houses of Parliament, who is the functionary who controls the messengers and police officers inside parliament.

Having written, there is no need for further contact with the Coaches branch or the Seargent at Arms. But you should ring up the Ceremonial Office, or arrange to go and see them if you can, to check things over not long before the day of the lobby.

Also write to the Whips' Office of the political party most likely to support your cause. They circulate a letter to all MPs in their party once a week, telling them what is happening in the following week, so that if you say you are going to lobby it will be included in that list and all the MPs will get to know about it. There are also a number of 'interest groups' among MPs. This means that all the MPs who are interested in, say, Nicaragua or pensioners, have meetings to discuss the subject and are on a mailing list for information about it. Some of these groups are all-party, like the group for pensioners; others are confined to just one party. An MP should be able to find out what groups there are for his/her own party at least, and one of these could help – if you are lobbying on their subject – to whip up interest and get press publicity. Be careful, though, that the group you are contacting is on the same side of the argument as you. For instance there is an MPs' group on South Africa that is in support of the present regime, not against it.

Booking a hall

People sometimes like to hold a meeting outside the House of Commons in conjunction with the lobby. Central Hall, Westminster (see 'Useful addresses') is the closest. It is expensive, very big, and not very accessible for the disabled, and it also has some restrictions like not allowing smoking and not letting you do your own catering. They are helpful, but will ask for a deposit. You could also try County Hall on the South Bank. If you are having a meeting, look at chapter 8 for ideas on how to organise it.

Telling people

As early as possible, once a date has been fixed, you need to send out the information to everyone who may be coming. As well as telling them **where and when**, give them **the facts** to lobby about so that they have time to prepare, and also a note about the **process of lobbying,** which is explained on pages 147–8. Also tell them that banners and placards are not allowed near the House of Commons, and that they must not hand out leaflets or sell newspapers while they are in the queue.

Coaches

If you have people coming down by coach, try to get people to tell you in advance how many coaches they are sending, as it will help you estimate your numbers. People coming in by coach need to know **where coaches can drop people off** – For the House of Commons, this is on the Embankment, a little way along – and about **coach parks**, where the drivers can go while waiting for their passengers. The police should give you a list of these for London. Otherwise, try the town hall or the library. Remind organisations to fix **a pick-up point** for afterwards and give them any helpful information. People should be asked on the leaflets to arrange a pick-up in one of the coach parks. Try to have a steward checking with the person in charge of each coach, as it drops off, that an arrangement has been made for pick-up, as people do forget about this. How to book transport is explained in chapter 6.

At the House of Commons

If the police are expecting a large lobby, they put barriers along the edge of the pavement by the House of Commons, and tape off part of the pavement: people then line up behind a sign saying 'Lobby Queue'. They then let people inside in small groups. They aim to have no more than 100 people in Central Lobby at a time, so once it is full they make you wait until people come out. If you have a letter from your MP making an appointment for a definite time, they usually let you jump the queue and go in. However, if too many people have been well-organised and got appointments, they stop using this system, and make everyone queue up. People are then only allowed to jump the queue if their MP comes out to fetch them. Make sure that the person in charge inside knows this is happening, and tells all the MPs who come along.

Once you are let in, you go past a security search and along a passage to a large room with passages leading off in all directions. This is the Central Lobby. There is a desk at one side where each person, or the leader of each group waiting to see the same MP, fills in a card saying who they want to see and why. Many people do not know who their MP is, so the steward here should have a list to show them.

The cards are taken by a messenger, who is a man in a tailcoat with a large medallion round his neck, and he goes off to look for the MP. They do not have modern devices like bleepers, so he wanders all over the building, putting his head round the door of different rooms, to see if the person he wants is there.

After what feels like an extremely long wait, you will hear your name called out. You then go up to the desk and either your MP is there, or you are told that s/he is not available. This could mean s/he is not in the building, or that s/he doesn't want to see you. Even if you are pretty sure it is the latter, there is nothing you can do about it; you are not allowed to go wandering around looking for an MP yourself, so you have to leave.

If your MP comes, s/he takes you away somewhere for a discussion. Often this is only one of the corridors running off the Central Lobby, where you either sit on a bench or stand around the MP in a crowd. This does not make it very easy to put your case, but you will need to make the best of it. Look at pages 139–40 for points about how to put your case. Remember, though, that you will not be able to bring banners or big display boards into the Houses of Parliament, which rules out taking in charts or large photos. Fit exhibits in a briefcase or large shopping bag. You could take a batch of smaller photos along to show the sort of problem you are describing. Try to have some material you can leave with the MP.

Publicity

See chapter 5 for how to send out press releases. There is no point in doing a mass lobby unless people are going to know about it.

Badges and stickers

Since you are not allowed to have placards or leaflets, you need something else to identify yourselves with your cause. Badges and stickers do this quite effectively, and having a lot of people wandering round central London wearing a particular sort of badge is one way to get noticed. Tell people they are available when you send out the instructions about the lobby, and also have some on the day to give to people as they join the lobby queue, or come off the coach, and also to hand to unsuspecting tourists or stick on the backs of the police. (Details about badges and stickers are on pages 55–6).

Stewarding

This is easy, until the police start creating problems. You need **at least one steward** on each of the following jobs:

- in the lobby queue;

- in the Grand Committee Room, if you are having a meeting there;
- in the Central Lobby; and
- to go between the different places taking messages.

Their main function is to answer questions from lobbyists, so they need to understand the set-up and the issues you are lobbying about. If stewards have official armbands; the police will let them go in and out without making them wait in the queue.

Deputations to councils

Many, though not all, councils have special arrangements for 'receiving deputations', either at the main council meeting or at some committees. This means that a group of people is allowed to address the councillors and answer questions about the subject they are concerned about. They are rather formal occasions, and can be intimidating. It is easier if there is a friendly councillor or officer in the room to give you moral support. **Sending a deputation should be done as well as lobbying the individuals**, not instead.

To find out how to send a deputation to your council, phone up the town hall or county hall. Ask to speak to the department in charge of administering the committees. Find out from them:

- what committee you should go to, and when it meets;
- how much notice you have to give – usually it is one or two weeks;
- whether the letter asking for permission has to be written in a special way;
- how many people are allowed to go;
- how long they can speak for – usually it will be ten minutes at most.

If a lot of people want to go, the extra ones can sit in the public gallery and watch. This will help the ones who have got to speak.

It is best to have only one spokesperson – although when it comes to answering questions you might want to bring in others. Prepare yourselves well, as suggested on pages 139–40, so that you make the best use of your time, and keep within the limits you have been set, otherwise you will irritate the councillors. They may well irritate you – by not paying attention, or even doing a crossword puzzle while you are talking. Try and keep your temper, however outrageous their behaviour, if you are trying to get something out of them.

Afterwards

Follow up in the way suggested on pages 140–1.

Checklist for lobbies

Why bother?

(1) Why are you having the lobby?	132
(2) What are you priorities?	133

People

Have people been given the jobs of:

- finding out who takes the decision? — 134
- when they will take it? — 134
- where you can meet them? — 134
- preparing briefing documents? — 138–9
- booking coaches? — 66–8
- contacting the people? — 137
- organising meeting room? — 138
- doing leaflets, posters, mailing to groups, and other publicity? — 29–48
- taking along exhibits on the day? — 139
- organising the stewards? — 143

Things to do

Confirm who it is you want to see 134

Arrange a meeting with them: 137

- Letters written confirming
- Reply received
- Phone call to check
- Thank you/confirming statements letter

Organise meeting room: 137

- Letter confirming
- Deposit paid
- Thankyou letter

Briefing material: 138–9

- Short leaflet written
- Longer document prepared

- Printed/duplicated
- Distributed to participants
- Handed over to those you are lobbying

See page(s) Date done

Exhibits prepared:

- Who is taking them?   139
- Getting them back afterwards?

Press contact: 60–5

- 1st press release sent
- 2nd press release sent
- Phone to see if they are coming
- 3rd press release after meeting

Publicity: 29–48

- Mailing to local groups
- Ad in local paper
    paid for
- Leaflets: how many?
    printed
    delivered
    paid for
- Posters: how many?
    printed
    put up
    paid for
- Banners and placards:
    Who is making them?
    How are they getting there?
    How are they getting back?
- Badges and stickers

Meeting afterwards/while lobby is going on
(see checklist for public meetings)

Coaches: 66–8

- Coach operator phoned
- Estimate received
- Confirmed by letter

- Booking form produced
- Distributed
- Money collected
- Receipts sent
- List of those going
- Final check with operator
- On day:
      map of where you are going
      list of people
      coach park
      something to raffle
      tip for driver

See page(s) Date done

On the day

Stewards: people available to
    look after lobbyists   143
    look after those waiting outside
- have you briefed them?
- have you got a briefing document?

Equipment: check you have
- exhibits   139
- toolkit   92
- first aid box   237
- leaflets to hand out   29–48
- clipboard for addresses/petition   154–172
- briefing sheets for stewards   117

Have you:

- organised transport?   139
- found a place to meet up beforehand?   139

Afterwards

- Notes written up?   137
- Crucial meeting attended?   141
- Thankyou letters sent?   140
- Bills paid?
- Borrowed/hired equipment returned?
- Was it worthwhile?
- Did you affect the decision?
- What is your next step?

11.

Petitions

Aims

Petitions by themselves are not taken much notice of by the people who take decisions. A local council may have 15 or 20 of them presented to it at each meeting. They will be referred to the committee that deals with the subject, and for many of them a standard answer will be sent, and that will be the end of it. However, petitions are much underrated as campaigning weapons. They can:

- act as a way in, to ensure that the issue you are interested in is put on the agenda of an official body;
- give you a chance to talk to people while you are collecting signatures; and
- give you a peg to hang other publicity events on when you present them.

- Seventeen-year-old Debbie and her friends want to get a youth club going on their estate. They decide on a petition, and take it round all the flats. At each door they explain why they need a youth club, which involves saying how many children there are on the estate, how little there is to do at the moment, how most of the trouble on the estate comes from boredom, and how they would run the club if they got it. They find, as they go around, not only a lot more kids to support them, but also lots of parents who agree to help them organise a public meeting after the petition has been handed over to the council.

Taking round something to sign has shown that they are serious and organised, and given a method by which they can take the next step of going public.

So why do **you** want a petition? Here are some examples of possible reasons:

- Alex lives opposite a factory where he knows dangerous chemicals are kept, and he does not think proper safety precautions are being taken. He wants to show the council, and the factory management, that people living close by are worried about the dangers involved, and he wants to make sure it gets discussed by the right council committee, so that something starts to happen. More people will sign a petition than will agree to write individual letters. The council's rules mean it will be considered formally by a committee. If it is followed up with a lobby they can make sure the issue does not die.
- Debbie's youth group, in the example above, are using their petition to get a problem known around the estate, and gather support for it.
- Tariq works in a law centre which the council are trying to close down. They say people locally do not know or care about it, and it is a waste of money. So the centre decides on a petition to show the council there *is* support, and they aim to get more people to sign it than voted for the councillors at the last election.
- Olly's group of pensioners are having a big demonstration about pensions. They want people to know it is going to happen, and they also want a way of finishing the demonstration. So they decide to take a petition to parliament and to go round all the lunch clubs and old people's clubs for signatures. This gives them the chance to make short speeches about their demands, and then they can present it to the MP at the end of the demonstration.
- Eva hears there are people presenting a petition next week to close down an adventure playground, because they say it is noisy and the kids cause trouble. So she and her friends rush round a petition supporting the playground, and present it at the same time, to reduce the effect of the hostile one.

Priorities

The various examples above have different needs. Tariq's petition needs to be very big, and to get a lot of press publicity. Alex's needs to be local and to focus tightly on the question that matters to them so that the council cannot fob them off with general answers. Eva's has to be organised very quickly if it is to be of any use. Olly and Debbie both need enough people who understand the issues involved to talk at length to different groups.

In addition, they all have some things in common. These are:

- the **wording must be right,** so people know what they are signing, and why, and feel they want to sign;
- they must **get the petition around** the people they want to sign it, and they must **get it back** as well;
- they must **present it to the right people**;
- they must do so **at a time** when it is likely **have an effect.**

The following section goes through these various points in detail.

Getting the words right

If you are doing **a petition to parliament,** there are certain (silly) rules you have to follow. If you do not follow them, your petition cannot be formally presented.

The top sheet of your petition has to be hand-written. The words that are underlined, in the example below, **have to appear in every petition**:

■ To the Honourable the Commons of the United Kingdom of Great Britain and Northern Ireland in Parliament Assembled; The Humble Petition of the Residents of Greater London Sheweth that the Bill proposing to remove the control of London Transport from the Greater London Council will mean a serious reduction in the quality of service available to London's travelling public, and increased fares. The proposal to move the funding of pensioners' bus and tube passes to the individual London Boroughs is a threat to free travel by London pensioners.

Wherefore your Petitioners Pray that the Bill proposing to remove the control of London Transport from the Greater London Council be withdrawn; And your Petitioners as in duty bound will ever pray &c.

Jo Smith   19 Bolingbroke Rd, SW19
Mary Davies   31 Roxburgh Grove, E3

All the other sheets **must repeat** the bit from 'Wherefore' to the end, followed by **only signatures and addresses,** nothing else. So any explanation or request for donations has either to go on a separate sheet, or be organised so that you can cut it off before you hand over the petition. So each extra page of the petition could be as follows:

Wherefore your Petitioners pray that the Bill proposing to remove the control of London Transport from the Greater London Council be withdrawn;
    And your Petitioners as in duty bound will ever pray &c.

Cut off here

Tick for further info.

Jim Daly 99 Cunningham Crescent, W12

Masoor Patel 23 Alma St, N9

Cut off here

Published by the Save London Transport Campaign, Printed by XYZ printers

For **a petition to anyone else**, there are no set rules. But the points you need to include are:

- who you are petitioning – it could be the council, an MP, the health authority, or anyone else who has the power to take the decision you want;
- who the people signing are – are they people living in Ashvale Road, or people living in Fernhall Ward, or people living and working in the city of Newcastle?
- a short statement of the situation; and
- a statement of what you want done about it.

You may need to spend a lot of time on the last two items. The words **have to be clear**, so no one is in any doubt what they are signing. The statement should be **as short as you can make it,** because the longer it is, the more likely people are to argue with particular bits and say they will not sign, or just not bother to read it because it looks too much like hard work. And **it must be a fair statement** of the case. If people say you have been misleading them and getting signatures under false pretences it will discredit your whole campaign.

Here is an example to show what is needed:

■ We the undersigned residents of Greater London, call upon the government to withdraw its Bill proposing to abolish the Greater London Council.

If these proposals go through, there will be a serious reduction in the quality of services available to London's public, and an increase in bureaucracy.

The proposal to transfer the financing of the arts from the GLC to the individual London Boroughs is a threat to this important service.

The GLC has done a good job in helping the arts in London. We demand that the GLC be retained.

	SIGNATURE	ADDRESS
1		
2		
3		
4		
5		
6		
7		
8		
9		

Numbered lines for each signature make it easier to count how many signatures you have got at any tiime. If you have a round number of lines on each page – say 20, or 25 – you can easily multiply them by the number of sheets you have got. At the bottom, say **what organisation has published it.** Use only **one side of the paper,** and have each sheet looking the same.

However, **if your main aim is publicising yourselves** through the petition, you could create something that looks completely different, to catch the eye of the press. One group of pensioners in Telford for instance, made a giant greetings card, 6 foot high, for their MP, setting out what improvements they wanted to see in the state pension scheme, and got people to sign that.

Getting people to sign

Passing a petition round at a meeting, or putting one up on a notice-board or leaving it on a table, will each get some signatures, but none of these methods really take any further the **aim** that should be behind petitioning, which is **to convince people that they should support your cause.** To do this, you need to make personal contact by **knocking on doors; standing on the streets,** and **stopping people** as they go into a meeting or collect their children from school.

This will give you the opportunity to explain your case properly. The size and purpose of your petition will dictate exactly where you want to go to collect signatures, and whether your group alone does it, or you ask a lot of other people to help. Using the previous examples:

- Alex and his friends arrange to meet on Sunday morning and each take one of the streets close to the factory, knock on all the doors and ask for support. Each of them has a few petition forms, and they hand them back to Alex in the pub afterwards;
- Tariq is trying to get 26,000 signatures, so he has to work much harder. He arranges for petition forms to go out in the Labour Party, Trades Council and Council of Social Services mailings, with a covering letter asking people to discuss the issue at meetings and send the forms back by a particular date. The committee also organise petitioning groups in the shopping centres each weekend.

In the street

Organising signature collections in the streets is very like organising the handing out of leaflets, which is covered on pages 44–48. It takes more nerve to go up to people with a petition, than simply to hand out a leaflet, especially if it is a cause to which they might be hostile, so several people should do it together. Have a stall (use a decorating table) or a poster display that will catch people's attention, and lots of leaflets about that issue, as well as badges and stickers. The signature-collectors can then hover near the table and approach people who look interested. If one of them gets in an argument, or is having a bad time from some obnoxious person, someone else can rescue them. Don't expect collectors to last more than a couple of hours at a time. They need to be supplied with:

- petition forms – enough not only to get signatures on, but to give in handfuls to enthusiastic people who offer to take them round their workplace;
- clipboards, or pieces of cardboard, to attach petitions to;
- polythene bags to cover them up with if it is raining;
- pens – check they work before you go out in the cold, and expect to lose several;
- something to drink.

Ask people if they have already signed, and don't let them sign more than once. They will often want to do so with the best intentions, but people can pour scorn on your efforts if they can point to names that appear twice.

If your petition is to be signed by people living or working in a particular area, you will have to stop others signing too. For a more general petition, this would not matter. For a local petition, therefore, either collect in a very local shopping centre, or knock on doors in the area instead.

Door-to-door

Taking the petition round people's homes is a good way of starting a discussion in depth about the issue you are concerned with. If you are looking for a chance to change people's minds, a petition gives you the excuse to knock on doors, and helps people to start talking to you in a way that simply asking for their views, without a bit of paper in your hand, does not. It is also easier to find helpers if there is something to show for their effort, even if it is only a list of signatures.

But it does **need careful organising** to be sure that every street gets done, and that no street gets done twice. It also takes **a long time,** involves a **great deal of talking;** and calls for **a lot of confidence about the issue** by your helpers.

Traditionally the best time to knock on doors and find someone in is early evening, between 6 and 8 p.m. or Sunday mornings. With the current level of unemployment, though, a great many people are also in during the afternoons, and this may be better because your helpers will not be so worried about going round the streets then, and also because people will be more ready to open their doors to people they do not know. If you arrange for the petitioning to go on at various times, people can come when it suits them best.

Leave out very affluent areas, but for many campaigns you will get considerable support from areas of good houses, where the well-off middle classes live.

Where to get together

If there is a room in someone's house available within the area, this will be comfortable; otherwise meet at some local landmark, such as a station or **outside** a pub. The person organising needs **a list of the streets** to be covered, and some **maps of the area** you are doing. Photocopy the right bits of the Ordnance Survey map from the library. You also need the equipment listed on page 160.

The group will first of all **need briefing.** Reminding them **why they are petitioning, what the issues are, where the petition is going, what you hope to get out of it,** and **how people can join.** Before you start petitioning, spend a bit of time putting a checklist on this together.

If you are meeting somewhere comfortable, the briefing can be done immediately before you go out; but if you have to meet on a cold corner of the street, try to do the briefing beforehand. Give a copy of the checklist to each helper, together with:

- copies of the petition;
- leaflets to go through doors if no one is there;
- a pen and a clipboard;
- a badge or a sticker as identification.

If you are intending to go back again to the houses where you get no answer, or where people are unsure about the question, then you need to keep a check on what happened at each house. The easiest way is to adopt the Labour Party's method of 'canvassing'. This means that you get hold of copies of the electoral register – from the Electoral Registration Officer at the Council. Political parties get a certain number free, other people can buy copies. Then either split this up into sheets or, if you are being really thorough, cut it up and paste it on cards, with columns for yes, no and maybe, and room on the back for notes. This then allows you to go back after your first canvass to the maybes and those houses where you could not get an answer. You can buy these cards ready printed from the Labour party, or make them yourselves.

Unfortunately many Labour Party people see canvassing as a race – how many doors can they get round before going to the pub. This attitude needs re-training so that a serious discussion is seen as important rather than time-wasting, and progress may be fairly slow,

The petition organiser will need to **allocate one or two streets to each person or group.** Some people will be anxious to go in pairs, while others will want to go by themselves. Those going alone should work on opposite sides of the street. This gives some protection to the nervous and enables the other person to rescue anyone trapped by a superbore who just goes on talking. Send experienced people to take the lead for the first few doors, and then to stand back and let the new person try his/her hand.

Occasionally very hostile people will want to argue and give someone a rough time, but more often they slam the door in your face. A more difficult problem is the person, often elderly, who has not seen anyone to talk to for weeks, and will invite you in, offer you a cup of tea, and talk for hours. It can be awkward to get away without offending or upsetting them; one way is to suggest they come to the next meeting, and offer a lift, if necessary; **make sure it is followed up afterwards.**

If people are working in pairs, try not to have two large men working together. They may in fact be very gentle people and not at all threatening, but this is not how it will look to the person inside the door. They are likely to have a high proportion of conversations shouted through letter boxes. Also, if you are working on a dark evening, do not ask women, alone or in pairs, to go to places where they will be afraid, such as ill-lighted dark-access blocks of flats. They will not be able to have a proper conversation if they are shaking with fear every time someone opens the door. Send a man and a woman together if possible.

An individual, or a pair working together will probably cover about 50 houses in one 2-hour session, which is about as long as anyone can take. Ask people:

- **to introduce themselves fully,** saying what group they are from, and what the petition is for;
- **not to waste time** on someone really hostile, who will not be convinced by whatever they say;
- **to offer leaflets,** posters and membership forms to anyone enthusiastic, and to make a note of their name and address so they can be followed up;
- after they have talked to the person who opens the door, to ask if anyone else in the house will sign the petition as well.

Entryphones, and houses full of bedsitters, are particular problems; you can either:

- hang around outside until a resident comes along; or
- push the bells until you get an answer, and then explain what you are doing and ask if they will let you into the block.

With a house full of bedsitters, it takes some nerve, once someone lets you in, to go wandering round knocking on unmarked doors, but if your petition is, for instance, about housing conditions, it will be essential to do it. Send people in pairs to bedsitter areas.

Afterwards

Fix a definite meeting place – this time it can be **inside** a pub. If you need to meet by someone's car, get people to make a note of the registration number before they go off. Suggest a time when they can give up without feeling guilty, but tell them to use their judgement about giving up earlier if they find no one will open the door to them once it is dark. Get everyone to tell the organiser;

- **how far along** their allocated street they got; if you gave them canvassing cards, these must be collected; otherwise tick off the streets that are done on the list.
- **how they got on** – what sort of questions did people have, and what issues were they raising?
- were there any points they could not answer, or where they felt the answer suggested was not convincing?

Change the briefing note before the next time people go out, if there are things that need covering.

Are there any **people to be visited again** with more literature, membership details or posters? **Allocate this work straight away,** as it will be easier.

If someone has had a particularly bad time for instance, having doors slammed in his/her face, the organiser will **need to offer support and encouragement.**

Count up the signatures from the evening's work before people finally leave, and announce a figure, as this will help everyone to feel they have achieved something.

Getting the forms back

If you have done a big mailing, or if you handed out petition forms

to several groups to collect signatures in different places, then
someone will need to spend time getting them back. Put a date
by which you want them returned on each form, or in the covering
letter.

Make the date a couple of weeks before your own deadline
because forms will continue to trickle in well after the given date.
The person doing this job should **keep a list** of where the forms
have gone, and **phone up or write** to each person asking for them
back, and **tick them off** as they come in. Some forms will never
come back, but the lost ones will not have been wasted, as they
will have made people aware of the problem.

Counting up

Keep a running tally as the forms come in. Keep an eye out while
doing so for any ridiculous ones. Some people think it funny to
sign themselves 'Mickey Mouse' or 'The Duke of Wellington'.
Cross these names out, and do not count them in your totals,
otherwise they will devalue the petition.

Who are you presenting it to?

A petition usually ends up inside the formal machinery of an official body. It may be presented by a councillor at one council
meeting, considered at a committee, and reported back at the next
council meeting. Usually it has to go via the official channels. That
is, usually only a councillor can present a petition to the council,
or an MP to parliament.

Having collected the signatures, therefore, you have to get it to
the person who can take this formal step for you, and can use this
stage to **get publicity,** to **lobby for your cause,** or **both.**

Usually, you want the petition to get to the people who can take
the decision you want, like a particular council committee, as in
the example of Alex's petition, on page 159, about the chemical
works. But it can also be that you are using someone who is really
irrelevant but will help you to get publicity for your cause.

- Olly's group, know the council cannot change the level of
  pensions but they might hand a petition to the council about
  pensions because that way they can get stories in the local
  papers.
- Debbie's group take the opportunity of the Minister of Education visiting the town to present a petition direct to him/her,

asking that the council should be ordered to open a youth club. They are pretty sure that s/he will not do so, but it gives them a peg to hang their demand on.

Most councillors and MPs will present any petition that people they represent ask them to whether they agree with it or not. So the local MP for the constituency, or the councillor for the ward, is the first person to ask to take charge of it. For other bodies, for instance district health authorities, office-holders do not formally represent different patches of the area, so ask the most sympathetic one to speak on your behalf.

Handing over the petition to the person who is going to present it can be done either well in advance, or just before the meeting at which it is going to be presented. **If publicity is important, do this in advance.** At the time of the meeting there may well be other petitions to go in too, and there will be other news coming out of the meeting. Choose the time that gives you the best chance of getting press coverage. On the other hand, if you are concerned **to lobby about your cause,** just before the meeting might be the best time, to catch the right person, or it might be the only time they are available.

Two or three people can simply **hand the petition over;** or you could invite **the person concerned to visit the area** that the petition is about, and hand it over at the end of the visit; or you could **hold a public meeting** about it; or you could have **a big demonstration** or a bit of **street theatre** as part of the hand-over.

Whatever you decide to do, **don't neglect publicity, and contact with the press** (see chapters 4 and 5). The important points to get in any press release will be:

- who will receive the petition;
- when it is going to be presented;
- what it is about;
- how many people signed it.

If the number of signatures does not sound very high, you can also include the proportion of people affected who signed. So a press release might say '80 per cent of parents with children on X estate signed the petition,' as this would sound much better than '200 people signed'.

Street theatre

Handing over a petition is one time when certain groups might want to put a lot of work into getting over a particular image by doing something that catches the eye, and the attention of the press, in fact, by having a little performance. It can be useful in other events as well. It need involve only half a dozen people, which makes it very useful for occasions when you are not going to get masses of people turning up, but it does involve careful preparation. A group doing this needs to be self-disciplined and reliable, as the absence of one person could be disastrous for them, while an ordinary lobbying group could still get by if they were one short.

If you are a larger organisation, give responsibility to a small group to go away and get on with it. Some groups manage very well without a convenor, but most do need one; that is, a person who will get meetings together, have a list of addresses, phone round to remind people what they have agreed to do, and so on. The group will need to work out:

- what it is doing;
- who is doing what;
- how you are getting hold of the things you need;
- how you, the clothes and the equipment, are going to get to the place you need to be;
- how you get it all home again.

What are you doing?

Look back at chapter 2, and decide what sort of image you want to get over. Get together preferably in a group, so you can bounce ideas off each other. Try to think of one or two words that sum up the major point of your campaign, then think of pictures you associate with them. For instance, **damp**: buckets of water/ mouldy clothes/ drips/ wallpaper falling off walls/ people with colds/ condensation/ public health inspector.

You could do something that involved using the back of a lorry as a float; or you could write and act out a little play. Look at the list of words and see what is most vivid and most practical. In the example of damp, for instance, you might cross off 'wallpaper falling off walls' because it would be too difficult to do; then you might want to cross off 'public health inspector' because it would not mean anything to anyone who had not already got damp. You might then decide to combine one or two of the other images, and have a group in mouldy clothes, holding handkerchiefs to their noses, handing over a petition.

Anything that reverses what we normally expect will be eye catching. People look at pensioners dressed in leather jackets and crash helmets; or at people in masks, or at people in animal costumes. The trick is to create the image that not only **catches the eye, but also carries a message about your campaign.** Hell's Grannies are saying to the public, through the press photos, 'We are going to make trouble if we don't get a better deal' without needing to have a lot of words spelling this out.

It helps if your group includes people with acting experience, but it is not essential; lots of people are willing to dress up and look silly for a good cause. There are all sorts of props a group can use. The group petitioning about the adventure playground could have a float on the back of a lorry, and have a group of 'fenced in' children on it. The pensioners who decide to come as Hell's Grannies could arrange to borrow motorbikes, if they could find someone to lend them, and have them parked near the town hall, so they did not have to take them very far.

Finding props

If you need special costumes – Victorian dresses, or animal costumes, for instance – try a local drama group, or a school or college drama department, or people who are good at sewing, before hiring from a theatrical costumier, who will be fairly expensive.

If you are using ordinary clothes, remember that things will have to stand out to be noticed. So the group campaigning about damp cannot simply wear the mouldy clothes they have got hanging up in their wardrobes; they need to paint on great streaks of mould-coloured paint for it to show up properly.

Try joke shops for masks, noses, moustaches and so on. Try your friends for other props – but if you want them to stay your friends, make sure you return them. Remember to insure anything valuable.

If something needs to be built – a fence round the children on the back of a lorry, for instance – you will need ordinary tools and the sort of materials that most do-it-yourselfers accumulate – two by four wood, nails, screws, bits of wire. Allow yourselves plenty of time and draw a plan of what you are doing before you start.

You will also need a ready-made 'caption' to your picture, so that people passing know who you are and what you are saying. You should have **banners** giving the name of the organisation;

and **placards** saying what you want, or what you are protesting about. You also want **leaflets** to explain to passers-by what you are doing and why, and a loudspeaker – or hand-held megaphone – to announce it. You will also need **press releases before** and **after** the event, and the people 'performing' should be well prepared for silly press questions like, 'Don't you think you're bringing your cause into disrepute by doing this?'

If you are doing a bit of acting, it will be easier if you know you are going to have some audience. If you are handing over the petition at the end of the march, you have a ready-made audience. If you have to create one, then everyone else not involved in preparing the gimmick must help with the publicity, and also bring their friends along.

If you are too shy

If everyone in the group is too shy to dress up in public, you could find someone else to do it for you. Get your children to dress up, or find a theatre group, or drama students at your local school or college (see page 109 for sources). It will then be very important to be sure you both have the same idea about the image you are trying to put across. It will not do if you want to appeal to people's sympathy and the group comes across as very aggressive; nor, for that matter, if it is the other way round. The petition organisers ought to have at least one discussion face to face (not on the phone) with the organiser of the outside group, to be sure there are no misunderstandings.

If you have got what you feel is a good image but no one to carry it out, ask yourselves again – is it really the right image? If you get saddled with it and it does not fit your group, is it going to help the campaign or do it harm? Taking again the example of the Hell's Grannies, if the pensioners' group decided that this was a terribly good idea but they did not have the nerve to do it, and found some real motorbike enthusiasts to make up their faces and wear grey wigs, this might be equally successful in getting press publicity. But a rather timid group of people would then have everyone thinking they were aggressive and militant, and they would have to live up to that for ever more. If you have thought about an image already, as suggested in chapter 2, this should help here.

Getting there

One of the things likely to put people off taking part in this sort of event is the problem of getting there, costume and all. You may have the nerve to be the back half of a pantomime horse outside the town hall along with a lot of sympathetic friends, without necessarily feeling able to change at work and travel in full costume on the 77 bus. There are two possible ways to get round this: **organise lifts** to the place you are going; or **organise somewhere to change** once you get there.

Another possibility is to organise a central place for people to change, and then borrow a minibus, or several cars, to get them from there to the point they need to end up at.

The same problem arises afterwards, when you are getting people home. You *can* be cruel and simply abandon them to make their own way back, but you will probably lose some valuable members of the group if you do. Try to organise a pick-up for them, or lifts with individual members of the group

After handing over the petition

At the time when you hand it over, the person receiving the petition may not know exactly when s/he will be able to present it. An MP, for instance, has to take the petition to someone called 'the Clerk for Public Petitions in the Journal Office'. This person says whether it is in order, and the MP then signs a list saying when s/he will present it. Make sure you find out when it is to be – **remind them** to tell you, and **issue a press release** timed to fit in with it.

If the petition is, say, to the council, it will usually be referred to the committee that deals with the subject. Find out when this meets, and decide what to do about it. Do you want to:

- lobby the councillors beforehand;
- send a deputation; or
- have a demonstration?

This will depend on the aim behind the petition. When you have decided, look at chapter 4. Use the progress of the petition as a reason for putting out **a further leaflet** about the issues involved. If there were particular queries that kept coming up when you were collecting signatures, this is an opportunity to answer them. Follow up afterwards in the same way as for a lobby (see pages 140–1).

Checklist for petitions

Why bother?

(1) Why are you doing the petition?	184–5
(2) What are your priorities?	155–6

People
Have people been given the jobs of;

- sorting out the right wording? — 157
- finding someone to present it? — 164–5
- preparing a briefing? — 138–9
- organising a session in the shopping centre? — 159–60
- finding volunteers? — 159–60
- organising a door-knocking session? — 160–3
- mailing petition out? — 159
- getting it back? — 163
- counting it up? — 164
- arranging what is happening on the hand-over? — 164–5
- doing the follow-up? — 137–41
- doing leaflets, posters, mailing to groups, and other publicity? — 29–48
- taking it along on the day? — 167–8
- organising the stewards? — 143
- doing press releases? — 60–5

Things to do

Prepare petition: — 157
- Work out wording
- Get it duplicated or printed — 60–5
- Distribute it — 159

Confirm who is going to present it for you.

Arrange meeting with them: — 164–5
- Letters written confirming
- Reply received
- Phone call to check
- Thankyou letter

For collecting signatures
- Get maps of area   160–3
- Copies of electoral register
    paste on cards or split into separate
    sheets
- Find meeting place
- Bring: petition
    clipboard
    pens
    posters
    leaflets
    badges for helpers
- Briefing leaflet written
    printed/duplicated
    distributed to volunteers

Organise handing over:
- Street theatre   163
- Other meeting organised   163

Press contact: 29–48
- Ist press release sent
- 2nd press release sent
- phone to see if they are coming
- 3rd press release, after meeting

Publicity: 60–5
- Mailing to local groups
- Ad in local paper
    paid for
- Leaflets: how many?
    printed
    delivered
    paid for
- Posters: how many?
    printed
    put up
    paid for
- Banners and placards:
    Who is making them?
    How are they getting there?
    How are they getting back?

● Badges and stickers
● Loudspeaker
● Props
● Vehicles
● How are people getting there?
● How are they getting back?

See page(s) Date done

On the day

When you are collecting signatures: 159–64
● People to organise:
　　where you are going
　　volunteers to help
● Have you briefed them?
● Have they got a leaflet?
● Have you collected information afterwards?

Have you 161
● organised transport?
● found a place to meet beforehand?

When you are handing over:
Have you: 164
● counted up the signatures?
● arranged to meet beforehand?
● made appointment with person doing it?
● confirmed?
● written press releases?
● prepared how you are going to hand over?
● got people there to watch?

Afterwards 137–40

● Meeting attended?
● Thank-you letters sent?
● Bills paid?
● Borrowed/hired equipment returned?
● Was it worthwhile?
● What is your next step?

12.

Conferences and schools

This chapter covers events – variously called conferences, week-end schools, or seminars – organised with the idea of having detailed discussion of policies you are putting forward. From the point of view of the organiser, there are three main types:

- residential ones, that last two days or more, usually over a weekend, where people expect to stay overnight in the place where the conference is being held;
- conferences that last more than one day, where people do not expect to stay overnight at the meeting place, though they may expect you to find somewhere else for them;
- day conferences.

All of these types can be large or small, and may involve mainly people from the local area or people from all over the country. Residential conferences have particular problems about the places in which you hold them, so that point is covered separately. It is assumed here that the conferences are being held over the weekend; weekday ones are much the same, except that the train timetable may be more flexible, the shops will be open, and so on. This chapter covers points of organising registration, sending out agendas, and other items which are much the same for all three sorts, but where size makes a difference. First, however, there is the question of why you should hold a conference in the first place.

One thing you can be certain of is that it will not bring in people who are not already involved in some way, either in your group, or in another similar one. There are people who do not have much to do at weekends, and seem to turn up at all sorts of conferences for the sake of it, but no one completely non-political is going to see a poster about a day conference on nuclear disarmament, for instance, and think 'Oh, that looks more interesting than doing the shopping' and wander in off the street.

Aims

What are the reasons for having a conference? Here are a few examples;

- Nick's CND group want to raise enthusiasm and plan a campaign over the next few months, in conjunction with the local Labour Party and trade unions, about arms manufacture in the area.
- Sue's Labour Party branch want to discuss in detail the council's plans for reorganising the local schools, and come up with an agreed policy statement at the end.
- Trevor's group has agreed to run the annual weekend meeting of the Playbus Association, which has groups all over the country who can only get to see each other, find out what they are doing, and decide on policy for the next year, at these get-togethers.
- Leila's groups of radical youth workers are writing a pamphlet about their views. They have each drafted papers and now want to discuss and criticise them before the person editing goes away to put the final draft together.

Not included in this list is the frequent, but not very good, reason for having an all-day conference – that the ordinary business keeps overflowing the meetings, so that you need a full day to deal with all the things that get left over.

If you have got into that state, the problem you have really got to solve is why your meetings are taking so long. Is it that some people are simply talking too much? Are people arguing endlessly about minor things because they really disagree about fundamentals, or simply dislike each other? If so, having a whole day or weekend will simply give them time to do more of the same. These are the problems that need solving, not just the overflow of routine business.

Priorities

In the previous examples:

- Nick's group needs plenty of publicity among the people who are likely to come, and a good big name speaker to get themselves off to a rousing start. They also need a place where they can break into smaller groups to discuss plans of campaign. They do not need to put high priority on socialising, though, as it will be people who see each other pretty often at meetings anyway.

■ Sue's Labour Party are likely to have a great many complicated resolutions and amendments. Unless they have a firm chair-person and a tight agenda, they may get bogged down altogether. They need to get the preparatory work right. All the branches should know about the conference and the education policy document that they are supposed to discuss, getting in names of delegates, getting resolutions sent in early enough to be circulated to everyone else. Then they will have to make sure that a careful record is kept of the conference and that the decisions it takes are sent to everyone so that there can be no argument about what is decided. They do not want to break into groups, and in order to keep people together at lunchtime, so that they can stick to their timetable, they need to organise food for everyone.

■ Trevor's group has quite a lot of formal business to get through, but it also needs to give people the chance to recharge their batteries, swop ideas, and generally talk endlessly about playbuses with other similar enthusiasts. So they need to mix full meetings (often called 'plenary sessions') with smaller groups which can discuss detailed problems. They also need to allow time for chat, and to arrange a good social at some point. To get some backing for their cause, since they always need to convince local councils about how important it is, they need to get an eminent speaker to start them off. And finally, since people are coming from all over the country, they need to hold the conference somewhere that people can get to easily, and they have to find beds or floors for the night.

■ Leila's group is small, and does not need very elaborate arrangements, but it does need somewhere comfortable to meet, and also to make sure that the draft papers are sent out early enough for people to read them. They also need to sort out where people will stay. It will be important for someone to take really good notes of the conference so that the editor of the pamphlet knows what all the various comments were.

Drawing up the programme

You will now have some idea of whether your conference simply has to get through a lot of business, or whether the socialising is just as important so that you want a more relaxed timetable.

Do a draft of the programme **very early in your planning**, because this will show you how much time is needed. You need to find a balance between stretching it out too long and cramming the timetable too tight. People will feel that they have been steam-rollered if there is no time for proper discussion.

Make a list of the different 'segments' you think you will have in the conference, and put beside each how long you think they will take. It is bound to involve a lot of guesswork at this stage, of course.

■ Nick's CND group have: they decide it will take:

A big name speaker	30 minutes
A general discussion of his/her talk	30 minutes
Workshops	2 hours
Reporting back from workshops	30 minutes
Putting together a plan for future action	30 minutes

■ Sue's Labour Party involves 20 branches, all of whom are enti-tled to send in resolutions. They cannot know how many will, but they can guess they will be on four main subjects.

They decide on:	which will take:
health	2 hours
social services	2 hours
housing	2 hours
education	2 hours
and their policy document on education	1 hour

So this makes 9 hours altogether

■ Leila's youth workers want a relaxed discussion, but they need to make sure they have got through all the papers by the end, and not got stuck on one. So they decide they should discuss each paper for an hour and a half, and then switch to the next one, even if they are not finished, leaving a little time over at the end to tie up any loose ends. As there are 8 papers this means 12 hours' work, plus an extra hour. They also know they want a social, which has to go into an evening.

If having worked out what you need to include, there seems to be simply too much business, you can either cut out something, or split up the conference into smaller groups. This will not be easy with a conference that is making formal decisions, because you run into problems about whether they can properly be taken by a small group, but a discussion conference can do this.

■ For instance, half of Leila's radical youth workers could be discussing one paper, while the rest are discussing another. That way, they could get through 16 papers if they really want to!

Big discussion conferences are often organised into 'streams' of the main subjects, so that sessions on employment, for instance, would follow one after another rather than overlap. People can then decide to go to all the sessions about a particular subject, or hop between several if they are interested in several things.

However, having decided what you have to fit in, you also have to look at the other limits on people's time. **Think about**:

- **where people** are coming from;
- **what other things** they have to do;
- **what is happening** around the conference.

If you travel a long distance to a conference, before you set out you have effectively decided that the weekend is a wash-out so far as doing the usual household chores and socialising is concerned. Either someone does them for you, or you do them on another day, so you will want to feel you are using your time effectively while you are away – for instance by starting fairly early. On the other hand, if you are going to a local meeting, you will probably try to fit your commitments round it. For those who go to work, Saturday is the day they do their shopping, go to the launderette, and change their library books. If you start too early, only those with someone else to do these chores (which usually means men whose wives stay at home) will be able to come at the beginning.

In the same way, at the end of the conference involving local people, those with children will need to go off and get their meal and put them to bed, and the sports fans will want to go home and watch the results.

On the other hand, for the people who have come from a distance, there will be nothing much to do after the conference sessions finishes except have a drink. So for this type of event you need to break up at the same time as the bar opens, so there is no hiatus when people stand around looking impatient and thirsty.

Do not expect them to go on conferring once they can start drinking.

The other point to think about is train times, and especially the trains from London. When does the first reasonable train get in, and how long will it take to reach the conference from the station? Like it or not, the trains will dictate when the conference actually will start.

Think about **starting** at about 11 a.m. depending on the local train service, and have a short session before lunch. If you arrange a Friday evening session, people will drift in gradually, depending on what time they can get away from work. You can start at about 8 p.m. on Friday, with a discussion going on till about 9.30 p.m. and then assume that everyone will go to the pub. This allows you to get the formalities and registration over, to get people settled in, and to start early on the Saturday morning. Do not try to take serious decisions on the Friday night, because a lot of people will not be there, or will arrive late and tired having come from work.

For a residential conference, once people are there and have stayed the night, you may as well start in the mornings about half an hour after breakfast, as people will not have anything else to do. On the other hand, if you have arranged for people to sleep on floors all over town, then many of them will be dependent on what time their hosts get up, and give them a lift to the conference centre. This may mean starting at 10 or 10.30 a.m. Some people will always be late and half asleep, whatever they do.

If you are having a social one night, assume people will be sleepy and provide plenty of coffee before the start next morning.

If people have come from a distance, you need to **finish** by mid-afternoon on Sunday at the latest, and possibly even at lunch-time, because the Sunday train service is so limited. Again, look at the train timetable, because people will anyway disappear shortly before the train that looks convenient for them. Offering lifts to the station, means you can cut it finer than if people have to wait for buses or order taxis. Possible timetables are:

Weekend

	Residential	*Non-Residential*
Friday	8 p.m. to 9.30 p.m.	8 p.m. to 9.30 p.m.
Sat.	9.30 a.m. to 12.30 p.m.	10 a.m. to 12.30 p.m.
	lunch	lunch

	2.00 p.m. to 5.30 p.m.	2 p.m. to 5.00 p.m.
	bar opens	
	dinner	
	8 p.m. social	8 p.m. social
Sunday	9.30 a.m. to 12.30 p.m.	10.00 a.m. to 12.30 p.m.

or

	11.30 a.m. to 1.00 p.m.	11.00 a.m. to 1.00 p.m.
Sat.	2.00 p.m. to 5.30 p.m.	2.00 p.m. to 5.00 p.m.
	bar opens	
	dinner	
	social	
Sunday	9.30 a.m. to 12.30 p.m.	10.00 a.m. to 1.00 p.m.

lunch for those who want it

One-Day Conference

10 a.m. Registration and coffee
10.30 a.m. Start
1.00 p.m. Lunch
2.00 p.m. to 4.30 p.m. Afternoon session

Having done this preliminary work, you are now in a position to decide the programme for your conference. Taking our original examples:

■ Nick's group realises they can do things in one day.
■ Sue's conference will need two days.
■ Leila's group could theoretically get through everything in two hard days' work, but if they want a relaxed atmosphere they need to start on Friday evening.

The final stage is to slot the different items in. Here you can make use of the high spots to make sure people come back from lunch on time, and to help create the atmosphere you want.

■ Nick's group put their big speaker on in the morning, immediately after the chair's introduction, as an attraction to get the conference started promptly.
■ Sue's put on the education policy document, which lots of people see as important, straight after lunch so they will be back for it.

- Nick's group start the workshops before lunch, and arrange for people to go back to the same ones afterwards, so that the groups will tend to go to lunch together, and will have ready-made openings to start talking.

When you get **close to your conference date,** have another look at the programme, and adjust it to take account of the issues or problems that have come up since.

Deciding on the date

In chapter 8, the question of good and bad times of year was covered, so look back at that. There are two chief problems that arise with arranging any sort of conference. First, **yours may clash with another conference.** This only matters if both are likely to involve the same type of people. You cannot find a weekend without some conference or other going on, but it would matter if the Child Poverty Action Group and the NCCL clashed, for instance, because there is likely to be lot of overlap. Check with other groups that might overlap, and ask people you know who go to a lot of conferences before fixing the date.

Second, **your conference may clash with a Bank Holiday weekend.** This happens particularly in April and May, which is a popular time for conferences and when there are three Bank Holidays (Easter, May Day, Whitsun) in quick succession. Watch out also for the Boat Race and the Grand National, which some people consider important. Later in the year you have to think about the Cup Final. (See page 107 for possible sources of information.)

Residential conferences

How many people are you expecting? Depending on this, possible places to hold the conference will be:

- educational places, such as colleges and university halls of residence;
- hotels;
- special conference centres and residential centres.

Big residential conferences – over 100 people or so, are pretty well restricted to colleges or university halls of residence, although you might be able to take over an entire hotel, out of season.

Colleges and halls of residence

These are only available during vacations, that is, around Christmas, Easter and the summer. The majority are quite comfortable and have gone into the conference business seriously, so they run fairly smoothly. You need to book up well in advance.

The bedrooms are rather bare and austere, with one bathroom for every eight or ten rooms. To keep down staff costs they often impose conditions like everyone taking their dirty plates back to the serving hatch after meals. This may be seen as unreasonable by stroppy people, and means the organisers will have to nag about it.

Hotels

Hotels are usually fairly comfortable, and will have all the facilities like bar, restaurant, parking space, and meeting rooms.

They are expensive, although if it is the off-season in a holiday area you may be able to get a block booking for much less than you expect. They are also commercial, so that they are probably not at all committed to what your conference is about. The staff could in fact be hostile to what you represent, especially if your group is not one of the orthodox political ones. Check them out carefully, preferably by finding another group that has used them – ask one of the sources on pages 17–19.

Check also if the hotels are **unionised** by ringing the local or regional office of the GMBATU or TGWU, which are the two main unions that organise hotel workers. Ask if the hotel is on the 'fair list'. If they tell you that it is not, ask them to recommend one that is. You could also ask for advice on where they hold their weekend schools and conferences.

There are also special centres owned by the Co-op, some churches and charities, and unions and the Labour Party. For instance, near Sheffield there is a large centre called Wortley Hall which is a country club geared for use by the unions and left groups, and there is a similar place near Leeds. Often you will only find out about these places by asking around, but also try the library, and the other places listed on page 17.

If yours is a small group that needs to get down to some hard talking (like Leila's group in the above examples) your main needs are to be comfortable and away from ordinary pressures. If you ask around your more affluent friends and acquaintances, you may find that they, or their parents, own a place in the country that you could borrow for a weekend. If there is not room for all of you, some people might be willing (or even keen) to camp in the grounds. A youth hostel, or a farm where they let out rooms, is another possibility, but try to use a place that someone already knows.

Children

It is not reasonable to expect people to leave their children at home, with a long-suffering spouse/partner. Those who like seeing their children simply will not come if you do not make provision for them. Think about:

- occupying them during the conference sessions;
- mealtimes;
- the evenings;
- night time.

Ignore residential places that do not take children, are grudging about them, or put on a massive extra charge. A good place will set aside a decent room for a creche, be willing to provide children's portions at mealtimes, and let children share the parents' room for a small extra charge. It will also offer arrangements for keeping an eye on the children in the evening – if necessary with voluntary help from conference participants and for heating up bottles for babies, and so on.

Make sure you put details of these arrangements on the publicity, so that people know they can apply. Even with this, you may find that very few people actually do bring their children to the conference, mainly because, understandably, the children tend to resist. The provision is worthwhile, though, even for a very few, to allow parents access on equal terms with everyone else.

Disabled people

The larger, and longer, your conference is the more important access for people with disabilities becomes. A small informal group may be able to get away with lifting a wheelchair up and down steps for a day, provided the occupant does not mind. A big conference that does not advertise wheelchair access means disabled people are kept out. Again, ignore places that do not have access to wheelchairs or are unhelpful. Boycotting them will be the only way to make them change, as it hits them where it hurts, in their pockets.

Ideally, you should arrange facilities for sign language for deaf people, but there are too few people with this skill to make this always possible.

Food

Catering in conference places tends to be fairly institutional and boring, but you have to put up with this. However, what about the people with special diets, particularly the largest group, vegetarians? You cannot expect them to survive a whole weekend on eating the 'meat and two veg' without the meat. Many places that say they cater for vegetarians actually only do omelettes or grated cheese salads.

If your conference is going to attract a good many (for instance, if it involves Quakers, Friends of the Earth, or Ecologists) try to find a place that will do interesting vegetarian food, and let them know in advance that there is going to be considerable demand. The Vegetarian Society (see 'Useful addresses') has a list of vegetarian hotels, but not of conference venues. If you phone them they may be able to give you some ideas of places in the right area, but they say the only way to be sure is to talk to the manager about it before booking. See page 187 for ideas on organising your own catering.

Problems can arise about deciding on numbers for your **first and last meals** – Friday night dinner or Saturday lunch, depending on when you are starting, and Sunday lunch. Ask on the application form whether people want the first meal, and only arrange it for those who say they do. Take a head count on Sunday morning of those who want Sunday lunch, so that they can tell the kitchen before they start preparing the food.

Drink is also important for smooth running of most residential conferences. Try to book a place that has a bar at lunchtime and in the evening, or that will let you run one. (See page 233 for getting a special licence.) Get the opening hours clear from the beginning, and especially whether you can have a late bar or not. If you can, say so in your literature.

People attending but not staying

If the conference is held, say in Manchester, then Mancunians will not want to spend the night in your centre, but will go home, So you will need to allow for some people who want to go into the session and to have tea, coffee, and meals, but do not need a bed. Remember to clarify this in advance with the centre and to negotiate a special price.

Deposits and cancellations

The management will probably ask for a deposit when you book, some of the money in advance, and charge a cancellation fee if you pull out, or have fewer people than you said you would. This is because they will have to buy food, arrange for staff and so on. This means that you must have some money available before you even start organising. If you have none of your own, will another group sponsor you or give you a guarantee?

Get clear, in a written contract, exactly what you are letting yourself in for. You may be able to negotiate better terms before you confirm the booking, but **do not be content with vague assurances.** The more you can get in writing of all the points above, the better. Try to insure yourselves against loss (see page 238).

Non-residential conferences

Here, the same issues arise for a day or a weekend conference, so they are covered together. Your choice of venue will be fairly limited at a weekend (see pages 180–1 for finding a place) and you may have to pay quite a lot, because you are competing with weddings, antique fairs, and jumble sales. This is particularly so in November and December, as it comes up to Christmas; and the caretaker and cleaners should be being paid overtime rates.

Remember to think about **facilities for making tea and coffee, serving lunch, and running a creche.** If the conference is large, and is going to break into groups, try a school or college building. If it is staying in one meeting, try a public hall. Especially in the winter, **check the heating before booking.**

Where will people stay

Although you have decided on a non-residential conference, if people are coming for a weekend from any distance away they will still need to spend the night somewhere. At many conferences, the organisers say they will find a bed or a floor for people to sleep in. This is a large and thankless task; be honest about your group's capacity on this; taking the responsibility on and then messing it up so that people have nowhere to stay, is worse than not agreeing to do it in the first place. If you are not finding people places, make this clear in the conference documents from the beginning. Get a list of hotels from the council's information service or tourist office, and send *this* out with the conference papers, instead. As some people will turn up without anywhere to stay, you could keep in reserve a few names of people or places who can help.

If you *are* taking the job on, one person should take full responsibility for it, with extra help as necessary. The first thing is to collect a list of people with beds and floors to spare. Do this through your own group's network of friends and contacts, and advertise anywhere you can think of:

- the Student Union, if there is one;
- any alternative bookshops;
- the local Labour Party offices;
- the newsletter of any local voluntary organisation you think might be full of helpful people.

As you get in names, put them on a card index, with a note of:

- how many people they can take – and the absolute maximum they can manage;
- any special conditions – a single woman may not want men to stay with her, or a non-smoker may stipulate that s/he does not want smokers;
- how to get in touch – will s/he be at the conference, or is it for the individual to phone the person concerned, or simply turn up there?
- what the accommodation is, bed or floor, and is a sleeping bag needed?

Even if you seem to have more beds being offered than you have demand for, do not turn anyone down.

If you are dealing with a large number of people, try to find in advance a head who will lend you a school, or a sympathetic vicar who will let you use the church hall as an overflow if necessary. If you are putting people in a place not normally used for sleeping, the local fire brigade will want to inspect it to know that it is safe, and that they can get fire engines there in an emergency. They will want you to have stewards awake on the premises overnight, fire buckets (metal waste-paper bins filled with sand) and torches in case people have to make a rapid exit at night. You ought also to provide facilities to make tea and coffee, such as an electric urn, catering packs of coffee/tea bags, milk powder, plastic cups, sugar and spoons – and rubbish bags for disposing of it all.

On the application form for the conference, you will need a section for people to fill in saying if they need somewhere to stay. This needs to cover:

- Name
- Sex
- Have you your own transport?
- Will you sleep on a floor if no bed is available?
- Have you a sleeping bag?

Then the real problem, of matching up the two groups, starts. Theoretically this should all be done in advance. In practice people simply do not fill in forms, they turn up on the day and announce they need a bed, simply assuming that it will appear. Get as much done in advance as you can though, to cut down the headaches on the day.

At the conference

The accommodation person needs a separate desk with a large sign above it, where s/he can sit with all the papers spread out, and deal with the requests as they come in. This desk will need to be kept going long enough to allow for latecomers, and then possibly re-opened in the early evening to deal with any crises.

Ask the guests to make contact, and come back and tell you if there are any problems – and keep your fingers crossed. Allocate the places furthest away to those with their own transport. Keep a map handy. If you can, photocopy enough maps of the area to hand out to people as they register. Give (or if you can organise things in advance, send) to each person who comes a card with their host's name, address and phone number written on it, and directions for getting there.

Where people have put down restrictions, a bit of tact and common sense will help you get round them, where necessary. A single woman who has put down 'no men' would probably not mind being asked to take a man and a woman together.

If there is a shortage, fill up the maximum people say they can cope with – after that, you will have to make appeals during the conference itself for more space. If all else fails, twist the arm of the rest of the committee to take home anyone who is left over.

Keep a list of all the places you send people to, and send the hosts a duplicated note afterwards thanking them for their trouble. This is less important if it is chiefly your own group members who have helped out, as they will all know each other anyway. But if you have had help from all over the town it will give your group a good name.

Food

You do not have to provide this; people can always use the local pub or chip shop. If you decide it will help the conference if you do give food, then only worry about lunches; people will expect to find their own evening meal on the Saturday. Don't forget vegetarians and non-drinkers when deciding what to provide.

Some places may have food on the premises; a college or arts centre, for instance, may have a canteen. Others, especially where a council has handed over the franchise to a private firm, may insist you use their own expensive caterers. Make sure you get all this clear when you book.

If you are allowed to bring in your own food, someone has got to organise this. There are various possibilities. **Groups,** mainly co-ops, **who specialise in wholefood catering** may help. If there is a local wholefood shop, ask there about the possibilities, or ask the various sources of information listed on page 17.

Voluntary help may be available. if there are people who like cooking, you could ask them to do a buffet, or something hot (like big pots of stew and rice) if the cooking facilities run to it. This will need checking in advance. If this would be too difficult or there is no one enthusiastic, do not push people to do more than they want. Settle for something very simple, like pies and beans, or large chunks of French bread, cheese, and fruit, plus cans of beer and fruit juice.

If you are unsure about numbers, ask at the beginning of the first session how many people want lunch, and rush out and buy extra provisions if necessary.

Providing food is easier if you split up the tasks: ask six people each to make one salad rather than one person to make six. Try asking people who are members of the group but feel unable to take much part in organising the conference, perhaps because of family commitments, to help out here. Don't make the sexist assumption that only women can cook, though, in asking for volunteers.

The   person in charge should ring round those who have agreed to provide something, a day or two before the event, and remind them what they have agreed to do. Give them a definite time by which the food should be there, remembering to allow for heating things up before the lunch-break if that is necessary. Ask people to take their dishes away as they leave, even if they are not washed, so that you do not need to go round and return them the next day.

You also need to check whether the hall has plates, glasses, cups, and cutlery. Use plastic or paper ones if not. You will need large plastic dustbin bags to put rubbish in, and, if you are serving tea and coffee at breaks, you will need tea, coffee, milk and sugar.

If there is washing up to be done, those slaving away behind the counter serving should not be the ones to do it. Shame a few of those taking part in the conference, or arrange an additional team.

If the food came free because of a co-operative effort in the group, you will not need to charge for it, but if you have paid for the supplies, work out how much to charge each person to cover your costs. You may be able to get things cheaper in bulk, if someone in your group has a cash-and-carry card, or by making an arrangement with a local baker or greengrocer.

If you are charging a registration fee for the conference, don't bother to charge separately for tea and coffee. If the conference is free, then 10p a cup is the going rate.

Creche

Delegate responsibility for this to one person and give them the resources to do it properly. The creche at a conference or public meeting is too often an afterthought. People who run them have horror stories of being expected to set up in hallways or rooms with unprotected radiators hot enough to burn children. Creches will never be very heavily used, because people will make alternative arrangements if they can, but they are crucial to give equal access for a minority. You need:

- a reasonably large clean room, in the same building as the conference; use a room in another building only as a last resort, as it makes it very difficult to fetch a parent for any reason;
- easy access to toilets;
- easy access to drinking water;

- no problems about making a noise;
- preferably, some safe, secure outdoor space.

Check the room when you book, and also first thing on the day of the conference. If it needs cleaning, this will have to be done before the children arrive.

Equipment

Possible sources are **a nursery school, playgroup,** or **another creche.** Are any of your members involved with one of these? In a very few areas, there are mobile creches with all their equipment packed in a van so they can be set up anywhere. (Check with one of the sources of advice listed on page 17 if there is one near you.)

Alternatively, a number of people can each contribute something; one person a climbing frame, another an easel and paints, another some toys, and so on. One person should be in charge of organising this, and remind people who volunteer the day before about it.

Whatever the source, you will need to make arrangements for equipment to be picked up and returned either with a large van, or in several journeys with a smaller one. Vital pieces of equipment are:

- **a first aid box** – buy one if necessary; and
- **a large tarpaulin,** or several smaller ones. Try to borrow them from people who go camping. They can be spread out on the floor, and the children can make as much mess as they like without causing problems for the cleaners.

Try to provide plastic aprons or overalls for the kids, but anyway suggest that they are sent in play clothes.

You will need **orange juice and biscuits** for the morning and afternoon. Lunches for the children can be difficult, as the children will all have different ideas about what is good food, and turn their noses up at what you offer them. On the other hand, taking them out of the creche at lunchtime can unsettle them, and parents do value that time for informal discussion. It really depends on how experienced your helpers are, and whether they feel they need a rest at lunchtime or not.

Close altogether before supper, so that the children are collected in good time.

Try not to put on a lower age limit, but if you really cannot cope with very small babies, say so in advance rather than struggle with them.

If you are expecting a large group of children you could take the older ones on an outing, which would be fun for them, and get them out of the way of the toddlers. A minibus, or a couple of cars, make it fairly easy, whereas going by public transport means counting frequently to check you have not lost anyone. A zoo, a museum, or a swimming bath are possibilities. For any outing, **you must get written permission from parents,** to protect yourselves if something goes wrong. Warn parents in advance if children need equipment like swimming things. If there are admission charges, collect the money from the parents when they bring the children.

Helpers

As with equipment, helpers can come from either professional or amateur sources. There are a few groups around the country who provide creche helpers as a voluntary project; the local library, or a women's centre will know if there is one in your area. Otherwise:

- some of the staff in a local nursery school or playgroup may be willing to work at a weekend. They are very poorly paid, so might well need the extra money;
- students on a nursery nursing (called NNEB) course at the local technical college or further education college might help;
- if someone in the group knows some playgroup staff, you could approach them.

If you cannot find anyone whose job is with children, try to find two or three nice parents and perhaps a couple of sixth formers, to take it on.

The 'going rate' for a playgroup helper is about £3.79 per hour. Organisations like unions who can afford to pay more should expect to do so, probably at the same rate of pay as day nursery staff.

Make crisis plans, in case the creche gets swamped with children – people you can ring up and ask to come over, or people who you know are coming to the conference who will not mind spending an hour or two in the creche if necessary. If all else fails, appeal for help during the conference. This often does not get too good a response, as people will not want to miss part of the conference, so you may need to threaten to close the creche altogether.

Registration

Except for the very small creche for a group who all know each other, registering the children so that you know who their parents are is vital. You may have one who is very unhappy and will not stop crying, or someone may get hurt. Giving the children badges can please them, and it helps you to identify them. Here is an example of a registration form, adapted from one used by Camden Playbox which is a mobile creche in London.

Registration Form

Child's name . . . . .Age . . . .

Parents' name and address
or person who brought child . . . . Tel . . . .

Where can parents be contacted (e.g. Room no.)? . . . .

Are there any special things we should know about your child (e.g. likes, dislikes, child's own word for toilet, toys or comforter special to her/him)? . .
. . . .

Health. Are there any allergies or illness? . . . .

Any comments . . . .

I hereby consent to . . . . receiving medical treatment if the creche workers or doctor think it is required as a matter of emergency and I cannot be contacted following reasonable attempts to do so, prior to such treatment being given

Signed. . . . . .Relationship to child. . . . .
Date. . . . .

Please bring a change of clothes in a bag labelled with your child's name. If at all possible, would parents of babies please bring a large carrier bag clearly labelled with the child's name, in which there are three separate bags containing: the milk/food your baby needs; a change of clothes; disposable nappies.

Try to get people to register for the creche in advance, and bring along the form with all these points already filled in on the day. Not everyone will, though, so at least one creche helper will have to spend the first half hour or so sitting at a desk registering children.

Babysitting

For a residential conference where there are children, pay for babysitters if your group can afford it, or organise a babysitting rota among those without children there, at least if there is a social going on, so that the parents can have a break. It need only involve each person for an hour or so – but you may have to put moral pressure on to get volunteers, especially among men.

Getting in bookings

This is another separate job for someone. If yours is a **delegate conference**, intended to take policy decision, you will need to send your publicity to all the branches and organisations entitled to send delegates, and to make sure they send back proper authorisation for that person to act on their behalf. This means having a long time-scale so that each branch can discusss the conference, who to send, the issues it raises and what policy they would like to adopt.

Allow long enough for at least three stages:

- to get into the mailing and get the branch secretary;
- to be put on the agenda for a meeting to be discussed;
- for the secretary to write back and tell you who the delegate is, and what resolutions they want.

This probably means two months, or longer if part of it is the August or Christmas break. Send reminders to those who do not respond, if you are eager to get full representation.

Publicity

If your conference is intended for individuals – so that it is in effect a prolonged public meeting – then your publicity will be much the same as for a public meeting (see pages 60–5 for details).

People do not book in advance for a local conference any more than they do for a public meeting; they simply turn up.

For a large national conference, you will want people to get tickets in advance. Tell them the basic details in all your publicity of **who, where,** and **why.** Put in **a ticket price,** a **deadline** for registration, and an **address for enquiries.**

If the conference is going to be a success, enquiries will start cominf in fairly quickly, and some will include money even before people have got the full details. Each person should be sent:

- the preliminary leaflets, including details of how to send in resolutions or papers for the conference;
- a registration form; and
- a receipt if they have sent money.

Below are two examples of registration forms, covering the points that were listed above, on pages 180–91. The first is for a delegate conference which is residential, and the second for a non-residential conference for individuals.

Registration for residential conference

This year's Annual General Meeting will be held at Barchester University on Saturday and Sunday, 3 and 4 April. Each branch is entitled to send one delegate.

Individual members of Vegetarians Against the Bomb are also entitled to attend, but not to vote.

Notes
(1) The building is accessible for the disabled.
(2) The registration fee is £4. This includes tea and coffee on both days.
(3) Accommodation is available in the University, and must be booked by 26 March. Lunch on both days, and dinner on Saturday, is also available if booked in advance.
(4) Creche facilities are available, but please book by 5 March so that adequate arrangements for staffing can be made.
(5) It is possible to attend the AGM without meals or accommodation by registering at any time up to and including the conference weekend, but it would very much help the administration of the AGM if those wishing to attend would register in advance by post.
(6) The conference will be open at 8 p.m. Friday, and finish at 1 p.m. on Sunday. No evening meal will be provided on Friday.

Registration
Branch Secretaries should complete this section and send it with the payment to Headquarters as soon as possible. (We can give refunds on cancellation provided we are informed by 21 March).
..........Branch nominates the following delegate for the Conference:
Name . . . .
Address . . . .
We enclose a delegate fee of . . . .
Signed. . . . . Date. . . . .

The delegate should complete this section.
I wish to book bed and breakfast on Friday/Saturday night at a cost of £10.75 a night.
I wish to book Saturday lunch/Saturday Dinner/Sunday lunch at a cost of £3.50 a meal.
I do/do not require creche facilities. If yes, for how many children and what ages?
I do/do not require a special diet (please specify).
I enclose a cheque/Postal Order/Giro for £. . . . .

Registration for non-residential conference

The conference on Fighting the Cuts will take place at Northampton Training College, City Square on 10 and 11 March, 1984. All members are invited to attend.

Notes
(1) Any individual can attend the conference on payment of the registration fee (£20).
(2) Lunch is available on both days, but must be booked in advance. A bar is available. Entertainment is being organised for Saturday evening, and will be publicised later.
(3) Creche facilities are available, but must be booked by 28 February.
(4) No accommodation is available at the college. We will, however, try to arrange accommodation in members' homes for those who cannot make their own arrangements. If you would like us to try to find accommodation for you, please fill in the final part of the form.

Registration
Please fill in this form and send it to headquarters as soon as possible. We can give refunds if cancellations are notified to us at least 3 weeks in advance of the conference.
Full name. . . . .
Address . . . .
I wish to register for the conference and enclose a fee of £. . . . .
Meals: I wish to book Saturday lunch/Sunday lunch at a price of £4.00 each.
Do you require creche facilities? Yes/No
If so, how many children and what are their ages?
Do you need vegetarian meals (sorry, no other special diets available) Yes/No
I enclose a cheque/postal order/Giro for £. . . . . .

Accommodation
Do you require accommodation for Friday/Saturday night?
Have you your own transport?
Will you sleep on the floor if no bed is available?
Have you a sleeping bag?

Some organisations print the registration form, along with the advertisement for their conference, in the newsletter, which helps to make sure that everyone knows about it. Put the registration form and the conference details on separate pages, so that if you send off the registration form you still have details of where you are going.

As the registrations come in, the person dealing with them may accumulate quite a large sum of money. For a big conference, open a separate bank account, and pay in a 'float' from the general account to begin with, to pay for the hire of the hall, deposits for accommodation, and so on. This can be paid back later when there is enough money in the conference account. This will mean that the bank will help you with accounting for the conference, as the bank statement will be a double-check on your own notes of where the money has gone. (See chapter 3 for details about looking after the money.)

Final details of the conference should go out to everyone who has registered, about two weeks before the conference itself.

Resolutions

If your conference involves these, you must include in the publicity, and on the forms, a note about the procedure people must follow. This should cover:

- who is allowed to send in resolutions – is it only branches, or individuals as well?
- whether there are any restrictions on subjects, for instance can things that have been discussed and decided last year come up again?
- the last date they can be sent in;
- who they should be sent to.

Lay down also that they should be typed, on one side of the paper only, to protect the sanity of the person dealing with them.

Keep to your deadline for resolutions, otherwise you will get complaints. If you are using the same sort of procedures as political parties and trade unions, the resolutions will then need to be circulated to all the branches and members, so that they can send in amendments. Again, you need a deadline for this. Once this is up, you then need to move quickly to get all the resolutions and their amendments together ready to circulate in the final mailing.

For other, less formal, conferences, people will continue to register right up to the deadline, and indeed after. If the place you are using is strict about needing to know numbers in advance, you will have to be too; this also applies to people who cancel.

On the day

Registration

If you are charging a fee for the conference, you need to know that only people who have paid are going to get in. For a delegate conference that takes decisions, you need to know also that only those who are entitled to vote actually do so. Therefore, people will need to **register** as they come into the conference. This is the time also to sort out the **creche, accommodation,** or **meals.**

People taking registrations should sit behind a table, with the lists and sets of tickets in front of them, with a large sign above each person saying what their job is. Have separate desks for delegates and visitors; if the press are coming you also need a **press desk** where copies of press releases are available. Different groups can be given copies of different coloured tickets or agendas to identify them. Give extra conference papers to people as they register.

Pooled fares

Pooling the fares means that people who have come from a short distance pay a share of the fares of those who have come a long way. This only works if people are being paid for by their organisations, or where they are a cohesive group who feel some loyalty to each other. Otherwise, they will just not own up. To run this system you need a desk at the registration stage where people write down on a list how much they have spent. You then work out an average fare. Those who paid out more than that get some money back, and those who paid out less give you some money. Allow a margin, when working out the average, for some defaulters. Get everyone to sign, say, by lunchtime on Saturday, and then arrange to collect or hand out some money at the Sunday session. You can do it all by post, but it gets rather bureaucratic.

■ Trevor's Playbus Association has 20 people who each paid £10 in fares, 20 who each paid £5, and 20 who paid nothing, and do not wish to claim.

The average fare being claimed is therefore £5. Those who have actually paid £5 do not pay anything extra; those who have not made any claim each pay £5 (or perhaps £5.50 to allow for defaulters) and £5 is paid out to each of those who paid £10.

Anchorperson

For a big conference, appoint one person to float around in the background of the registration area, without a specific job, to deal with queries and crises, and give that person authority to make spot decisions.

Pursuing speakers

Arranging speakers for a conference is very like arranging speakers for a public meeting (turn to chapter 8 for details of this). However, there are extra problems if you are asking people to provide papers about their speeches, either before or after the event, expecially if you are intending to turn them into a book or pamphlet. People, especially academics, tend to be very bad at putting things down in writing. The more experienced they are as speakers, the worse they will be at this, because they will probably talk from notes or just off the top of their heads. If you **want something written** from them

- tell them so when you first arrange for them to speak;
- say how long it should be, and in what form – a full text of their speech, or just notes;
- give them a definite date to send it in by (tell them a date two weeks before you really need it!);
- remind them when it does not appear, and keep on politely until you get it.

For a conference that is raising new and important issues, or one where people are going to have to choose between different options, sending out summaries of what each speaker is going to cover in advance will help people take in the information. Try to produce papers that look attractive and easy to read, as this will increase the chances of people actually reading them. If there is any other reading material to go out, for instance copies of a policy document, send it at the same time. Make sure you have some spare copies of all the papers at the conference itself, for the people who have lost theirs.

Other helpers

Organise in advance a chairperson for each session (see chapter 8 for this). If your conference is making policy decisions, you need people to take notes. Split this up with a different person for each session, because it is hard work. Tell the volunteers that it will also mean **writing the notes up afterwards,** and give them **a date to do it by.**

If you are splitting into smaller groups, each group will need a chair and a person who will take notes and report back to the full meeting. The jargon word for the note-taker is 'rapporteur' (the French for 'reporter'). At many conferences, the first ten minutes of each workshop is taken up with people looking at each other and no one volunteering for these jobs, but you can avoid this by asking people in advance to do them. You will need to check on the day itself that they have turned up, and quickly find someone else if they have not.

Ask all those who have agreed to take one of these roles to come to a particular place before the conference starts or during the lunch break, so that you can go over things and check where the groups are.

Other items

For much of the organising, a conference is just like a public meeting, except that it goes on longer. Turn to chapter 8 and look at the sections on:

- stewards
- taking a collection
- stalls
- setting up the hall
- public address systems
- decorating the hall
- afterwards.

Try to organise enough helpers to give each one a rest. If your resources do not stretch to this, at least rotate the jobs, so that people are not outside the meeting room, sitting on a bookstall for instance, throughout the whole conference when they would like a chance to listen to the discussion.

Videos, films and slide shows

It is very common to have a slot for a show at a conference or public meeting. The **advantages** are:

- it can be a starting point for discussion;
- it can teach something, perhaps in a light-hearted way;
- it can be a break from hard thinking, and refresh people.

But there can be **disadvantages**:

- many films and videos are not very good, or not very suitable for your purpose;
- the equipment often goes wrong;

- people will be passive rather than actively participating;
- people can relax too much, or even go to sleep.

If the show's message needs thinking about, this may not be the best approach. So only plan for a show as a central part of your programme if you are sure it is right for what you want to do, and plan carefully for the discussion afterwards. If there is a show which may be interesting for some people but is not going to provoke discussion, arrange for it to be run during the coffee break or during the lunch hour. Those who want to can watch without taking up the time of the others.

Video is better for small numbers, because people need to be close to see the screen properly. Probably only about 20 can get round the usual monitor. Run the show twice, rather than cram too many people in.

Where do you get them from?

There are a number of organisations which distribute the films and videos that other people make. The British Film Institute publishes *Films on Offer* which is a complete catalogue, every other year (see 'Useful addresses'). A local film society or arts centre might already have one. If you know what film you want, the BFI information department will be able to tell you over the phone where to get a copy. Two other useful organisations are Concord Films Council who distribute films for many left organisations, and The Other Cinema (see 'Useful addresses').

The BBC also make many of their better programmes available. The films and videos that local groups make as part of their campaigns may only be available locally, and you will probably hear about them by chance. Ask people in your local arts centre, resources centre, or trades council, if they know of any. There is a *Directory of Independent Video Tapes,* available from libraries.

Try to book shows that someone in your group has seen and is sure are both relevant and of good technical quality. However interesting the subject matter, people used to the commercial cinema and televsion get very irritated with programmes where you cannot hear the words or the speakers have no heads.

Telephone the distributor to check that **the show you want is available when you want it,** and then write confirming. Some distributors ask for a deposit, and possibly also for the hire fee in advance. The figure they quote will not usually include VAT, so you will need to add that, at 15 per cent, and the cost of carriage, to find out how much it will be altogether. In November 1983, hiring *The Atomic Café* cost £45, plus £6.75 VAT, plus £5.50 carriage by Securicor – a total of £57.25.

Distributors usually use Securicor, which means someone has to be in to accept the parcel. **Open it as soon as it comes,** to check that it is the right film.

It is your responsibility to get it back properly wound and undamaged, and again someone will need to be there when it is collected.

Equipment

When you ring the distributor, check on the type of equipment you need. Films are generally 16 mm, very occasionally 8 mm. There are several different types of equipment for videos, of which the main ones are VHS, Betamax, and U-matic, so it is especially important to check what format the programme you are hiring fits. Before confirming and committing yourself to paying any money, make sure you can get hold of the right projector or video machine. Possible sources are:

- a local youth club, college or school;
- the local education authority (the school should be able to tell you who to ring at the education offices);
- the regional area arts association;
- a local film society; or
- a local trade union office.

You will need either to be shown how to operate it, or to persuade the lenders to send along someone who already knows. If you are on your own, make sure (and double-check) that you have fool-proof arrangements for collecting and returning equipment.

For a film and slide show you also need a screen. You could improvise one with a sheet, but it will look amateur. You will also need:

- A take-up spool (which should come with the projector, but check);
- an extension lead with the right plug on;
- a screwdriver;
- spare fuses;
- spare bulbs – make sure you are shown how to put them in;
- tape to stick down the wires so they do not trail.

The room

Make sure that it blacks out properly, especially if you are running the show in daytime or early evening. Try for a room with a low ceiling, a carpet, and soft furniture, not only because it will be more comfortable, but also because it makes the sound quality much better. Check that there are **power points**, and what plugs they take.

Always have a trial run beforehand. With a film, check that it is correctly placed in the projector, that the sound is coming out properly, that the image fits the screen, and that it is properly in focus. Put the projector as high up as possible, so that people's heads do not get in the way of the screen. Try also to get the speakers high up – say about shoulder height – so that the sound does not get lost. With slides, check that they are in the right order, and the right way up. Give yourself enough time to run the show through – and time to rewind – before the audience arrives.

When you are ready to start, have someone else turn off the lights when you signal, and ask the same person to turn them on again if something goes wrong. Once the film starts running, the projectionist may need to adjust the sound, as a full room absorbs sound more than an empty one. Even though you have seen the show before, stay by the equipment – it will go wrong if you turn your back! Once the show has finished, turn off and leave the equipment until the end of the discussion. It is very distracting to have someone noisily packing up while you are trying to talk about the show's message.

Discussion

The discussion will get off to a better start if the person leading it has seen the show before, and has prepared a speech which ties in with it. If possible, prepare and put round in advance a brief note of what the show is about, and the questions it raises.

The person leading the discussion should be at the front as soon as the lights go up, and launch straight in so that the audience do not have the chance to think about leaving.

Entertainments

Conferences that go over a weekend frequently have an entertainment to keep people happy over the Saturday night. Possibilities, depending on the size and purpose of your conference, are;

- a theatre group or cabaret;

- a gig with a live band;
- an ordinary party with people bringing a bottle.

Make clear to people what it is they are getting, especially if it has a definite starting time like a theatre show. After the end of the Saturday afternoon session people tend to relax and have a drink, and then go off for a meal with their mates. The bulk of the people may not get back until 9 p.m. or later, which is fine for a bop, but not if a theatre group turned up at 8.30 and played to an empty hall.

It is not worth trying to organise anything for a local conference where people are all going home after the sessions. Arrange a social event on another evening instead.

The following sections go into the different types of event in detail.

Theatre group

Be careful about who you get. Some groups are just bad; others will not fit the theme of your conference, though if you are planning it simply as entertainment this may not matter so much. Good community theatre groups are also expensive, as the members have to earn a living. An evening could cost between £200 and £400. Even if they agree to do the show for their travelling expenses only, if there are half a dozen actors this will mount up. You could think, therefore, of **opening the show to the public;** or **charging for entrance,** perhaps with a reduced rate for conference-goers; or **applying for grants** to reduce the cost.

There is unfortunately no central source of information about shows. There is a *Directory of Alternative Theatre,* which your library should have, but it may be out of date. Use it to make initial contacts by ringing a few of the people listed in there and asking if thay have a suitable show, or know of people who do. There are not many people involved full-time in this area, so they tend to know what each other is up to. Try also the Touring Officer of the Regional Arts Association or the Arts Council in London, to see if there is a group touring your area anyway. (Other possible sources are listed on page 109.)

A group will need:

- reasonably strong lighting for the stage, and possibly black-out for the audience;
- 8 – 10 electric sockets for their equipment;

- access for their scenery, usually room for a Transit van to back up close to the hall, without too many steps or narrow corridors to carry it through;
- somewhere to park the van close by so they can load up again easily;
- a room to change in;
- access to the stage to set up in advance.

Setting up may take an hour or so. Plan a gap between the conference and the show, if they are using one of the meeting rooms. They will also need time to clear up afterwards before the place is locked up and the caretaker goes home.

Check all these points with them before you confirm the booking. Also check that both sides have the same understanding of the point of the evening. Is it simply entertainment, along with a bar, or is there intended to be a serious discussion afterwards? The two do not mix, so settle for one or the other. Also check with them how long the show is, and tell them what sort of people the audience will be. If it is going to include people who will be offended at swear words and the show includes a lot, you could either get the group to tone it down, or book a different group.

The group will also appreciate it if you offer:

- help with unloading and clearing up, especially if they are having to get up flights of stairs;
- a meal before or after the show; and
- beds for the night.

Some theatre groups print their own posters, with a blank space for you to fill in with details of the particular performance, but most do not. They might, though, have examples of posters that have been printed for other performances of the same show, so you can use the same material. You can also follow through the same images on leaflets and tickets. (See chapter 4 for ideas on publicity.)

Working out a ticket price

Calculate the budget for your entertainment before confirming your booking; if it does not look as if you can possibly break even try something more modest. Here is an example of a budget.

- Atara is booking a theatre group for the Playbus conference. She takes into account:

the fee for the group	say £200
hire of the hall	£50

| hiring other equipment | £50 |
| cost of publicity | £50 |

As it is going to be open to the public, they are applying for a grant from the local arts association (see below) and she thinks they can get the £200 fee covered in that way, which leaves £150. The hall holds 100; this means that if it is full, they need an average ticket price of £1.50. But it may not be full; if they assume 80 seats are filled, they need to average £1.87 per ticket. They cannot charge the same rate for everyone; the people coming to the conference will complain, when they have already paid a fee, and it will be too high for unwaged people. So they decide to charge £2.50 to the public, and £1.50 to people at the conference and to the unwaged. Assuming half the audience is not paying the full rate this will give them £160.

As this example shows, there are quite large risks in this. If more unwaged people, and people from the conference come than Atara has expected they will make a loss. So you need to know how you are going to meet any shortfall. Can the conference budget itself cover this, or the group that is behind the conference, or can you find someone, who while not wanting to get directly involved in organising is willing to act as a back-up? One of the organisations you have applied to for a grant, who has turned you down, might be willing to give a guarantee instead. What about any profits – where should they go?

You may decide you do not want the people coming to the conference to pay at all. But do the budget exercise anyway, to ensure that you have covered the costs properly within the overall ticket price for the conference.

Grants

There is a fairly well-established system of grant-giving to theatre groups, through the regional and local arts associations. For theatre groups that they know already (which means people who are already on the grants list) they will give a grant according to a scale they have worked out, for each performance. Ring up the regional arts association and ask to speak to the person dealing with community arts, and ask them how you apply. They may impose special conditions on you, and also ask for their name to go on any posters.

The council's Recreation Department may also be willing to

help with part of the fee. They can often hand out small amounts of money without having to go through too much bureaucracy. Try also the local Co-operative Society which covers your area; ask for the 'member relations officer' or 'political secretary'. They have political funds which they can use if they think it is a good cause.

Another idea is to ask another local organisation, like the Labour Party or a group interested in the same area as yours, to sponsor it and share the costs, risks, and possible profit. This gives an extra outlet for the tickets, and more people have a motive for selling them and making the show a success.

Try all these suggestions, as some may well not come off.

If the show is a success, then when you write your thankyou letters, write also to the people who gave grants, saying how good the group was. It will help them next time they apply for grants.

Cabaret

Most of the points above also apply to cabaret groups. In some of the larger and more commercial conference venues, a singer, stand-up comic or group is offered by the management as part of a package deal. While this can save a lot of trouble, it has its pitfalls: s/he may be very bad; or s/he may be quite insensitive to the type of organisation you are, and therefore be downright offensive, for instance, by making sexist jokes at a women's conference. If so, you will have people walking out.

It may seem crazy to turn down free entertainment, but do if it is going to cause trouble – it can mess up the whole conference.

Parties and socials

If you decide to have a really lively bop, think about:

- the likely tastes of the people who are coming – will they want reggae, 1960s nostalgia, or old-time dancing?
- how riotous you want the evening to be, and thus how much work you want the conference to do the next morning. If you have a late bar, people will go on drinking even later, and suffer the inevitable results!
- what facilities you have got – in particular, if the building you are in has other people staying and there is no alternative venue, having a big loud party will be very unfair on those who do not want to come, and on any children. One possibility is to find a room in a local pub.

A commercial conference centre may have a resident band – usually not very good – or a disco. The students' union at a university or college may be able to tell you about a good one. Otherwise, it will be a matter of relying on local knowledge and asking your more musically aware friends who they think is good. Try not to get anyone too extreme, as the music will probably be disliked by as many people as like it.

As with the theatre, you will need to work out a budget to see how much it will be costing you. Bands can be decidedly expensive (£250 or so a night) and conference participants are more likely to object to paying for a ticket for this than for a theatre show. You could open it to the public and advertise heavily (see chapter 4 on publicity). This will make it a rather different sort of event, at which your conference participants may well be outnumbered. You will have to steward it well, in case the local troublemakers turn up. There may be a risk if your conference involves, for instance, gay people or ethnic minorities, that it could be a target for extreme right-wing groups.

Much of the profit from a social comes from the bar, so decide who will get that money. If you hold your event in a pub or social club, with a permanent licence, or if you ask a local publican to come and do the bar for you, s/he takes the money, although you may be able to negotiate a share. If you are running the bar yourself you need **an occasional licence** (see pages 233–4 about getting one, and for other points on running a bar).

Selling drink without a licence is illegal. Selling raffle tickets, which people then hand over for a drink, is often used as a way round this, but it is also illegal. The police are not usually troubled about small socials in the local community centre, but if for some reason they are called out, they could prosecute you. Make sure you do have a licence if you are running a bar in a large public hall, or advertising a social publicly. The alternative is to get everyone to bring a bottle so that you do not need to sell drink.

What about food? Will people eat before the social, or come straight there? At a minimum, you will need crisps and peanuts. You may want to stretch this to include bread and cheese, or to offer more serious food. (Look back at pages 187–8 for ideas on how to organise this.)

If you are not providing much food, tell the people in advance, so they know to eat elsewhere.

Getting the room ready

If you are using one of the conference rooms for your entertainment or social, someone will have to do some furniture moving to get it ready. Will you have to organise this, or will the centre staff? Establish this in advance, when you first book. If it is your responsibility some people will have to commit themselves to do this. In any case, people will need to be there from the time the event is scheduled to start, even if no one else is. Someone also needs to be allocated to look after the entertainer you have booked. This person needs the authority to rearrange the programme if someone does not turn up, and to stop an act if it is offensive or bad.

Clearing up afterwards

You need to decide in advance who is going to do the clearing up and when. Has it to be done that night, or can it wait until the next day? If you are having your social in a room you are also using for your conference, clear up that night, rather than come in to stale cigarette smoke and empty beer cans next day. If it is up to you to do the tidying, try and organise people in advance, but expect some of them to sneak off, and be prepared to strong-arm a few others to help. Check in advance what cleaning materials are available, and bring anything extra that you need, and lots of dustbin bags to shovel the rubbish into.

At the end of the conference

There will be all sorts of papers and bits and pieces left, as well as bits of lost property which someone is going to have to sort out. Scoop everything that needs keeping into a large box, take it home and decide what to do with it at your leisure.

Follow-up

If the conference was making decisions, or planning to publish something afterwards, you will still have a lot left to do:

- The notes of the discussion may need writing up and distributing.
- A record may have to made and circulated of the resolutions passed.

● The papers presented to the conference will have to be prepared for publishing.

Find people in advance to do all these tasks. The group that did the organising will probably have to carry on meeting to make sure they are done. Where it is a matter of writing up notes, only one person who made the notes will be able to read them, so ask them to do this, even if they cannot type them up into final form. Press them for this work as quickly as possible. If they go back to their scribbled notes a month later, they will not be able to make head or tail of them.

You could tape-record the conference. If so, make sure you have enough tapes for the whole time. Transcribing them is a long job, and needs someone good at audio-typing, so make sure it can be done before committing yourselves.

Try to get speakers to hand their papers over to you on the day, as soon as they have stopped speaking, to save trouble chasing up. If you are publishing them, let the speakers see a copy of the final typescript, and ask them to make any amendments, but give them a deadline and say specifically that if you do not hear from them by a particular date you will assume it is alright.

Checklist for conferences

Why bother?

(1) Why are you having the conference?   174–5
(2) What are your priorities?

People

Have people been given the jobs of:
- finding and booking a place?   180–1
- organising the mailing?   192
- organising the creche?   188
- organising speakers?   197
- organising entertainment?   201
- sorting out the follow-up?   207
- finding stewards?   198
- doing leaflets, posters, and other publicity? 60–5
- registering people on the day?   195
- doing press releases?   29–48

Things to do

Work out timetable for conference.   178–9

Find venue: 180–4
- Check details on:
    cost
    children
    disabled
    special food
    bar
    cancellations
- Pay deposit
- Letter confirming
- Reply received
- Phone call to check

Registration form: 193–4
- Drawn up
- Duplicated/printed
- Mailed out

See page(s) Date done

Special bank account?   194
   Food: 187
- Who is providing?
- Who is bringing?
- Arrangements for heating up
- Washing and clearing up

   Creche: 189–1
- Room found, checked, confirmed
- Equipment
- Helpers
- Registration form
- Orange juice and biscuits
- Payment for helpers
- Getting everything back to owners
- Insurance

   Places to stay: 184–6
- Rooms found
- Church hall:
     fire precautions
- Heating
- Stewards to stay awake
- Breakfast

   Accommodation form: 184
- Sent out
- Card index drawn up
- Maps provided
- Person to do allocation on the day
- Emergency arrangements

   Show: 198–201
- Found
- Quality OK
- Booked
- Delivered
- Checked
- Returned
- Paid for

- Equipment:
  found
  how are you getting it?
  how is it getting back?
  take-up spool
  screwdriver
  spare fuses
  spare plugs
- Room black-out
- Screen
- Comfortable chairs
- Power points
- Access for setting up

Social: 201–6
- Group or disco found
- Booked
- Paid for
- Budget done
- Room checked
- Power points
- Occasional licence
- Who is setting up?
- Who is clearing up?
- Tickets organised
- Publicity

Press contact: 29–48
- 1st press release sent
- 2nd press release sent
- Phone to see if they are coming
- 3rd press release, after meeting

Publicity: 60–5
- Mailing to groups
- Ad in paper
  paid for
- Leaflets: how many?
  printed
  delivered
  paid for

● Posters: how many?
    printed
    put up
    paid for

See checklist for public meetings for other things to remember.

On the day

Registration desks: 195–6
● for delegates
● for visitors
● for press
● for accommodation
● for pooled fares

Stewards: (see public meetings checklist for their jobs)   198
● Person in charge of creche   189–1
● Person in charge of food   187

Clearing up afterwards organised?   207

Afterwards   207–8

● Notes written up?
● Speaker's contributions collected?
● Resolutions sent out?
● Publications done?
● Bills paid?
● Borrowed/hired equipment returned?
● Was it worthwhile?
● What is your next step?

13.

Festivals, fetes and bazaars

Campaigning can be fun, and a great many more people get the message if it is. Most people do not like going on marches or to public meetings; you have to be dedicated to start with to do those things. It is the people that are not dedicated that you need to reach. If you find yourselves planning a march or demonstration with no real idea behind it – as with the May Day March in the example on page 99, which was happening because it had happened for years – stop and think whether something like a festival might not be more exciting, and reach more people. Festivals are good for making people in an area aware that a particular organisation exists, and what it does – for instance, a Trades Council or a new community centre. The message of the festival needs to be simple, so that it does not get lost among all the other things going on. A 'Save our Hospitals' Festival could work; an 'Anti-Privatisation' one probably would not.

A full-blown festival is unlikely to make much money for your group – you will be paying out a lot for entertainers, and so on if it is to be any good. A smaller fete or bazaar with less outlay to start with is better for fund-raising, and can have a political content, so long as you keep it simple. There is no need to separate fund-raising and campaigning events.

As various events involve a lot of the same problems, they are all covered in this chapter.

Aims

Here are some examples of why people hold these events:

- Monica at the Doddingworth Community Centre organises a small festival every September for the people on the estate, to publicise the plans for the centre, and other local groups who take stalls, after the summer break. It is the one time when the grim square in the middle of the estate looks cheerful, and it is enjoyable, especially for the children.

- Judith's Trades Council runs a much larger festival each summer in the park. They want to promote the idea that trade unionism can be fun, and to undo some of the harm done by hostile press coverage, as well as creating a good day out that is not commercial or too expensive for ordinary working-class people. They also want to give individual local groups the chance to publicise themselves and raise funds.

- Shabir's Labour Party have a bazaar every Christmas which is their main fund-raising event, so they rely on it for money to carry on political activities the next year. More people come to it than all their public meetings put together, so they want to put across a good positive image to people, and also to show what they do.

- Dave's Health Emergency Group are organising a small fete in the grounds of their threatened hospital, to publicise the campaign locally and to raise funds for it.

Priorities

Taking the examples above:

- Monica wants to keep the event as local as possible. Her publicity needs to concentrate on the estate, with leaflets through doors and posters in the lifts. She needs to encourage those who cannot come to the festival at least to drop into her centre and see what it does. She wants to get the people who already use the centre to run stalls and provide refreshments, and for local organisations like the Adult Education Institute and advice centres to provide displays of what they do. She needs to work out how to decorate the square to look good, and to provide a lot for the children. She is not particularly interested in making money, although they must break even. Because many of the people on the estate are very badly off, as much as possible that is on offer should be cheap or free.

- Judith has to put a huge amount of work into publicity, in places throughout the Borough where working-class people will see it. She has to arrange lots of entertainment and sports that adults as well as children can enjoy, and persuade all the local groups to book stalls and co-ordinate their activities. She needs also to get lots of food and drink around to contribute to the atmosphere. As the Trades Council will be spending a great deal of money, she needs to get grants or guarantees to cover this where possible, in case the whole thing is a flop.

■ Shabir's priority is raising money – the Labour Party do not want to spend more than they can help. They want to have things given to them to sell – but not junk because of the importance of a positive image. They also want a very bright and cheerful display, for the same reason, making plain that it is a Labour Party event. They need to do a lot of publicity throughout the whole constituency, even though people may only come from nearby, so that people see that the Labour Party is not just about boring meetings.

■ Dave's Health Emergency Group is small, and their priority is saving the hospitals. They need to get other people to do the stalls, as a good way of showing their support. The group itself will concentrate on a display about the work of the health service, and what they are trying to save. As they want to make some money, they will have to persuade the stall holders to give them a cut of their profits and to run a raffle and tombola stall to pull the cash in. Their publicity needs to get across the dual message of what the fete is and what the campaign is.

Where to hold a festival

In many cases, the idea behind the event will also dictate where to hold it. Monica's group, above, can only hold it in the square on the estate. Other groups, like the Labour Party, will have a choice. The first thing to take into account is, do you want it **indoors or outdoors?** Indoors at Christmas and outdoors in the summer is standard, but what you do at other times depends on **how big a risk you want to take.** Arrange events that are happening on dates like May Day when the weather is uncertain, in places that have both a big hall and an outdoor space – if you can find one – so that you can hedge your bets against rain. This will only work where the building and the open space are right next to each other – people will not carry their stalls and goodies half a mile, nor will the customers bother to go that far. If in doubt, play safe and stay inside – unless yours is the sort of festival, like Judith's which has to be outside to be worthwhile. You can insure against rain (see page 238).

If you decide on **outdoors**, do you want to use **a public park, square,** open space like a **common,** or **waste ground?** A park or recreation ground may be expensive, but it is likely to have **toilets, water** and **electricity supplies** laid on. If you use waste ground for a big festival, and do not have these facilities, you will have to pay for them to be brought on to the site, or for people to tap into the supply in nearby buildings. If you use the site which the circus or the flower show always hires, the supplies are likely to be there already (see below).

You must find a site **the right size.** A few stalls will look lost in a vast space, but good in a small one. Be pessimistic rather than optimistic about the number of stalls and people that you will get. It is better to look too crowded than empty.

A site should ideally be **near a shopping centre and public transport.** Get people handing out leaflets in the shopping area for a couple of weekends before, to give publicity for your group as well as for the event.

Make sure your site is **accessible for the elderly, the disabled and people with prams and children.** They will make up a large proportion of your customers. So it should be on ground level, or flat.

Think also about **toilets, facilities for making tea, water, public address system,** and **fire exits.** Can you decorate the walls of an indoor site?

Is there **access for vehicles** bringing in equipment, and for emergency vehicles if there is an accident?

Make sure you book your space long enough to allow for setting up the stalls and decorating them at the beginning, and taking them down afterwards.

If you want to hold the festival in the streets you must get permission from the local authority.

Look back at chapter 9 about booking open spaces, and chapter 8 about booking a hall. Check who is expected to clear up afterwards – yourself or the park or hall staff (see pages 122–3).

Services

Public parks usually have pipes and electricity supplies to tap into fairly easily. In the street, or on waste ground, it will not be so easy and may cost a lot of money. **Electricity supplies** can be laid on by:

- linking up to a house or shop's supply;
- linking up to a lamp post;
- hiring a generator.

Always use professional electricians, even though it means you will have to pay. Electricity is dangerous.

Temporary **water supplies** have to be arranged through the Water Board (look in the phone directory). There is no fixed scale of charges – it depends on the length of time the service is needed, and whether the work has to be done at weekends. You will be asked to sign an indemnity form, absolving the board of any responsibility. Make sure your own insurance covers it.

Police

The police must be told well in advance if you are expecting a crowd, especially if you want any streets to be closed, or if you are taking a procession, or pram race, along the road to start the day off. They may offer to have a stall and hand out stickers about how wonderful they are. Do you want this? If not, decline it tactfully.

When to hold it

Festivals, fetes and bazaars can be held at times of the year when other events are not successful:

- near Christmas
- during the summer;
- on Bank Holidays

In fact, they are better held at these times.

One of the chief problems will be **what else is going on at that time?** The last two weeks of November and the first two weekends of December are peak times for fund-rasing events. The local library, or Council of Voluntary Services (see chapter 3), may know about some of them, but not all, so, at this time of the year, it is bound to be a bit of a gamble whether you clash with someone else. The rest of the year is clearer, but avoid clashing with events like carnivals, the Cup Final, or the Lord Mayor's procession.

Another problem is getting **helpers.** August Bank Holiday is theoretically a good time for a fun event, but not if your helpers are all on holiday themselves. If you fix your date far enough in advance some people may be willing to adjust their holiday plans. A weekend during the school term should mean that a lot of people with children are at home – but avoid half term because people go away then.

Once you have a date, let the library, the newspapers and anyone else who might be planning an event know, before you do your general advertising, so that other people do not fix dates to clash.

Pre-planning

Start your pre-planning **a long time in advance.** Judith's Trades Council held their first festival sub-committee meeting just before Christmas, for a July festival.

Notes of the first committee meeting, 9 December

Present: Calum, Hugh, Dick, Judith

(1) We agreed that the date for the festival would be Sunday 10 July, in the park.

(2) We agreed that each of us would take responsibility for 'overseeing' three of the areas of work, as follows:

Calum: transport
       site management
       stewards

Dick: food
       stalls
       beer tent

Judith: street theatre
       kids' activities
       sport

Hugh: publicity
       rock music
       other music

We further agreed that we would take responsibility for finding people to be in charge of each of the areas, and invite them to the next meeting. The purpose of this two-tier system is to avoid what happened last year when, if the person responsible for a particular area was unable to come to a meeting, the rest of the committee did not know what was happening and could not discuss it.

(3) Finance. We agreed that Judith would act as Treasurer to the Committee. The grant application has to be in as soon as possible, and it was therefore agreed that Judith would prepare the budget and Dick would prepare the wording for the form.

(4) Equipment. We drew up a shopping list which Calum agreed to check with Parks Dept to see what they can supply, and tell Judith before the grant application goes in.

Once everything has been started, there will be a couple of months in the spring when not much needs to be done, except checking on progress while people get on with their own little tasks.

At their next meeting in January, the committee need to have each person report progress in their patch, Judith to set out her budget, and then a session where the group throw around as many ideas as they can, which get followed up or dropped as impracticable. So the notes of this second meeting may run:

(6) *Other ideas for the day*
(a) We get the community newspaper to do a special festival issue (Hugh to contact).
(b) We ask the Labour Party to do an exhibition (Dick to contact).
(c) We ask CND to do a 'Borough after the Bomb' exhibition (Judith to contact).
(d) We ask the Women's Photo Co-op to do an exhibition for/ with the Trades Council (Calum to contact).
(e)We try to involve the kids from the local school in doing some kind of display (Hugh to contact).
(f) We hold a big raffle on the day with decent prizes (Judith to work on this as part of her finance job).
(7) *Any other business*
We should all remember this year that it takes two days to clear up afterwards!

Get your publicity out as early as possible (see chapters 4 and 5).

Financing a festival

Budgeting

Some commitments, such as booking a park may have to be made before you work out your budget, but do **a rough budget as early as you can,** and keep an eye on it during the next few months. Get an idea of the various costs by talking to people who have run other events, or by ringing up various groups and contractors and asking how much they charge, without making any commitments at this stage. Once you have made the budget, keep an eye on it. If costs seem to be higher than expected, you will have to take action either by making savings, or finding more money.

Here is Judith's budget for the festival. As you can see, it is not very detailed, but it does give the committee an idea of the framework they are in. The committee make it a rule that the relevant person for each activity must not commit themselves to anything that will bring them above the ceiling figure, without first asking permission from the others.

Expenditure	£	*Income*	£
Compere	100	Fees from stall bookings	250
Rock bands	700	Raffle	250
Other entertainers	700	Council grant	3,630
Kids' area	275		
Theatre group	500		
Sport	200		
Petty cash	100		
Sundries	200		
Administration	200		
Public liability insurance	40		
Equipment	1,115		
Total expenditure	£4,130	Total income	£4,130

Do not forget to budget for **administration before the festival.** Letters and phone calls will mount up.

Grants

Apply for grants, at least three months before the festival, to help with your costs. In some parts of the country it would almost be out of the question for something like the Trades Council to get a grant from the council; in others they may. Some areas have big festival weeks, during which there are events in the city centre, and different neighbourhoods can get money for their own small festivals at the same time. There are two tiers of local government in most places, and they may not be under the same political control, so apply to both.

Before writing off, phone up:

- the Council Recreation Department;
- the Council department dealing with youth clubs – start with the Education Department;
- the regional and local arts associations;
- the local sports council, if there is one.

Look back at chapter 3 for ideas on how to find these organisations.

If they say they are the wrong department, ask who you should go to. Councils organise their affairs in all sorts of strange ways. It may, for instance, be the Housing Department that would give grants to tenants' associations for festivals.

When you have tracked down the right people ask them:

- what sort of amounts are given out;
- the procedure for applying;
- whether there is a special form to fill in;
- the last date by which you must apply.

Put in for as big a grant as you can justify, as it may well get cut down. Check whether they expect you to put in applications to other people as well. Often, grant-giving bodies will concentrate only on one aspect of the festival. The sports council might be willing to help with the five-a-side football league, while you might get money for hiring inflatables from the council's Recreation Department.

If possible, apply to someone for a **deficit grant.** This means that they agree to make up the balance of the cost, after all the other sources have been tapped. They will only do so, though, if they are satisfied your budget is sensible and you have a reasonable chance of making a success of it.

The form to fill in may be complicated, and designed for people who are applying for long-term grants, rather than for one-off events.

If there are things which you think need saying but there seems no place to put them in, write a letter to go with the form. You could take the form along to the CAB or one of the places listed on page 17 and get their help, or phone up the department and ask for guidance on what should be put down.

Some organisations or departments may be able to lend you equipment more easily than giving you a grant. The council's Recreation Department might have tables, chairs and sports equipment, and might lay on water and electricity at a special rate. The Youth Service might have some costumes, tents, or a minibus. Look at the list of equipment on page 235 and see what you could ask them to lend you.

Other sources of grants or sponsorship were listed on page 204. You might be able to get sponsorship for something specific from somewhere as a form of advertising. A local sports equipment shop might pay for a football competition, for instance. But beware of **sponsors who might embarrass your group.**

■ Large and Nasty Builders Ltd are in the middle of a controversial redevelopment scheme. The community group that has fought against it all the way are running a festival. Large and Nasty offer to put up a beer tent with their names all over it 'to create goodwill', but the committee decide that it will make it more difficult for them to carry on the fight, which is presumably why Large and Nasty wanted to do it. So they turn them down.

If, say, a month before the event you have not got sufficient promises of income to cover your costs **cancel or reduce the scale.** Try not to make final commitments until you are sure the money is there. If you find yourself faced with cancellation fees, explain in a pleading letter what the problem is, and they might forgive you all or part of it. If people are being slow or sticky about giving grants, try lobbying the decision-makers (see chapter 10 for ideas).

Budgets for fund-raising events

For these, the budget has the additional purpose of deciding whether the event **is going to raise enough money** to be worthwhile. This is especially important if your group has been doing the same thing year after year. The cost of the hall may have risen gradually, along with printing costs, so that in the end you are putting in a lot of effort for a very small result. Here is Shabir's budget for the bazaar:

Estimated expenditure	£	*Estimated income*	£
Hiring the hall	194	Plant stall	20
Printing draw books	42	Groceries	40
Newspaper advert	36	Bric-à-brac	100
Prizes for draw	185	Bottle stall	100
Gratuities	10	Tombola	50
Insurance	10	Good-as-new	50
Leaflets and posters	51	Home-made sweets	
Total	334	and cakes	220
		Second-hand books	80
		Santa claus	25
		Programme sales	50

Games	200
Draw books	500
Other raffle	50
Donations	200
Total	1,705

This is based on the previous year's experience. If your group is starting from scratch, see if you can find someone from another group who can tell you what to expect in your area. The budget above shows **the two needs** for this type of event; good publicity so that people come, and enough to sell. If there is nothing worth buying, people will get annoyed and not come back next year. A good rule of thumb is that you should cover all your advance costs before the event by:

- selling raffle or draw tickets (see pages 240–1);
- selling space in souvenir programmes;
- getting donations from people;
- holding a smaller event (a social or jumble sale perhaps) a few weeks beforehand.

Souvenir programme

For any of the events covered in this chapter, you can raise extra revenue by selling advertising space in a souvenir programme. Some organisations, both commercial and other, authorise local management or officials **to advertise locally**, but insist **that donations** have to be agreed at a higher level. Charitable bodies can pay for advertising space to non-charities, but cannot usually give straightforward donations.

Allocate the job of souvenir programmes to one person, or a group. They should draft a letter to anyone they can think of, which would need to cover:

- what the event is;
- who is organising it, and why;
- what the programme or brochure will look like;
- how much it will cost to advertise; and
- who will see the advertisements.

Put in an order form, showing what size of advertising space you are offering, and whether you require blocks or artwork (see chapter 4 for an explanation of these). Stress the goodwill the organisation will get from it, and use the same letter to ask for straight donations of money, goods, or prizes for the tombola or bottle stall.

You can send this to anyone you think might help, and then follow up on the most likely ones. Try shops and commercial firms, other community groups, trade unions, schools, college student unions. Look in the local Yellow Pages, or try other sources of information in chapter 3 to find addresses.

If one of your aims is to publicise not only what your organisation is doing, but also other groups in the area, you could offer them preferential rates, or even free advertising, and ask them to put in the information about themselves as well as the usual 'best wishes from X' message.

Sell these programmes in advance, as well as on the day. Number each one, and use the numbers as the basis for a lucky programme draw late in the afternoon so that people stay a while.

Here is an example of the front page of a programme:

DODDINGWORTH ESTATE

FESTIVAL

23 June, 10 a.m. to 5 p.m.

This programme costs 10p and is number 434

Tear off this piece and hand it in at the Lucky Programme Stall. This will go in the draw to be taken at 3 o'clock. Prizes are:

1st, Box of Chocolates
2nd, Teddy Bear
3rd, Record Token

Best wishes to the Festival from Wandsworth WEA. Courses start 15 Sept. Contact WEA Secretary, 53 Turpin House for details.	Best wishes from Jo's Fish and Chip Shop, The Best Chips in Town.
We wish everybody a good day at the Festival *Jack and Mary Jones, Licencees, The Merry Sailor Pub, Doddingworth Road*	*The NUPE Caretakers' Branch send their best wishes to all the tenants on Doddingworth Estate.* Come and see our exhibition at the NUPE stall.

You could have a list of events and stalls, a plan of the area, and an explanation of what your organisation is, inside; and then more advertisements, or more useful information, on the back. The programme could be duplicated, or printed quite cheaply, as long as it is nicely done.

To sell it in advance, you will need to have it ready some weeks ahead. **Think about how you are going to distribute it.** Possibilities are:

- getting groups to sell it at their meetings;
- asking each individual concerned to take a certain number, and sell them to their friends;
- selling them door-to-door (see the section on canvassing, page 160 for how to organise this).

This is advertising as well as fund-raising, so use the method that will get at the people you most want to attract:

- the Trades Council could get delegates to sell the programmes at their own union branch meetings and around the workplace, after talking about the festival;
- the Doddingworth group could knock on doors all over the estate.

If you do not want, or could not cope with programme sales, try at least to get advertisements in the leaflet that you are going to hand out or push through doors about the event, so that you cover its printing costs.

What is going to happen

At that first meeting, you will have worked out the sort of thing that you want to have going on, and now people have gone away to organise them. The different things you may need to cover are: **entertainments; sports; stalls; food and drink.**

Entertainments

If you are fund-raising, you can charge for some or all of these, but try to keep the charges below commercial rates. **Have a mix of entertainments** which cater for a wide range of people. If the event is big enough, you can have different things going on in different places, at the same time. **Use local talent where you can,** not just big name speakers or entertainment. Contact, for instance:

- the local school steel band;
- an ethnic folk dance group;
- senior citizens' concert party.

Having made the contact, write confirming what you think they are going to do, so that if there is any misunderstanding it can be sorted out now. Check particularly how much time they need to set up and rehearse. Then, shortly before the event, write again, giving them details of:

- their place in the programme, and how long they have got;
- where and when they should turn up;
- who they should report to; and
- what financial arrangements you have made – expenses only, a fee or nothing at all.

Most groups will want to be paid **before they leave** that day, so make sure someone is in charge of a float from which they can pay out for this. Get a receipt for each payment. If you involve local people, their friends will come and see them, so you know at least you will have some audience. Warn them, though, about the conditions: performing in the open air, or in a tent, in front of an audience guzzling pork pies, is not easy.

If people are dressing up, they will need a tent to change in. Organise the bookings so that there are no embarrassing clashes like senior citizens undressing in close proximity to the Kung Fu youth group.

If your festival is going on into the evening, try and put one of the most attractive acts on between 5 and 6.30 p.m. to keep people there. This is the point when they tend to drift off and not come back.

Think about noise if you are near buildings. Tell local residents about the festival, and involve them in the planning so that they are less likely to object. If you can get round this problem, you may want to have an evening bop with good loud dance music. This means finding:

- a decent group or disco;
- floodlights; and
- a really big sound system.

Someone who promotes bands locally or the record shop all the real rock fans go to, should be able to tell you where to hire one. Make sure the electricity supply on your site is powerful enough, before booking them. You are unlikely to get any reduction, as these are very commercial outfits. (See page 206 for booking bands and discos.)

All the entertainments will cost money. If you are expecting them to stay around a while, run off some vouchers, especially for any child performers, giving them entitlement to food worth 25p or 50p.

Have an anchorperson to keep the whole thing going. A well-known figure can draw the crowds. Judith's group got one of the presenters from the programme 'Black Londoners'. Some celebrities will come to openings, but not stay all day, and some of them charge quite a lot. (See pages 85–7 for ideas on finding celebrities, and page 122 on the role of the anchorperson, and also page 115 on stewarding the stage and the performers.)

Sports

Another way to get lots of people involved is by running sports events for them to take part in, as long as you have enough room. Try to get the real experts to organise them for you. Some ideas are:

- **Five-a-side-football competition.** Is there a local league you can involve? Half a dozen short matches can be fitted into an afternoon. You need equipment, pitches, referees and teams. Try to have these mixed, not boys only.
- **Fun Run,** for the healthy people – try a local athletics club or a few jogging fanatics, to organise this, You might be able to get a local newspaper to sponsor it, in imitation of the *Sunday Times.* You need to organise a course, get them started, and make sure that first aid and cold drinks are available.
- **Greasy pole.** Two people sit on this and whack each other with pillows until one falls off; or people climb it to try and retrieve the prize at the top. In one area, the Fire Brigades Union organised this.
- **Tug-of-war** – not just confined to men.
- **Martial arts display.** Is there a local club? They could also demonstrate women's self defence, or run a class.
- **Welly throwing.** Anyone with a loud voice could organise this. The only difficulty is finding enough welly-boots, and getting them back to their rightful owners later.

- Slow bicycle races, or children's wheelie or BMX races. The local cycling club might do this.

There are also 'school sports-day' type activities – **three legged races, sack races, egg and spoon races** – which can be quite fun if everyone is feeling sufficiently silly at that stage. Persuade a few school teachers to organise these.

If you have a particular message you want to put across, like peace or saving the health service, you can do this by linking-in the sports events. You could have:

- **a tug-of-peace** instead of a tug-of-war;
- **a trial of strength** against the judges;
- **a sponsored run over 'political hurdles'** in support of the threatened hospital.

You could also have slide-shows with a political content – throwing wet sponges at someone dressed as Mrs Thatcher, for instance.

Children

If you have room for a special area for children, with inflatables, pony rides, children's theatre or puppets, happening all through the day, this will allow parents to leave them there for a while and go off on their own. You might be able to organise a special area for very small children, with creche helpers who will take responsibility for them for an hour or two at a time (see pages 188–92 for creches). Try asking:

- primary school heads;
- the Recreation Department;
- the library;
- the Education Department;
- people who run summer play schemes;

about good children's entertainments available in your area. Try to get some idea of both the quality and the content before booking – Punch and Judy is very offensive to many women's groups.

Members of your group, or friends may have the equipment for popular things like face-painting and badge-making, and surprising people turn out to have a talent, once you ask around, for walking on stilts or dressing up as clowns or Santa Claus. Try to have some of these people **walking around** your festival or fete, rather than just staying in one place, to catch people's attention if they are beginning to get bored.

Inflatables (huge plastic cushions full of air, that children bounce up and down on) are usually popular. The Recreation Department at the Council should know where to hire them locally. You need a generator, mounted on a lorry, to keep up the air supply, and smooth grass, or a smooth floor, to put them on. You also need a lot of adults around, to ensure that children do not overload the cushions and burst them, and that they do not get over-excited and hysterical. **Don't let adults join in** – they will be too heavy.

Again, **confirm in writing** with people what they have agreed to do, where and when. Adapt the letter on page 231 to cover this.

Stalls

If you want other organisations to take stalls you will need them **to book in advance;** if stalls are going to individual members of your group, or branches of it, you will need them to **commit themselves firmly in advance** as to what they are doing. Produce a booking form, and give one person the responsibility for chasing up those who do not reply. Send out the initial letter two months or so in advance, and ask your contacts in these groups to make sure the matter is discussed. A month or so before the event, send out another letter to those you have not heard from, and follow this up with phone calls. Both letters should include:

- **details of what is planned for the festival** – what sort of entertainments and events are going on;
- **what sort of numbers** you are expecting;
- **suggestions** about what sort of stall would fit in with your ideas.

Here is an example of the second letter and booking form for Judith's festival:

■ Dear friends,

Some time ago we circulated a wide range of trade union and community organisations, inviting you to book a stall at the Trades Council Festival in the Park on 10 July. A considerable number of stalls have now been booked, but we have not had a reply from you, so we are writing again.

We now have more details of the attractions at the festival, including two major rock bands, music and dance from Africa,

Ireland, the Caribbean and Latin America, lots of children's entertainers, a tent full of real beer, and much more. The theme is Peace and Jobs, and the emphasis is on having a good time. Last year over 20,000 people attended, and this year's event promises to be much larger. It is a good opportunity for publicising campaigns and work that you are involved in, and for fund-raising. Selling food and snacks, and crafts made by your members, can help the funds, and a display of the sort of work you do will help to publicise it. If you would like a stall reserved, fill in the form below and get it back to us as soon as possible. Ring Sue on [phone no.], if you want to run a food stall. . . . .
. . . .
Please reserve . . . . . stall(s) for . . . . organisation.
Contact address and tel no . . . .
We intend to use our stall(s) to . . . . (display/fund-raise etc.)
We enclose a cheque for . . . . made out to Trades Council Festival
Stall hire rates: Fund-raising £5
                 Displays £3
Return as soon as possible to Festival Committee (stalls) [address].

Two things need pointing out about this. First, **people planning food stalls** are asked to contact one of the committee. This is to make sure that there is a good variety of food, and also to make people aware of the public health regulations. (These are covered in more detail on pages 231–2.) Second, the committee is charging for stall hire. You would not do this if it was only branches of your organisation involved; but you might charge more if the aim was to fund-raise for your own group. Even if your main interest is in giving people a good time, it is worth having some fee, as once people have paid something they feel committed to the event, and are more likely to turn up.

Once people have booked, they will need to know:

- that you have had their booking and their money;
- that they will be allowed on the site to set up the stall, before the general public comes in;
- where they have to go and what time, and any other points about the arrangements.

Here is an example of a letter that gives all this information:

■ Dear Stall-holder,

Thank you for booking a stall at the summer festival. I acknowledge receipt of the sum of £........ in payments. Bring this letter with you, as it will allow you past the gate before the festival starts. I enclose a map of the festival area.

Please note the following points:

(1) You will be allocated your stall on arrival in the park by the stewards on duty. Trestle tables will be stacked beside the pavilion; please collect them from there.

(2) Please try to arrive to set up your stall between 9.30 and 11.30 in the morning. All vehicles must leave the festival area by 11.30 a.m. The only parking facilities in the festival area are for vehicles displaying a registered disabled sign. There is some parking available just by the bridge entrance to the park, but this is open to the general public, so first come first served.

(3) Enter and leave the park by the bridge entrance.

(4) The festival runs from 12 noon to 6 p.m. No vehicles should return to collect stall materials before 6 p.m.

If you have any difficulties, or anything you want to discuss, contact the committee at the above address and phone number.

Food and drink

You can have stalls selling soft drinks, sandwiches, salads, hamburgers, or whatever you want. People, especially children, eat an amazing amount on a day out.

There are some firm public health regulations you need to follow. The local Public Health Department (sometimes called Environmental Services) will tell you about them, and may well have a list of regulations to show you. They would prosecute a voluntary organisation only if there was a case of bad food poisoning, or if there was a peculiarly officious inspector around.

You may not be able to comply with every regulation, but it helps to know what they are. They are called the 'Food Hygiene (Markets, Stalls and Delivery Vehicles) Regulations 1966'. The main points are:

- stalls must be clean and in good condition;
- each stall must have the name and address of the people running it displayed – or the name of the secretary, if it is an organisation;
- each stall must have a covered rubbish bin;

- food must be kept at least 18 inches off the ground, unless properly protected;
- all the equipment in contact with food must be kept clean;
- people's hands and clothing must be clean, and if anyone has a cut or graze, it must be covered;
- stalls must have first aid facilities available, including water-proof dressings;
- wrapping paper must be clean, and food must not be put in any containers from which there is a risk of contamination;
- people serving food should not smoke;
- food which is unwrapped or uncovered should be kept covered while waiting for sale; stalls selling unwrapped foods must also have separate handwashing facilities with a supply of hot water.

This last regulation is the most difficult. In practice, no one will worry much about you selling home-made cakes and bread, or pots of jam. The things to be careful about, because they can go off and make people very ill, are:

- meat
- fish
- things with cream in
- ice cream.

Make sure food is freshly bought, or freshly out of the freezer, on the day you use it. **Don't keep things warm for long periods.** If you are grilling burgers or sausages on a barbecue, heat the coals well beforehand so that things cook quickly. Keep children away from the hot area. The profit margins on hamburgers are not great compared to the trouble of standing over a hot barbecue for hours on end, and you might do better to negotiate with the hamburger, ice cream, or baked potato vans that are bound to come to the edges of your site, and let them right into the area in return for a share of the takings.

If you have the use of a building, even if the rest of the festival or fete is out of doors, keep the food in there, so that you will be able to organise hand-washing facilities and proper storage of the food. The hotter and sunnier it is, the more people will welcome the chance to go inside and sit down.

If your own group is not doing the food, but you are inviting other local organisations to come in and set up stalls, ask them on the application forms to tell you what they intend to sell so that you do not have three stalls selling toffee apples and no one selling sandwiches.

Give each group a copy of the public health regulations, and ask them to abide by them. If a public health inspector does come wandering round, one of the organisers should try to get his or her name. If you are worried, contact a councillor afterwards and ask him/her to find out if a prosccution is likely, or speak to the chief public health inspector. Get advice from a lawyer (see page 16 for how to find one) and if possible be represented in court.

Beer tent

It is now much easier to get an occasional licence to run your own bar or beer tent, under a statute called the Licensing (Occasional Permissions) Act 1983. Previously, most beer tents and bars at events like these have been technically illegal. You apply to the local licencing justices for the licence. Get the address of the clerk to the justices from the library, and then phone up and check exactly what information you must provide. The application has to be in at least a month before the function. No organisation can have more than four occasional licenses in a year. Ask for the license to run for half an hour longer than you strictly need to allow time for people to finish their drinks and clear up. If you have a licence for extended hours, for instance throughout the afternoon, you will be popular. But have you got enough helpers to control drunks?

You have a legal power to chuck drunks out and refuse to serve people provided you do not discriminate on grounds of race or sex. You are committing an offence if you serve people under 18.

The drink usually comes from local wholesalers or breweries. For a small bar, you could, instead find someone with a wholesale cash and carry card, which could be a sympathetic local shop-keeper; or find someone who runs a social club who is willing to get supplies cheaper for you.

The most difficult problem is knowing how much to order. You may be able to arrange the barrels on sale or return, but this is not always possible even if you have not opened the barrels, because the beer will have been 'vented' and so cannot be re-used. People drink very different amounts depending on the time of year, the venue, and the type of event. Ask for advice from someone who has organised a festival locally, a friendly publican, or the local CAMRA (Campaign for Real Ale) branch.

If you are worried about having supplies left over, err on the side of caution and make up for it by buying larger numbers of cans, on sale or return; you may be able to sell some to the organisers at cost price at the end. Beer and soft drinks are easier to serve and cope with than wines and spirits. Lager should come in cans not barrels, as it can get very fizzy and difficult to draw from the barrel. Barrels need covering with sacking, and kept damp by a hosepipe, in order to keep them cool in hot weather. Check how far in advance they have to be delivered. If the tent has to be stocked some time before, think about security until it is opened up. If necessary find volunteers to sleep in the tent overnight to guard the beer.

If you are running the bar yourself, you will need to find equipment – ask the wholesaler or brewery, or local pub – and also staff.

Make sure you **keep it simple,** have **plenty of help,** and don't **keep any one person on the bar too long.** Even trained people make mistakes when they are serving large rounds for hours on end; untrained volunteers will tire quickly.

Keep the prices in round numbers – rounded up rather than down – like 50p for a can, to make change-giving easier. Make sure one person, preferably with experience, is in control.

Plastic glasses reduce the risk of breakages, but as people are even more likely to walk off with them than glass ones, or to dump them in the bin, charge a deposit of perhaps 10p a glass, and refund it when they return the glass. Organise people to go round frequently, both inside and outside the tent, collecting glasses and clearing away cans, so that the place does not look too sordid. You also need a water supply from a standpipe for washing up.

Equipment

As soon as you know what sort of things are going to happen, and before you start booking people, think about the equipment you are going to need. The best way to work this out, and to find where to get it, is to go and talk to the council Recreation Department, the local Horticultural Association, or whoever puts on the annual show that most areas have. This might well involve being friendly to someone like the Rotary Club, but they will probably be delighted to share their knowledge with you. Often, there will be one contractor who always does events on the site you are using, and you will simply need to discuss with him what you want.

A public hall may already have much of the equipment you need –
find out from the hall manager.

For a big festival, you may need some or all of the following:

tent	stages
tent pegs	paper towels
mallets	sound system
trestle tables	PA system
toilet rolls	poles for PA cables
signs	scaffolding
bunting	walkie-talkies
crash barriers	solid tables
chairs	pallets
lighting (including	standpipes
cables and bulbs)	bags
trolleys	fire extinguishers
fencing	first aid box
plastic table cloths	screwdrivers
extra litter bins and bags	drawing pins
inflatables	
floor coverings	
hammers	
pliers	
string	
coat rack (for performers' tent)	cash bags/boxes
safe/strong box	money aprons
stewards' armbands	
external telephone point	
dartboards (for beer tent)	
transport (minibus and flat-bed	
lorry including petrol	
expenses)	
power supply	toilets

Go through the whole list and decide what you can do without,
If the council run a big show themselves, they may well be able to
lend or hire you much of this.

■ Judith persuaded the council to lend her group:
   120 trestle tables
   2 large stages
   50 crash barriers
   150 chairs

lighting, cables and bulbs
fencing
pallets
standpipes (for water supply)
portable toilets
extra litter bins and bags
coat racks
armbands
strong boxes, cash bags and money aprons

If they are not able to help then think about who else is likely to make use of the things you want. Try for example:

- youth groups who go camping, or people who organise flower shows, or if you are desperate the army, for tents;
- the WRVS for tea urns and trestle tables;
- churches or political groups for tables and chairs;
- a brewery for pub games;
- a school or sports centre for sports equipment;
- a big shop for cash boxes and a strong box.

Ask the police where you can hire crash barriers locally (they may even own some) and also items like portable toilets.

If you borrow things that are complicated to set up or get working, like tents or a PA system, try to get the people you are borrowing from either to come along and help you sort them out, or at least give you a demonstration of how the thing works.

To hire, try Yellow Pages for contractors or commercial hire shops. Find out what they have, reserve it, and then carry on looking for better sources for as long as you can cancel without any costs.

If something is planned which **absolutely depends** on a piece of equipment for success, then track down the equipment before including the event in the programme. You need a greasy pole before people can climb one, for instance. **Make sure that anything you improvise is safe;** scaffolding should **never** be improvised. Check with the people you book for entertainment and events what they have got, and what they need, and add things to the list if necessary.

If you are not sure of the quantities you need of things like tables and fencing, get too many rather than too few. The extra ones can be stacked somewhere out of sight.

Work out **how you are getting things there, how long they will**

take to set up, and **how you are going to get them away** afterwards. If you are hiring, you will probably pay by the day, so **how soon can you get them back?**

With each major item you need to:

- track it down;
- check how much it costs, and the terms on which you are getting it;
- agree it with the group (unless they have given you discretion);
- confirm by letter with the person you are getting it from;
- remind them shortly before the event.

Start with the items most likely to be in short supply. Big tents, for instance, are going to be booked up well in advance for August Bank Holiday, when everyone is having shows, so you must get in early. You may need to pay a deposit. Check on the latest date you can cancel. The friendlier you are to the suppliers, the more help you will get out of them in return.

First aid

Always have a first aid box handy, however small your event. For a large event, have a first aid tent or room – it can also be the place where lost children are brought. People who have been trained as first aiders at work could staff this. St John's Ambulance and the Red Cross will provide teams of people to help at big public events. Ask at the local library, or phone their London headquarters, for the address of the local branch. Book them in advance and **phone to confirm that they are going to come** a day or so before. While they say they do not charge, in fact they do expect you to make a 'donation' to them.

You cannot avoid accidents altogether, but you can reduce the chances by getting someone – perhaps a person who is a health and safety representative at work – to do a safety check before you open. Look out for:

- trailing wires;
- sharp projections;
- things people can trip over, like guy ropes, manhole covers, odd planks of wood;
- holes people can fall into;
- structures – is your stage safe?

Keep the site tidy. If you have any gas cylinders or petrol cans in your equipment these should be in solid brick enclosures, under lock and key.

Insurance

Hopefully, nothing will go wrong. If it does, it could be very expensive for you. As a safeguard, you need several types of insurance: **all risks,** to cover loss or damage of any equipment, whether hired or borrowed; and **third party,** or **product and public liability insurance** – that is against any member of the public being injured during the festival. You can have unlimited coverage, or up to a particular figure. It cost Battersea Trades Council £40 in 1983 for cover up to £500,000. This may seem a huge amount, but if a tent collapsed on a number of people you could easily have claims up to this level. You will also need **employers' liability** insurance if you are paying anyone, for instance bar staff. You could be legally responsible if they got hurt. This cost the Trades Council £5 in 1983.

Check the insurance on any transport you borrow or hire. If it is not separately covered, add this to the policy. It will be cheaper if you restrict the number of drivers.

You may be able to organise this insurance through the council which should make it cheaper. If not, get an insurance broker to arrange it. Ask a well-established voluntary organisation who they deal with. You may find the council will insure you for some things and not others, so you will end up with policies from both the brokers **and** the council. If nothing goes wrong, afterwards you may feel you have wasted your money, **but it is crucial.** Make sure you have in writing exactly what you are covered for, before the day.

For outdoor festivals or fetes, you can insure against rain, but it is quite expensive, and fairly restrictive. You will be paid if the day is washed out by a downpour, but if it is overcast and miserable, so that no one comes, you will not get any money back. Work out the maximum actual loss you could make (that is, the amount you have actually spent out) not what profit you are hoping for and ask a broker how much it will cost to cover for that; then decide whether to bother or not.

Site layout

Draw a plan of your site or building early on, for the committee to work on, showing how you think things are going to fit. Someone needs to be responsible for up-dating this as new activities get planned, so that you do not have two things planned for the same space at the same time. Finalise this just before the event, and give copies to the stewards in charge of the site on the day, so that they can tell people where to go. Mark things like toilets, first aid, and lost children, clearly. Also give the stewards copies of the programme you are handing out to the public. If it is very detailed, do a special fuller one for the stewards as well.

You also need a **list of stalls booked,** and a **plan of where they are each to go,** for the person in charge of sorting out space on the day. The people on the gate, who will be letting in stall-holders before the general public come in, will also need a list, to check in case anyone forgets their letters of confirmation. If some people do not turn up, spread the other stalls out more to fill in the spaces.

Think in advance about decoration. If you want an overall theme running through the festival, you need to provide the decoration to go with it.

■ Dave's Health Emergency Group paint their slogan on long rolls of wallpaper, with the name of the group that has booked each stall underneath. They get the groups to pin these to the front of the stalls. They also ask people to wear their campaign T-shirts and badges while serving behind stalls.

The organisers must arrange for:

● the different activity areas to be marked out;
● tents to be erected;
● staging to be set up, and PA system to be put together and got working;
● sports or entertainment areas to be got ready.

Some of these things could be done the day before, if you have access to the site. You might be able to hive them off to the people running the specific activities, so you could ask the football league to sort out the pitches for the five-a-side football – but you will still need to keep an eye on it and help out with workers if necessary.

Stewards

Get people to commit themselves **in advance** to stewarding, and if possible **have a meeting a few days before** to discuss duties. Ask people to steward for an hour or so at a time, as a whole day will be too tiring. Get some people to come early, and as many as possible to stay late to clear up. The tasks that need covering are:

- letting in vehicles and people coming in to set up;
- ensuring the site is laid out properly and things are in the right place;
- taking money at the door or gate, if you are charging entrance;
- patrolling the area in case there is any trouble;
- picking up rubbish as you go along;
- looking after performers and contestants, (see page 115 for how to steward the platform);
- staffing a central Information Point, and keeping an eye on essential equipment and money;
- selling raffle tickets and handing out leaflets about the organisation.

Combine this last task with general 'patrol' duties as it gives people a reason to wander around and therefore they feel as if they are doing something. Keep a number of people around the beer tent and any children's areas or music areas, as these are likely to be where trouble arises, if anywhere. Tell the stewards in advance what you want them to do if there is a crisis; make sure they know where to send messages, as fast as possible – probably to your central Information Point. (See page 116 for the advantages and disadvantages of walkie-talkie systems.)

Raffles

If you sell raffle tickets in advance to pay for the costs of organising your festival, the draw should be on the day of the festival itself so that you can sell tickets to the crowds as well.

The law on raffles and lotteries under the the Lotteries and Amusements Act 1976 is quite strict. The police do not often prosecute, but it is just as well to know when you are breaking the law. There are three types of 'lottery' (the word is used to cover raffles and draws as well):

- **small ones,** which are just part of some other entertainment like a fete or dance. The sale of tickets happens in the same place as the draw. The prizes must not be worth more than £50 altogether, and the draw should not be advertised;
- **private lotteries** where the sale of tickets should be

restricted to members of the organisation, and the tickets must be printed, with a price marked and a name and address of the 'promoter', who is a named individual in charge of the lottery. The prizes must also be listed. Tickets must not be sent through the post;

● **public lotteries.** The organisation doing these must register with the local authority and has to submit an account afterwards showing the amount collected, the expenses, and the prizes paid out. Tickets must not cost more than 50p, and are not supposed to be sold to people under 16. They must not be sent to non-members through the post.

If you are planning a big raffle or draw, phone up the council first to find out which department you have to register with, and check through the detailed rules with them. The printing job is a specialised one, as it involves numbering all the tickets. Look in the Yellow Pages, or *Exchange and Mart,* or phone up local printers and ask if they can do it. You need the tickets at least two months before the event, to give you time to sell them.

For a raffle to be successful, you need a lot of good prizes, either in money or goods. For your pre-sales, get supporters, both individuals and groups, each to take a batch of tickets. The hope is that they will buy themselves what they do not sell. Keep a list of who has tickets, and chase them up for unsold tickets, stubs, and money a week or so before the event. Then sell all you have left on the day. Put the prizes on display to encourage people to buy.

Have the draw late in the day, so that people will stay for it, and try to get a celebrity or someone who people will regard as impartial like the MP, to draw the tickets. Produce a list of who has won as quickly as possible afterwards and circulate it to people who sold your tickets

You can buy various ready-packaged fund-raising activities like pontoon tickets, draws where you can win pink teddy bears, and others, from various promoters. Look in the Yellow Pages or *Exchange and Mart* for addresses. The profits to the promoters are probably higher than yours, and the drawback is that you must buy and pay for the complete package, which might be 500 pontoon tickets at a time. If you can only sell 250 of these, you will not make any money. Other good fund-raising stalls are tombola and bottle stalls, or games like 'Test Your Weight' or 'Find the Key of the Door'. Ask around other groups and see if they have any of these they can lend you. Make sure you get them back.

You might also be able to get a funfair on the site; this would mean the stall-holders would keep the takings and give you a donation. Ask anyone you negotiate with if they are a member of the Showmen's Guild, because they have various standards which the operators have to comply with. Ask the council's Recreation Department if they know how to get in touch with a funfair. Make sure you settle:

- how many rides and stalls there are to be – you will not want the site to be swamped;
- the price of rides – make clear that it is not to be raised during the day;
- the date of arriving at and leaving the site, and times of operation;
- whose responsibility it is to clear up afterwards;
- what facilities are necessary – fairs usually have their own generators, but they need a water supply.

The money

You are likely to end up with quite a lot of cash around. The groups that have hired stalls are likely to want to keep their own money separate.

If there are parts of your own organisation running stalls, the money will be at less risk if you collect it in centrally every so often. Send two large fearless-looking people around together, carrying a shoulder bag into which they put the notes. They should give each person a receipt for their cash, and this then acts as a record of how much they have made. Collect all the loose coins in at the end, again giving a receipt.

Set out in you final accounts what each stall took; it makes people feel more of a personal sense of achievement, and it also shows you, and anyone who asks your advice in future, what stall or events make money. You may want to keep something on if it is fun, even if it does not make much money – but scrap those that are neither fun nor profitable.

If you are going to get a large sum of money in, find somewhere in advance to keep it overnight, and make sure it goes to the bank in the morning. You might be able to use the safe in a school, or a union office, or someone in business might have a key to a night safe in a bank, or you could arrange this specially with the bank, or another friendly organisation. When you have made the arrangement, it is wise to keep quiet about it.

At the end

Even if the park or hall staff are doing the main clearing up, you will still need to get everything you have borrowed or hired back to its rightful place. It will need quite a lot of people to take down tents, fencing and staging. You may be able to leave things overnight, provided your helpers are willing to come back next day. It might be better to clear it all up at once and have done with it.

When you have recovered, **do a report and a detailed set of accounts.** Send a copy, together with a thankyou letter, to any organisation that gave a grant or sponsored you. This will make it easier to get grants next time. Send thankyou letters to anyone who helped organise things for you, so that they will come back next time too. Keep a list of the names and addresses of all your contacts – it will help you, or anyone else who decides to organise something similar, another time.

Finally, **decide if it was fun or not,** and whether you got across your message. If not, why not, and what could you have done to ensure you did?

Checklist for festivals and fetes

Why bother?

(1) Why are you having the festival/fete?   213–4
(2) What are your priorities?

People

Have people been given the jobs of:
- finding and booking a place?   215
- organising a mailing to stall-holders?   229
- organising food and drink?   231
- liaising with the police?   217
- sorting out electricity, water, toilets?   216
- organising entertainment?   225–6
- sorting out site layout?   238
- doing a budget?   220
- finding equipment?   234
- finding stewards?   239
- doing leaflets, posters, and other publicity?   60–5
- doing press releases?   29–48
- arranging a beer tent?   233

Things to do

Find suitable date: 217
- tell people

Find venue: 215
- Has it got services?
- Do you need police permission?
- Have you negotiated hiring?
- Paid deposit
- Filled in booking form
- Confirmed booking

Budget: 222–3
- Who is drafting?
- Estimates from people?
- Who can you get grants from?
- Put in applications
- Chase up to see what has happened

Souvenir programme: See page(s) Date done
- Letter to groups 223–5
- Follow-up
- Printed
- Distributed
- Paid for

Entertainments: 225–7
- Contact with local groups
- Sort out place in programme
- Payment?
- Noise problem dealt with?
- Sound system
- Floodlights
- Disco/group
- Anchorperson
- Food vouchers
- Equipment for each act
- Dressing tent

Sports 227–8
- Thought about ideas
- Contact with local organisations
- Who is organising what?
- Letters written confirming
- Equipment needed

Children 228–9
- Entertainment
- Creche (see conferences checklist) 189–91
- People walking round the site
- Lost children's tent

Stalls 229–30
- Booking form
- 2nd letter
- Phone calls
- Letter of confirmation/receipt
- Details of arrangements

Food and drink

See page(s) Date done

- Public health regulations 231–3
- Copies issued to all stall-holders
- Water supply
- Rubbish bags

Beer tent

- Occasional licence applied for 233–4
- Decision on quantities
- Prices
- Equipment
- Glasses
- Drink
- Volunteer helpers
- Clearing up afterwards

Equipment:

234–8

- Listed
- Recreation Department asked
- Other sources asked
- Hire shops
- Getting it there
- Getting it back
- Insurance
- Putting it all up
- Safety check
- Cost
- Bills paid

Insurance

238

- Public liability
- All-risks
- Employers' liability
- Transport
- Rain

Site layout:

238–9

- Plan drawn up
- List of stalls booked
- Decoration
- Tents/staging/fences put up

	See page(s) Date done
Press contact:	
● 1st press release sent	29–48
● 2nd press release	
● Phone to see if they are coming	
● 3rd press release, after event	

Publicity: 60–5
- Mailing to local groups
- Ad in paper
     paid for
- Leaflets: how many?
     printed
     delivered
     paid for
- Posters: how many?
     printed
     put up
     paid for

Raffle: 240–2
- Permission from local authority
- Tickets printed
- Distributed
- List of who has got them
- Prizes
- Person to do draw
- List of who has won

Money: 242
- Bags and money boxes arranged
- Collectors organised
- Receipt book
- Safe place to put it
- Where are you keeping it overnight?
- Counting it up and accounting for it

On the day

Stewards for: 239–40
- Letting people in early
- Setting up tents and equipment
- Taking money at entrance

- Patrolling area
- Picking up rubbish
- Looking after performers and entertainers
- Selling raffle tickets and handing out leaflets
- Staffing beer tent
- Collecting money off stalls
- Staffing information point

List of equipment: 234–8
to bring
to take away

Suppliers:
All turned up?

Afterwards

- Accounts done?   243
- Report written up?
    sent to grant aiding bodies
- Thankyou letters sent?
- Bills paid?
- Borrowed/hired equipment returned?
- Was it worthwhile?
- What is your next step?

Part 3
Disasters

This final section is intended to give some idea of what to do when things go wrong. All the way through this book points have been made that, hopefully, will mean the disasters will not happen. In summary the important things are:

- give individual organisers clear responsibilities;
- hold regular committee meetings where you check what each person is doing;
- get things in writing and double-check;
- make sure you know the law; and if you know you may break it, have a friendly lawyer available;
- insure wherever you can;
- have enough stewards;
- have a safety check;
- have first aid available;
- know where a phone is (and have some 10p coins available).

However, things can still go wrong. This section has a list of them, and suggestions for how to cope. They will not fit every case, but they may give you ideas for other things to do.

No one comes

Salvage what publicity you can. Send out your press releases anyway, with appropriate changes. Instead of, 'Speaking to a packed meeting last night', you can say, 'Speaking to a meeting . . .' Take photos of the platform, rather than the rows of empty chairs.

If there is food or drink to dispose of, ring

- a children's home;
- a playgroup;
- an old people's home;

and see if they will take it. Or sell it to group members. Or get someone to put it in their freezer, and decide what to do with 10 dozen hamburgers later, when you are less depressed.

Thank everyone who was going to speak or perform anyway. Don't let them feel it is their fault – you may need their help again.

Work out why no one came. Was the issue just not interesting to people? Or was the issue all right but the publicity bad? Or the site? Or the day? Agonise over it a bit. It will stop another disaster. Remember the fault is more likely to lie with you than with the public. (See below on making a loss.)

The meeting is disrupted

The chairperson on the platform is going to have to decide whether **to abandon the meeting**, or **to struggle on**. It may well look worse from the platform than from the floor. If there seems no hope of your speakers making themselves heard, **ask them what they want to do**, and if they agree to give up, do so.

Surround the disruptive group with stewards – but don't let them start a fight. If it looks as if they can escort them out peacefully, ask them to do so.

What about **calling the police**? This is difficult and depends partly on who is doing the disrupting. The left will sympathise if you call the police about the National Front, but not if it is a group of anarchists causing the trouble. Someone else, a member of the audience, may call the cops even if you do not. Once they are there, you may as well use them to solve your problem, rather than get into an argument with them as well.

If there is damage done while evicting disrupters, **you will have to pay for it**. Check that your insurance covers this. If so, put in a claim. Own up to whoever you have hired the place from. If you try to hide the broken chairs under a lot of others, you will probably be found out, and then you will not be allowed to use the place again, and other people might be stopped as well. (See page 81 about the law on refusing entry to a meeting.)

An individual will not stop heckling or making long speeches

Stay calm, try and make a few cracks back that will **get the audience laughing**. Do not be abusive – you want them on your side not the heckler's.

If someone is going on and on, **say politely** something like,

'Now, you have had your chance, can you let someone else in?' or 'Why don't you let Mr . . . take up the very interesting points you made?'

Give him/her **enough leeway** and hope they will **get tired and shut up**. When you think the audience have lost patience with the heckler, get a couple of stewards to escort them out, and not to let them back in again.

Someone you do not want to be there turns up

Ask him/her quietly to go away, explaining your reason; it is possible s/he has genuinely not realised the difficulties s/he was making by being in on a confidential discussion.

If this does not work, once the meeting starts, **explain to the audience** what the problem is, and **ask them to vote** whether to allow the person to stay or not. If the audience agrees s/he should go, get a couple of stewards to escort him/her out, and then ensure there are people on each door to stop him/her coming in.

If the person is refusing to leave and you do not want to make a scene, or do not think you can carry it through, **freeze him/her out**; ignore any remarks s/he makes, and pretend s/he simply does not exist. You have to be very thick-skinned to withstand this for long.

In the last resort, **close the meeting.**

Your speakers or entertainers do not turn up

If you have some warning, even a few hours **telephone around and find a substitute.** (Try one of the sources on pages 85–7). Or can you **rearrange the programme** so it does not show so much?

If you do not have any warning **ask the preceding speakers to go on for longer,** in the hope that s/he might still come; or see if **someone else, already in the audience, can step in.** Only politicians and entertainers will be able to do so with no notice. If a crisis seems likely to arise, send a note down to X in the audience saying 'If Jo Bloggs does not turn up, can I ask you to say a few words?' which at least gives him/her a chance to scribble a few words on the back of an envelope.

If it is the big name everyone has come to hear who has let you down, **decide as a group how unscrupulous you are.** If you think you will not make yourselves so unpopular that your campaign suffers as a whole **do not let on until the audience is in the hall.** With a bit of luck, they will stay and hear the other speakers. Give the impression, without actually lying, that you have only just heard about the cancellation. If you haven't the nerve to do this, **cancel, or go ahead with another, different sort of meeting.**

Don't make the other speakers or entertainers – the ones who **did** turn up – **feel undervalued.** They are important too. **Thank them anyway,** just as much as if the meeting had gone ahead as planned.

Valuable equipment gets lost

It does not matter if this was borrowed or hired; **it is still important.**

Put out **an appeal** to all the groups involved, and **publicise the loss,** perhaps through a letter to the local paper. The person who pinched it might have a conscience – it is worth trying.

Notify your insurers.

Organise a fund-raising event as soon as possible.

People get arrested

Let their **friends or relatives know,** as quickly as possible.

Appeal for **witnesses** who saw the arrest, and what was happening just before.

Find out **where they have been taken.** Do they need a change of clothes?

Try and find out (through a lawyer) **whether they are going to need bail.** If so, find some reasonably affluent people to help with this.

Read *Trouble with the Law* (see 'Useful books') for **procedures in criminal courts.**

If you think something is going wrong, **make a fuss.** Contact someone 'respectable' – a vicar, a JP, an MP, a trade union official – and ask them to take the case up and **find out what is happening.**

There is a bomb scare

Call the police, if they are not there already. There is no room for ideological hang-ups – just dial 999.

Do what they tell you. Usually, this will be to evacuate the site. Having done so, **do not let people come back too soon** – there might be another bomb. Allow at least half an hour before people return.

Someone gets hurt

Appeal for a doctor over the PA system.
Call an ambulance quickly.
Do not let people crowd round. Make sure access is clear for emergency vehicles.

Find out **who the person/people are**. Make sure someone – a friend or relative if available, otherwise a steward – goes with them to the hospital. Contact friends or relatives as quickly as possible.

Find out **what happens to the injured person. Send them a letter**, flowers etc.

Tell the insurance company.

Write a statement of what happened, and track down witnesses if necessary. You may need them if you are sued for negligence, or if there is a criminal prosecution.

It rains

Did you **insure against it?** If so, **put in your claim.**

Discuss with any outdoor speakers or entertainers whether **they want to cancel altogether, or cut their act short**. They may not want to go on at all in front of a thinning, damp, audience.

Is there **anywhere you can move to**, lock, stock and barrel? Make a few phone calls to local church halls, the students' union of a local college, any community centre.

The event makes a loss

Make a list of your debts and decide how much money you do have.

Pay first the people who you might want to use again, or who might turn nasty: the council; commercial hirers. Individuals might have to wait for their money.

See if there is **any organisation which will give you a grant or a loan** (see page 220 for ideas).

Send out a financial appeal to your supporters, and to anyone else you think might be sympathetic.

Decide what went wrong, so it does not happen again.

Have another fund-raising event – having learnt from your mistakes.

Anything and everything else

Most of all, **don't panic**. Make a joke about it and perhaps people will think you planned it this way all along.

GOOD LUCK

Useful addresses

British Film Institute
81 Dean Street
London W1V 6AA
Information Department
tel: 01-437 4355

Campaign for Nuclear Disarmament
11 Goodwin Street
London N4
tel: 01-263 4954

Campaign for Real Ale (CAMRA)
34 Alma Road
St Albans
Hertfordshire
tel: 56 67201

Central Hall Westminster
Storeys Gate
London SW1
booking tel: 01-222 8754

Police Ceremonial Office
Cannon Row Police Station
tel: 01-434 6135

Police Coaches Branch
Room 618
Tintagel House
Albert Embankment
London SE1

Concord Films Council
201 Felixstowe Road
Ipswich
Suffolk
tel: 0473 715754

Department of the Environment
(for booking Trafalgar Square)
tel: 01-212 3128
(for booking Hyde Park)
tel: 01-212 3833

House of Commons
London SW1
tel: 01-219 3000

Labour Party
150 Walworth Road
London SE17
tel: 01-703 0833

Law Centres Federation
164 North Gower Street
London NW1
tel: 01-387 8570

Legal Action Group
28a Highgate Road
London NW5
tel: 01-267 0048

London ICOM
245a Coldharbour Lane
London SW9
tel: 274 7700

**National Association of
Citizens' Advice Bureaux**
110 Drury Lane
London WC2
tel: 01-836 9231

**National Council for Civil
Liberties (NCCL)**
21 Tabard Street
London SE1
tel: 01-403 3888

**National Council for Volun-
tary Organisations**
26 Bedford Square
London WC1B 3HU
tel: 01-636 4066

**National Graphical
Association**
Graphic House
63/67 Bromham Road
Bedford

The Other Cinema
12/13 Little Newport Street
London WC2
tel: 01-734 8508

Press Association
Fleet Street
London EC4
tel: 01-353 7440

Report
411 Oxford Street
London W1
tel: 01-493 7737

**Services for Community
Action and Tenants**
31 Clerkenwell Close
London EC1
tel: 01-253 3627

Shelter
157 Waterloo Road
London SE1
tel: 01-633 9377

Trades Union Congress
Congress House
Great Russell Street
London WC1
tel: 01-636 4030

The Vegetarian Society
53 Marloes Road
London W8
tel: 01-937 7739

Useful books

Accounting and Financial Management for Charities, Bloom and Norton, n.d.

Hilary Blume, *Fund Raising,* Routledge and Kegan Paul, 1977.

Civil Liberty: the NCCL Guide to Your Rights, Penguin, 3rd edition, 1978.

Community Action Magazine, PO Box 665, London SW1X 9D2. A few years ago CA published a set of Action Notes on things like running committees, and organising street festivals. A local resource centre may have back copies.

Cousins, *Teach Yourself Book Keeping,* Hodder and Stoughton, 1975.

Mike Gapes (ed.), *The Activist's Handbook,* Labour Co-ordinating Committee.

Gilley (ed.), *Sunday Times Self-Help Directory,* Granada, 1982.

Housing and Campaigning, A Shelter Guide, Shelter, 157 Waterloo Road, London SE1, 1983.

How to Manage your Money, If You Have Any, Community Accountancy Project, 34 Dalston Lane, London E8, 1983. This is written especially for Hackney people, but has ideas that other people would find useful.

How to Organise for Victory, The Labour Party, 1982.

Local Festivals Manual, Hackney Festivals Support Group, 380 Old Street, London EC1V 9LT, 1983. This is written specifically for Hackney people, but has ideas that can be used anywhere else.

The Long Creche, National Child Care Campaign, 1981. This contains basic information on organising a creche.

John McIlroy, *Strike! How to fight. How to win,* Pluto Press, 1984.

Denis MacShane, *Using the Media,* Pluto Press, 1979.

Grainne Morby, *Know How,* Pluto, 1982.

NCCL Fact Sheets, National Council for Civil Liberties. This is a series of small sheets in a pocket-size plastic folder; there are sheets on arrest, police questioning, demonstrating, and so on.

Daniel Plesch, *What Do We Do After We've Shown the 'War Game',* CND, 1982.

Publicity Information Guide, Islington Bus Co., Palmer Place, London N7, 1983. This is written for Islington people, but useful for others; the same organisation publishes other fact sheets on screen printing, fund-raising, etc. which are also quite good.

Release, *Trouble with the Law,* Pluto Press, 1978.

Jonathan Zeitlyn, *Alternative Print Handbook,* Penguin, 1983.

Index

accounts, 19, 23, 243

Acts of Parliament: Abortion Act 1967, 133; Criminal Damage Act 1971, 126; Criminal Law Act 1977, 126; Licensing (Occasional Permissions) Act 1983, 233; Metropolitan Police Act 1839, 102; Prevention of Terrorism Act 1976, 73, 102; Public Meeting Act 1908, 82; Public Order Act 1936, 81, 101–2; Race Relations Act 1976, 26; see also Police and Criminal Evidence Bill

addresses, 13, 14, 15, 257–8

advertising, 5, 6, 51, 53–5; see also publicity

advice, 16

affray, 72

alternative directories, 14

arrests, 72–4, 123, 254

badges, 14, 56, 120, 148

bail, 73, 254

balloons, 56

bank accounts, 19, 22–3

banners, 102, 120–2, 142, 144, 167

barbecues, 232

bars, 206, 233

bazaars see festivals, fetes and bazaars

beer tents, 233–4

breach of the peace, 69–70

by-laws, 16, 45

cabaret, 205

caterers, finding, 14

Citizens' Advice Bureaux, 16

citizens' band radio, 117

Clerkenwell Green, 106

coaches, hiring, 23, 66

colleges, 181

community newspapers, 41, 55

community print shops, 32, 41

community theatre groups, 109

conferences and schools: accommodation, 184–7, 196; aims of, 173–4; anchorperson, 196; bookings for, 192–5; chairperson, 197–8; checklist, 209–12; children and creches, 182, 188–92, 196; disabled people and, 182–3; entertainment, 201–7; equipment, 189–90; failure, 251–6; films, 198–201; following up, 207–8; food, 183, 187–8, 196, 206; helpers, 197–8; non-residential, 178, 184–8, 194–5; notes, 197–8, 208; organising, 198; parties, 205–7; places for, 180–2; pooled fares, 196; priorities, 174–5; programme, drawing up, 175–80; publicity, 192–4; registration, 188, 193–6; residential, 173, 178–9, 180–4, 193, 206; resolutions, 195; slide shows, 198–201; speakers, 197; tape-recording, 208; theatre groups, 202–5; timetables, 178–9; timing,